Language Change in Child and Adult Hebrew

Language Change in Child and Adult Hebrew

A Psycholinguistic Perspective

DORIT DISKIN RAVID

New York   Oxford
OXFORD UNIVERSITY PRESS
1995

OXFORD UNIVERSITY PRESS

Oxford   New York
Athens   Auckland   Bangkok   Bombay
Calcutta   Cape Town   Dar es Salaam   Delhi
Florence   Hong Kong   Istanbul   Karachi
Kuala Lumpur   Madras   Madrid   Melbourne
Mexico City   Nairobi   Paris   Singapore
Taipei   Tokyo   Toronto

and associated companies in
Berlin   Ibadan

Copyright © 1995 by Dorit Diskin Ravid

Published by Oxford University Press, Inc.,
198 Madison Avenue, New York, New York 10016

Library of Congress Cataloging-in-Publication Data
Ravid, Dorit Diskin.
Language change in child and adult Hebrew : a psycholinguistic
perspective / Dorit Diskin Ravid.
p.   cm.
Includes bibliographical references and index.
ISBN 0–19–508893–X (cloth).—ISBN 0–19–509036–5 (pbk.)
1.   Hebrew language—Acquisition.   2.   Hebrew language—Variation.
3.   Hebrew language—Inflection.   I.   Title.   II.   Series.
PJ4544.85.R38   1995
492.4—dc20   93–41770

1 3 5 7 9 8 6 4 2

Printed in the United States of America
on acid-free paper

To Arik and Ruth—
Thank you.

Contents

Technical Notes

Hebrew forms are represented here in broad phonetic transcription, with consonantal roots indicated by means of the historical elements attested in conventional orthography. For example, the verb form pronounced *hizik* 'harmed' is based on the historical root *n-z-q*. Verb forms are given in the traditional form—the 3rd person masculine past tense—unless otherwise indicated. Words have main stress on the final syllable, unless marked otherwise by an acute accent on the penultimate syllable, e.g. *xófeS* 'freedom'.

The following symbols stand for specific phonemes:

The voiced pharyngeal fricative is denoted by *y* ; The voiceless pharyngeal fricative is denoted by *H;* The voiceless palatal fricative is denoted by *S;* The voiced fricative is denoted by *Z;* The voiceless palatal affricate is denoted by *C;* The historical emphatic alveolar stop is denoted by *T*. An apostrophe indicates what is today pronounced as an intervocalic glottal stop before a stressed vowel, e.g. *bo'er* 'burning', *ka'av* 'hurt', although in the first word this symbol stands for the historical voiced pharyngeal fricative, and in the second for the voiceless glottal stop.

Noun and adjective patterns are given in the form of a consonantal skeleton, representing root radicals, with additional affixes, e.g. *miCCaC*, standing for *miklat* 'shelter', root *q-l-T;* and *mitbax*, 'kitchen', root *T-b-H*. *Binyan* verb patterns are given in their traditional form, with the Hebrew root *p-y-l* meaning 'do, act', standing for the root radicals. For example, *Pi'el* is the verb pattern shared by *limed* 'taught', *sikem* 'summarized'.

Inflections are marked using the following abbreviations: Pa = Past Tense, Pres = Present Tense, Fut = Future Tense, Inf = Infinitive, Tr = Transitive, Int = Intransitive, Pas = Passive, Sg = Singular, Pl = Plural, Masc = Masculine, Fm = Feminine, Pr = Person.

Language Change in Child
and Adult Hebrew

1

Background

1.1. INTRODUCTION

The study of language acquisition has taken on a new meaning in the last decade. When seen as part of the study of other forms of language variation across time and space, such as dialects and sociolects, as well as the study of pidgins and creoles, it provides us with a new understanding of how language evolves and what directs its development.

My study was undertaken with a view to conduct precisely such interdisciplinary research, focusing in particular on inflectional morphology. Its purpose is to trace language development from childhood to adulthood, to explore strategies of language acquisition, and to characterize variation in the spoken Hebrew of speakers of different ages and socioeconomic backgrounds. The study thus touches on various interrelated issues: It raises general questions in developmental psycholinguistics as well as themes specific to the acquisition of Hebrew. And it relates to the development of Modern Hebrew as an ancient tongue recently revived and now undergoing accelerated processes of change.

Sources of Variation in Contemporary Hebrew

Contemporary Hebrew is a language with a unique history. A Semitic language with ancient roots and one of the longest written records known to us, it lay dormant, though not dead, for more than 1500 years, its speakers dispersed throughout the world (Rabin 1972). Hebrew ceased to be generally spoken around A.D. 200 due to extralinguistic historical cir-

3

cumstances. However, it continued to develop even when no longer functioning as a native tongue (Ben Hayyim 1985). Medieval Hebrew, for instance, represents a rich and heterogeneous array of language types and language use, religious and secular poetry and prose deriving from both Biblical and Mishnaic Hebrew, heavily influenced by contemporary Arabic. It was a literary language serving a multitude of functions, and it underwent lexical and grammatical change, e.g. the rise of nominal and adjectival suffixes *-ut* and *-i* as in *enoS-ut* 'humanity' and *enoS-i* 'humane' (Ben Hayyim 1985, Goldenberg 1978, Kutscher 1982).

Even greater variety marks what is called "Modern Hebrew," which came into being as a result of what is known as "Revival of Hebrew" (Blau 1981b, Rubinstein 1981, Sivan 1976). This in fact took place in two phases: Hebrew was first revived by the adherents of the *haskala* or "enlightenment" movement at the end of the 18th century as a modern secular literary language which derived simultaneously from Biblical and Mishnaic Hebrew, as well as from Aramaic, Medieval Hebrew and Yiddish (Even-Zohar 1986, Kutscher 1982). The second phase in the revival was the re-introduction of Hebrew as a spoken language in pre-state Israel (and very marginally in Eastern Europe too—see Kloisener 1964) at the turn of the century (Kressel 1984). Within as little as a generation Hebrew became a spoken vernacular, native to a large group of speakers; by the 1950s it formed the mother tongue of second and third generation native speakers of Israeli Hebrew. Contemporary Hebrew is thus the non-linear product of a number of historical layers, as well as of various literary sources and contact languages, both Semitic and non-Semitic. Foreign influence extends to components of lexicon and grammar, which accounts for much of the lexical and grammatical variation found in it today (Bendavid 1967, Ben Hayyim 1953, Blanc 1957).

Nonetheless Biblical Hebrew continues to constitute the major source of Israeli Hebrew morphology and vocabulary.[1] In this respect, Hebrew has remained a basically Semitic language characterized by tri- or quadri-consonantal roots that combine with verb or noun patterns to form new words (Berman 1987c, Blau 1981c, Gesenius 1910, Ravid 1990, Sivan 1963). Thus the Biblical root *s-H-r* 'trade' underlies all the following: *saxar* 'traded', *nixxar* 'was traded', *soxer* 'merchant', *sáxar, mixxar* 'trade, commerce', *saxir* 'tradeable', *sxora* 'merchandise'. In the domain of inflectional morphology, Contemporary Hebrew still displays the highly bound nature of Biblical Hebrew. Nouns are marked for gender and number, and they occur either in a free form or in a bound genitive form, e.g. *Safan* 'rabbit', *Sfan-im* 'rabbit-s', *Sfan-a* 'rabbit,Fm', *Sfan-o* 'his rabbit', *Sfan nisayon* 'an experimental rabbit = guinea pig'. Adjectives agree with their head nouns in number, gender and definiteness, and demonstratives agree with their head nouns in number, e.g. *ha-rakdaniy-ot ha-muxSar-ot ha-éle* 'These talented,Fm,Pl dancers,Fm'. Verbs agree with their subjects in number, gender and person, and are also marked for tense, e.g. *ha-dovér-et nas'-a* 'the spokesperson,Fm went away,Fm'.

While the morphology of Contemporary Hebrew is mostly Biblical, its syntax resembles Mishnaic Hebrew in several respects, including the three-way tense system, the extensive use of full-fledged subordinate clauses with finite verbs, and the predominant SVO order in verbal clauses (Avineri 1964, Bendavid 1967, Berman 1978a, 1980a, Rosén 1956, Rubinstein 1981). The exceptional history of Hebrew is in itself a source of variation, which is why Hebrew has a number of parallel constructions, none of which has been rendered obsolete by the others, e.g. *bigdey ha-mélex; ha-bgadim Sel ha-mélex; bgadav Sel ha-mélex* 'the king's clothes' (Ravid, Shlesinger & Sar'el 1985); rather they complement each other and are used in distinct semantic, syntactic and pragmatic contexts, constituting part of the linguistic competence of the Modern Hebrew speaker (Rosén 1977).

It is not only the ancient history of Hebrew that is a source of current variability, but its recent history too. In itself a "linguistic miracle" that many refused to accept (and some still doubt), it took a surprisingly short time to revive a language that had been dormant for so many generations (Blau 1981b, Harshav 1991, Izre'el 1986, Wexler 1990). Modern Hebrew has served as the sole language of teaching at all levels of education since 1914, and by 1920 was already being spoken as a mother tongue by Jews in pre-state Israel (Fellman 1973). However, the population of Hebrew-speakers did not remain constant. After the first two waves of immigration which established the core of Jewish settlement at the turn of the century, further waves arrived before, after and during World War II, bringing the total number of Jews in pre-state Israel in 1948 to some 600,000. These took in double their number in the years immediately following the establishment of the State of Israel, when large concentrations of Jews immigrated to the Jewish state (Bachi 1957, Schmelz & Bachi 1973). Since then, immigration waves have been coming in more or less every ten years, with the last wave of Russian and Ethiopian Jews bringing in more than 400,000.

The Hebrew-speaking community in Israel has thus always constituted an extreme case of an immigrant society, with Modern Hebrew the only common means of communication: each new wave of immigrants brought its own language with them, with a consequent intensification of the "languages in contact" situation on the one hand, and a consolidation of the colloquial vernacular they all had in common, on the other. While the immigrant parents painstakingly study Hebrew, many of them never becoming proficient, their children invariably join the widening circle of native speakers.

This extreme variability in the linguistic competence of Hebrew-speaking children and adults is one of the factors responsible for the accelerated change that Hebrew has undergone in all facets of its structure. In all areas, forms and usages attested to occasionally in earlier stages of the language have become a widespread and productive part of the grammar of current Hebrew (Goshen-Gottstein 1951). This diachronically motivated multistratum nature of Contemporary Hebrew forms the background to three further sources of variation: the discrepancy between normative requirements and linguistic usage; the evolution of two sociolects, and the natural tension between the speech patterns of members of different age groups.

Normativism and Linguistic Reality

A primary source of variation in Contemporary Hebrew is its revival by literate adults—writers, journalists, scholars and teachers, committed to the reconstruction of Classical Hebrew as a living language. Thus the revival of Hebrew is closely linked to the revival of the Jewish people as a sovereign nation in Israel, and is hence heavily loaded emotionally.

The writers and journalists to whom the task of rejuvenating Hebrew fell directed their efforts towards shaping the new Hebrew according to declared principles of reliance on historical Hebrew writings, and enriching the vocabulary with new roots and items taken from other Semitic languages, mainly Arabic and Aramaic (Bar-Adon 1977, Blau 1981b, Kutscher 1982, Rabin 1972, Rosén 1956, 1966, 1977, Sivan 1976). Bitter controversies arose among the revivers of Hebrew concerning such issues as the introduction of foreign loan words, the type of pronunciation to be adopted,[2] and the general Semitic purity of the language (Avineri 1964, Fisherman 1985, Ornan 1977, Tené 1985).

The other major agents of rejuvenation in Modern Hebrew were the teachers who insisted on using Hebrew as the only language of instruction in institutions of learning at all levels throughout the country. By the onset of World War I they had won their fight against the use of Yiddish, French and German as primary languages of instruction (Kimhi 1928, Fellman 1973, Ornan 1985).

In 1890 Hebrew scholars, teachers and writers headed by E. Ben Yehuda established the Hebrew Language Council, which was replaced in 1953 by the Academy of the Hebrew Language, an official organ of the State of Israel (Akademia 1950, Léket Te'udot 1970, Medan 1969).

The revival of Hebrew was thus carried out by literate adults, in the main native speakers of Indo-European languages, proficient in Classical and Medieval Hebrew, and eager to direct the newly revived language into channels appropriate to what they viewed as its "true" spirit (Avineri 1976:11–13). However Hebrew first came to life again in the schools, where children and adolescents learned it from their teachers; and at home—since by the 1920s the language already had native speakers, those who were born in pre-state Israel or who had come to the country at an early age. And what these youngsters made of the language in the schools, streets, villages and neighborhoods was not always in accord with what the adult planners had envisioned (Bar-Adon 1963b).

Modern Hebrew took on a shape which in many cases deviated from the norms set by those who were the official agents of its revival. This was especially true in the domain of morphophonology, since speakers lacked a phonetic frame of reference for speech (Izre'el 1986, Rosén 1956:113, Tené 1985). For example, originally natural phonological classes such as the gutturals, the emphatics and the so-called *béged-kéfet* group of stop/spirant alternants lost phonetic motivation in Contemporary Hebrew usage (Ornan 1983, Rabin 1940, Schwarzwald 1976). In addition, several phonemes had coalesced together (e.g. the Biblical glide *w* merged with the spirant version of *b,* yielding in both cases *v*). As a result, the morphophonemics of Contemporary Hebrew emerged as a different entity from that represented in Biblical and post-Biblical writings.[3] Teachers, scholars and other official language planners perceived this as a very unfortunate state of affairs, and devoted considerable effort to preventing or reforming what they took to be a torrent of solecisms and incorrect usages. As early as the 1920s and the 1930s, there appeared articles vilifying the deplorable state of children's language, and suggesting ways of correcting it (Avrunin 1924, Barles 1937, Dolzhansky 1937). These writings dealt almost exclusively with morphophonemics and the lexicon, and rarely lingered on matters of syntax.

The discrepancy between normativistic demands and the natural development of Modern Hebrew has not lessened with the years. Special attention has been addressed to teaching "correct" language at school and through the radio and daily newspapers (Bendavid & Shay 1974, Dotan 1985, Rabin 1959). School grammars have the expressed aim of correcting students' language, to the point where formal instruction in Hebrew grammar is treated as a means of correcting deviations in the usage of students (see, for example, Léket 1972). Most of the corrective effort focused on morphophonology rather than syntax or vocabulary (Kremer 1980). Hebrew speakers' use of their language, and especially the precise formulation and inflection of words, is constantly criticized and corrected during their school years and beyond. But despite explicit teaching according to the official norms, the growing Israeli vernacular has persisted in following trends that violate those norms (Goshen-Gottstein & Eitan 1952, Manzur 1962, Rabin 1977, Rosén 1953).

One result of this friction is that native speakers suffer from what may be termed "a basic insecurity" with regard to their native tongue. Even highly-educated, literate speakers are not at all confident about what constitutes the "correct" form of very common, every day Hebrew words e.g. *mezik* or *mazik* 'harmful'; *moxek, móxek, maxak* or *máxak* 'eraser'.

In the last decade, developments in general linguistics and in sociolinguistics have led Hebrew scholars to re-examine their basic approach toward this problem, leading them to claim that normativistic criteria should be applied mainly to the written language, and that the language spoken by young people should be left alone. A speaker's language should be "appropriate" rather than normative, changing according to the pertinent register (Davis 1976b, 1978, 1981, Kaddari 1986, Nir 1974, 1977, Rabin 1981, Sar'el, Shlesinger & Ravid 1986). This, in a sense, represents a re-evaluation of the role and nature of language planning in contemporary Israel compared with earlier periods in the revival of spoken Hebrew. This approach has not gained ground among the die-hard establishment Hebrew teachers, although it has led in certain circles to a distinction between "normative" and "standard" usages (Donag-Kinrot 1978, Rabin 1986, Rosén 1953).

The friction between official demands for "purity" in the language, and the daily violations of these norms is a primary source of variation in Modern Hebrew and as such is directly relevant to this study.

The Rise of Two Sociolects in Modern Hebrew

Israel is too small and Modern Hebrew too young for local dialects to have formed, despite the (somewhat artificial) efforts in this direction at the beginning of the century (Bar-Adon 1975). However, social stratification in Israel has led to the emergence of rather distinct sociolects with characteristic morphophonological and syntactic properties. These sociolects can be ranged along a continuum, from the usage of literate upper- to middle-class speakers to that of largely uneducated, lower-class members of the speech community.

General research in sociolinguistics in the last two decades has focused on the characteristics of urban lower-class sociolects in the West. One extreme view is that uneducated speech is impoverished, less well organized and less correct than literate upper-class speech. This view stems in part from the work of the British sociolinguist Basil Bernstein, who originally characterized the speech patterns of lower-class and middle-class children as "restricted" and "elaborated" respectively. The "restricted" code is typical of spoken language, being context-bound and implicit, relying less on verbal explanation and being open only to a narrow interpretation that stems from the immediate context. By contrast, the "elaborated" code, identified with literate middle-class speakers, is explicit, context-free, oriented towards universalistic meanings, and requires an elaborated verbal explanation since non-verbal context-bound cues are missing. This code is necessarily identified with written or formal registers, and is suited to academic, school-type language which requires a wide range of structures and levels of usage (Bernstein 1970).

Bernstein's ideas have been taken by educational psychologists to mean that lower-class children are impoverished in their means of expression, and differ from middle-class children in the organization of their cognitive processes. Proponents of the "deficit theory," as it is termed, related the restricted language code to inefficient problem solving, a lack of need for logical evidence, and an episodic, chaotic grasp of reality. This is turn has a cumulative effect that results in a discrepancy in learning abilities between established and lower-class children (Bereiter & Engleman 1966, Blank 1970, Deutsch 1965, Hess & Shipman 1968, Jensen 1969). Bernstein himself warned in later writings that the restricted code should not "be misinterpreted as simply poor language" and that the sociological and linguistic picture is far more complex than indicated before (Bernstein 1970:37, 1975).

The issue of social class differences in the language of children has been addressed by linguists and psycholinguists who regard language development as part of the genetic inheritance of every individual member of the species, so that children are led to the eventual mastery of any input language (Berman 1984b, 1986c, Bickerton 1981, Maratsos 1982, Slobin 1982, 1985a). The role of input is taken to constrain children to the specific language, dialect or sociolect that they happen to be exposed to, but not to endow them with a linguistic system that is superior or inferior to that of other children.

In a series of studies, researchers have shown both middle- and lower-class children to possess well-ordered, highly structured systems that may *differ* in certain structural aspects (Furrow & Nelson 1984). They found no consistent difference in cognitive complexity and communicative success in the speech of children from a variety of environments, with different research designs and elicitation procedures and in different age groups. The language of working-class British children and of lower-class black children which served as the basis for many sociolinguistic analyses, is shown to constitute tightly structured sociolects with their own rules and constraints (Labov 1972b, Labov & Harris 1986). Likewise, Williamson (1986) found no evidence that the minds of socially disadvantaged Mexican children were in any way "impoverished." In fact, many of the language problems encountered in schools by speakers of Nonstandard sociolects derive from mother-tongue interference, a claim that assumes the existence of *two* well-structured language systems (Baratz 1970, Williams 1970a). By establishing non-threatening test and interview situations, researchers have demonstrated that lower-class speakers use both the restricted and elaborated codes successfully, and that literate usage is not always isomorphic with carrying over a message explicitly and economically. In short, uneducated sociolects are *different,* not *deficient* (Edwards 1975, Kay 1977, Stevenson et al 1978).

This controversy has had a powerful impact on Israeli thinking (see, for example, Cais 1981, 1983, Davis 1976a/b, 1981, Kemp 1984, Minkowitz 1969, Stahl 1977). Educational sociologists in Israel have noted certain syndromes in what has come to be termed the "deprived" population—in Hebrew *te'uney tipúax,*[4] literally "requiring cultivation." These syndromes include failure at school, lack of motivation for learning and problems in the ability to conceptualize and to think abstractly. The earlier literature of the 1960s and the 1970s associates such educational problems in lower-class children with their type of language usage, which is designated as "poor" or "deficient" (Eiger 1975, Frankenstein 1972, Minkowitz 1969). Much of the analysis in later literature relates to pragmatic measures such as style, fluency, vocabulary content, and the communicative success of children's language, rather than to its more purely structural properties. Those measures are taken as evidence for the conceptual or cognitive differences between middle-class and lower-class children.

A number of Israeli scholars have gone into detailed empirical research on the subject, but most of these studies unfortunately lack formal linguistic analysis.[5] Thus Stahl (1977) relies almost exclusively on *written* materials to establish the difference between the language of middle-class and deprived children as that of a literate vs. oral tradition, a distinction close to that of Bernstein's elaborated vs. restricted codes; Shimron (1983) tests the *communicative* competence of children from two socioeconomic backgrounds to find similar differences. Using much the same measures of analysis, Cais (1981) presents conflicting evidence: in her samples of the *spoken* language of 12-year-olds, boys of both socioeconomic backgrounds used both sociolinguistic codes as frequently. However, a study with more formal linguistic orientation, which studied the *spoken* language of children from two ethnic origins, finds significant statistical differences between the two populations (Vidislavsky 1984).

By contrast, Davis (1976b, 1978, 1981) makes the necessary distinction between general cognitive or conceptual properties on one hand, and structural or formal properties of language, on the other. He fails to find differences of the first type in samples of the *spoken* language of children from well-to-do and deprived backgrounds; what Davis does point out is that there are grammatical and stylistic differences between the two populations, noting especially the use of durative marking on the verb in lower-class children and their inability to switch to formal registers.

Recent studies have focused on a wider variety of linguistic domains in addition to the usual stylistic and syntactic measures using more precise statistical instruments. For example, both Kemp (1984) and Schwarzwald (1976, 1981) find that higher-class speakers perform better in tasks requiring academic language proficiency: Schwarzwald's study of morphophonological properties of familiar vs. rare verbs reveals statistically significant differences between established and disadvantaged subjects in the number of normative responses; Kemp finds that students from established backgrounds do significantly better in language tasks relating to language as a formal-problem space and consequently requiring context-reduced communication (Karmiloff-Smith 1979, Olson 1977).

In sum, the literature reviewed, both in Israel and abroad, points to the existence of two major sociolects of differing socioeconomic backgrounds. While researchers disagree on the cognitive and conceptual consequences of these differences, most of them agree that the uneducated sociolect is characterized by (i) different structural properties from the literate sociolect, and (ii) inability to access a wide variety of language registers that are typical of the type of language required at schools.

A second source of variation in Contemporary Hebrew is thus a social one. The gap between the Hebrew usage of literate speakers and normative requirements increases due to the existence of a Nonstandard sociolect even further away from normative demands (Davis 1981, Nir 1977, 1981). Below I consider an illustrative example.

The preposition governed by the verb *Siker* 'lie = tell a falsehood' in Hebrew is a sociolinguistic variable. The official grammar-book form is *Siker le-* 'lied to', while the dominant colloquial usage is *Siker et* 'lied Acc'. A third variant is the Nonstandard *Siker al* 'lied on', typical of uneducated speakers. Thus, not only does colloquial usage not conform to puristic demands, but it also drives a wedge between the official form and the third uneducated option.

Age Differences in the Speech Community

While the friction deriving from recent historical and social factors seems especially typical of Modern Hebrew, a third source of linguistic variation is a general feature of all living languages. This is the natural tension which arises between the language of different age groups in a given speech community, due to the related effects of *maturation* and *literacy*. The speech of preschoolers will differ from that of school-age children by virtue of the latter being able to read and write; and the onset of puberty, with accompanying cognitive maturation, sets the language of preadolescent children apart from that of adolescents and adults.

Literacy and cognitive maturation go hand-in-hand to cause fundamental changes in the linguistic organization in children aged 5–7. By the age of 5, children have mastered what Karmiloff-Smith (1979) terms an "utterance grammar," concentrating on sentence-internal features and constructing a number of separate "mini-theories" about the grammar of their native tongue. It is only after age 5 that young speakers organize these separate mini-systems into coherent systems of relevant options, and go on to the level of expanded discourse, acquiring procedures for operating on spans of cohesively related structures (Karmiloff-Smith 1983, 1986a, Scott 1988).

These changes in the child's linguistic apparatus are due to both cognitive and language-specific maturational factors. Cromer (1976) shows that younger children rely heavily on non-linguistic, communicative cues, while older ones pay attention to linguistic cues such as surface word-order and yet older ones reorganize linguistic knowledge in such a way as to incorporate underlying structure factors (Johnston 1985). Children first view language from "outside," employing general cognitive strategies to explore linguistic events, gradually focusing on the formal properties of language, first from the surface, finally perceiving its underpinnings.

In her pioneering study C. Chomsky (1969) demonstrates this move from general, superficial knowledge of syntax, relying on the juvenile Minimal Distance Principle, to an understanding of the different deep structures involved, between the ages of 5 and 9. In much the same way Israeli researchers have found that school-age children still progressively acquire syntactic structures between the ages of 6 and 12, and linguistic maturity is achieved only after age 12 (Berkowitz & Wigodski 1979, E. Ziv 1976). In this context, "linguistic maturity" means overall grammatical command and the ability to resist misleading cues in the process of decoding incoming information.

A similarly developmental treatment of the child's semantic system is found in Bowerman (1978, 1982a/b). Her analysis of the word-choice errors of 5-year-olds suggests that children construct a series of successive theories which are then integrated within a common, generally applicable framework around age 5. According to Bowerman, this development has little to do with communication, and more with the maturation of language as a complex object that children learn to regard as distinct from themselves, one more aspect of the environment to be explored. The gradual growth of this understanding is what makes the school-going child distinct from the younger preliterate speaker.

According to Berman (1985, 1986a), the major difference between younger and older children's language is the fact that preschool children's knowledge of grammar, though no longer context-dependent, is still too rigidly grammaticized. They also favor such juvenile strategies as Transparency (one-to-one mapping between formal markers and semantic content) and Formal Simplicity (minimal modifications of a basic stem form) (Clark & Berman 1984). By contrast, older children pay more attention to conventions of use, having a greater variety of structures and lexical items at their disposal. They are more sensitive to productivity of structures in colloquial usage on the one hand, and to school-type grammatical rules on the other; schoolchildren's knowledge of lexical exceptions and idiosyncratic information increases, making them aware of register variation, conventions of usage, and stylistic options in the language of their speech community.

Developmental factors of general cognition and of particular linguistic abilities thus account for many of the changes in the language system of the growing child (Menyuk 1977). Another important factor that characterizes this transition is the impact of literacy (Nelson 1988, Nippold 1988b). That literacy has wide-reaching implications for cognitive development has been shown in a variety of studies. Cook-Gumperz & Gumperz (1978), Torrance & Olson (1985) and Wells (1985) all stress the importance of literacy for successful functioning in school. Stevenson et al. (1978) point out how age and schooling interact to produce higher levels of performance on a variery of tasks. One such effect is children's growing ability to handle the decontextualized language of the classroom (Donaldson 1978).

By learning to read and write schoolchildren gain more, a new dimension to language knowledge, since the *written* language necessarily involves linguistic awareness, the "objectification" of the *spoken* language (Aronoff 1985). Acquisition of literate abilities evokes contemplative linguistic capacities: The child must consciously distinguish between speech units of various sizes—phonemes, syllables, words, sentences—that are represented by corresponding units in the writing system (Ehri 1985, Perera 1986,

Smith 1986). Metalinguistic knowledge thus necessarily accompanies the initial phases of the acquisition of literacy. Moreover, the more deliberate, planned nature of the written language, and the possibility of reviewing and rewriting enable literate speakers to differentiate their written from their spoken language, and to construct organizational principles and literate strategies that focus on abstract, non-context-bound information (Tannen 1985).

Literate speakers thus acquire two important features of written discourse: *integration*—the tight organization of devices that result from deliberate planning of discourse, and *decontextualization*—the spatiotemporal divorce of sender and receiver of communication (Kalmar 1985, Givón 1979b, Ochs 1979). This in turn forces the speaker/writer to select carefully from the many options now available, including a differentiated vocabulary (in English, for example, more lexical items of Latinate origin), a variety of conjunctions for integrating ideas into complex clauses, and different registers and genres of written texts, which necessarily have an effect on the spoken usage (Corson 1983, Olson 1985).

Literacy has an even greater significance for speakers of Hebrew. Reading non-vocalized texts enhances the reader's awareness of a major typological property of Hebrew—the primacy of consonants. Most nouns and adjectives, and all verbs in Hebrew consist of a consonantal root which serves as the semantic and formal core of the word, and which combines with a relatively limited set of morphological patterns termed *binyanim* (verb patterns) and *mishkalim* (noun and adjective patterns). These provide vocalization and (in many cases) additional affixes, and they expand the meaning of the core root, thus serving as a primary lexical word-formation device (Berman 1987c, Gesenius 1910, Ravid 1990). The primary weight of consonants in the structure of a Hebrew word is augmented when learning to read, since Hebrew writing is generally consonantal, with vowels indicated by diacritics, termed *nikud,* literally "pointing." Except for poetry, texts for very young readers and for second language learners, texts are typically unvocalized, and the reader is expected to reconstruct the full word according to context and rules of grammar, something which all proficient readers of Hebrew do easily and automatically (Allon 1984). For example, the root *q-d-m* 'to precede' occurs in a three-letter sequence spelled קדם, in which each letter stands for a root radical. This consonantal core may be associated with any of the following vowel patterns:[6] *kédem* 'east'; *kódem* 'before'; *kodem* 'previous'; *kadam* 'preceded'; *kidem* 'promoted'; *kudam* 'was promoted'.[7]

In addition to the largely predictable nature of Hebrew vowel patterns, Hebrew writing reflects another major feature of the language: the highly bound nature of Hebrew morphology. Many grammatical formatives occur as inflectional affixes on words, represented in the writing system as letters that attach to the beginning or ends of words (Blau 1981c). A Hebrew reader may thus encounter a string of the form וכשבזרועותינו *uxSebizro'otéynu* 'and-when-in-our-arms' in a text, and not think twice about it. Becoming literate in Hebrew necessarily means becoming metalinguistically aware of the highly bound nature of Hebrew morphology, and especially of the consonantal skeleton of Hebrew words, including which consonants are more likely to be affixal or root radicals.

Literacy, then, is a powerful tool at the disposal of the proficient Hebrew reader: deep-rooted typological properties of the language which are intuitively recognized by the preschooler are rendered more accessible by the writing system (Bentur 1978, and also see Badri 1983, Omar 1973 on Arabic, another Semitic language). Moreover, learning to read and write resolves opacities inherent in Modern Hebrew phonology. Knowledge of spelling motivates the otherwise unexplained behavior of what seems to be the same phoneme in different environments, since Hebrew orthography preserves most of the distinctions that have been neutralized or lost in Contemporary Hebrew (Berman 1981a, 1981b, Sandbank 1992). Thus a first grader was able to tell me that the final letter of the word *savéa* 'full, satiated' was ע , standing for the voiced pharyngeal fricative which does not exist in his accent. The child, in effect, was able to reconstruct this abstract phoneme by comparing his knowledge of phonology with the orthographic system, since ע entails a final insertion of *a* (compare *savéa* 'satiated' to, say, *ra'ev* 'hungry').

The school-going child is clearly different from a preschooler both cognitively and linguistically: some differences are due not only to general cognitive and linguistic maturation, but also to the effects of literacy. An analogous gap exists between the prepuberty child and the adolescent. Puberty is the precursor of formal operational thinking: cognitively, the adolescent differs from the younger child in the development of such abilities as formal logic, scientific reasoning, and hypothetical thinking (Flavell 1985, Menyuk 1977, Piaget 1926).

At the same time, the onset of puberty ends the "critical" period for language acquisition (Goldin-Meadow 1982, Lieberman 1984). Research has shown that a good deal of language development is still underway at the end of elementary school, during middle childhood and beyond, up to adolescence (C. Chomsky 1969, Legum, Kim & Rosenbaum 1978, Palermo & Molfese 1972). It is only by the teenage years that the speaker attains linguistic maturity, with full mastery of the native tongue reached at the endstate phase of language development (Nippold 1988b). For instance, innovative usage of less common and familiar noun compounds is found in Hebrew only from school age and onwards; full command of complex syntactic processes such as pronominalization and relative clause formation is not reached before age 12; mastery of gerunds is achieved only beyond age 12; and it is only adults who attain a full grasp of narrative discourse (Berkowitz & Wigodsky 1979, Berman 1987c, 1988, Mayrose 1988, E. Ziv 1976).

The language of adolescents and young adults is characterized by a peculiar dichotomy: constant and prolonged exposure to linguistic norms at school is countered by the thrust to maximal use of socially stigmatized forms and slang terms. Starting from second grade, Israeli schoolgoers are taught *dikduk*—literally, "being precise,"—formal instruction in grammar (which includes topics in Hebrew morphology, such as pattern, root and inflections, and traditional syntax and parsing). In the higher grades students are also taught diachronic grammar. Finally, the school-leaving examination in Hebrew grammar requires students to reconstruct historical roots that often have little surface realization in Contemporary Hebrew (Tal 1980). For example, they are taught formal methods for detecting that the historical root underlying *hegen* 'defended' is *g-n-n*. As a result, the intuitive knowledge that Hebrew speakers have of formal properties of their language is extended and supplemented in school. These grammar lessons have a further purpose: drilling students in puristic requirements, so that they should be able to choose correct forms, following prescribed rules that they have learned by rote (Berman 1981b, Schwarzwald 1978, 1981). As a result, an educated speaker is often able to select a "correct" form when asked to, though he/she may not use it in everyday speech. By contrast, an uneducated speaker may not be aware of the required form at any level of usage.

Mature literate speakers also differ from the preadolescent in having a wide array of formal language styles and registers at their disposal, as a result of having been exposed to written texts from all periods of Hebrew. Students first learn to read and write in Modern Hebrew, but from second grade onwards they have almost daily classes in reading original Biblical texts with the aid of a glossary. In addition, school readers at all levels contain texts in all styles and varieties of Hebrew, including Mishnaic and Medieval. Young readers will early on encounter works written in Biblical or Mishnaic styles, so that they become familiar not only with varieties of Contemporary Hebrew, but also with styles and genres from previous periods which they can understand and even produce when required (Berman 1982b). This results in the context-reduced, academic type of language proficiency required at school that Kemp (1984) found 75% of her literate subjects to possess. This promotes their proficiency at coining blends, clipped forms and acronyms, which requires metalinguistic awareness of the written mode, and is prevalent from teenage years only (Ravid 1990).

The same youngsters are concurrently open to peer-group influence at its peak, at an age when speech too becomes a symbol of in-group membership (Romaine 1984). Thus, though teenagers may be aware of conventions of "good" or "correct" usage, they are also the ones who typically initiate new slang terms and who deliberately violate those formalities. For example, the Modern Hebrew tendency to make mass nouns countable is especially apparent in young military (18–22) circles, e.g. *neSakim* for grammar-book *néSek* 'weaponry', *rexavim* for *réxev* 'pool of cars'.

In sum, a third source of variation in Contemporary Hebrew is the gap between age-graded strata of native speakers. While the literate school-going child has access to linguistic resources nor available to the preschooler, there is a similar discrepancy between linguistically and cognitively mature adolescents and younger prepuberty children, on the one hand, and those same innovating, norm-violating adolescents vs. more conservative adults, on the other (Avineri 1946).

Three contemporary sources of variation thus obtain in Modern Hebrew: normative demands that conflict with linguistic reality, different sociolects deriving from social and educational factors, and the natural divergence engendered by chronological age. These three sets of factors underlie a range of variables of spoken Hebrew, discussed in 1.2 below.

1.2. LANGUAGE VARIATION AND MODERN HEBREW

Classification of Varieties of Spoken Hebrew Usage

The terms applied to different varieties of Hebrew usage are highly controversial, used with different denotations and connotations by people of different orientations and convictions (Givón 1976, Kaddari 1983, Rosén 1956). The following characterize classes of speech usage in current Israeli Hebrew:

Hebrew Language Establishment (Henceforth HLE)—Individuals and organizations that publicly prescribe forms they consider appropriate in usage, and proscribe others. The HLE includes the Hebrew Language Academy (Akademia 1950), organizations such as *kéla* (The Hebrew Language Foundation), and individual teachers and language consultants in official institutes, such as Israeli Television.

Norm—Pattern, type, representative of a group when judging other examples. This is a statistical term used in the present study when based on quantitative findings of this study. However, when associated with "Normative," it has the meaning of "form prescribed by the HLE."

Normative—Refers in this work to the usage prescribed or approved by the HLE.

Standard—Description of Hebrew usage typical of educated adult native speakers in Israel.

Nonstandard—Uneducated speech; usage considered unacceptable by educated adult native speakers of Hebrew, typical of uneducated persons.

In using these terms in the study, the discussion is confined to *spoken* Hebrew alone, thus ruling out not only fiction and expository prose, but newspaper and textbook usage of the kind characterized as *ivrit beynonit* 'Middle Hebrew' (Ben Asher 1973, Sivan 1976, Rabin 1958), and the subject of relatively wide study (e.g. Landau 1980, Sar'el 1984, Shlesinger 1985).

Deviant Phenomena in Spoken Hebrew Usage

The different sources of variation in Modern Hebrew have given rise to three main types of morphophonemic phenomena which constitute "deviations" from normative requirements: *Transient Phenomena, Nonstandard Deviations* and *Language Change*. Below each of these types of "errors" is characterized:

Transient Phenomena

These are developmental errors, universally judged as unacceptable by adult native speakers, regardless of their socio-economic background. Such errors are found *only* in the speech of young children, and they disappear fairly early and completely. Bar Adon terms these deviations "primary or initial creations" or "temporal creations" (1971:305). Berman (1983, 1984a) places these errors in the early period of "interim schemata," where childish strategies are adopted in order to deal with opaque sets of formal alternations. Kaplan (1983) encountered many such forms in her study of development of morphological categories in children 2–3;6. Levy (1980) describes such occurrences in the development of number and gender in her son, Arnon. However, no single study presents a thoroughgoing analysis of these different types of childish errors.

Examples of Transient occurrences discussed in this study are the following:

   (i) Use of the *miCaCeC* pattern to denote present tense where end-state grammar makes no distinction between present and past tense forms, e.g. *mikanes* for standard *nixnas* 'enters', *mariv* for standard *rav* 'fights'.

   (ii) Collapsing roots ending in historical glottal stop and *-y* in past tense, so that *y*-final roots behave like ?-final roots, e.g. *kanáti* for standard *kaníti* '(I) bought', root *q-n-y* (compare *karáti* '(I) read', root *q-r-?*).

   (iii) Formation of non-standard pronominal inflections on prepositions, e.g. *miménax* for standard *mimex* 'from-you,Fm' (compare *miméni* 'from-me'), or *alo* for standard *alav* 'on- him' (compare *Selo* 'his').

   (iv) Avoiding changes in the inflected stem, e.g. *magévet/magévetim* for standard *magavot* 'towels'.

   (v) Adding a third root radical where only two occur on the surface, as in *soxétet* for standard *soxa* '(she) swims', root *s-H-y* (compare *soxévet* '(she) drags', root *s-H-b*).

Nonstandard Deviations

These are deviations from the standard variety of spoken Hebrew, as defined in the classification above. These deviations are typical both of children from all socio-economic backgrounds as well as of uneducated speakers at all ages. In both these groups, Nonstandard errors occur with great frequency. The bulk of such deviations eventually disappear from the speech of middle-class children, but typically persist in the uneducated sociolect. Occasionally some of these forms occur in middle-class usage, but this tends to be sporadic and restricted to a limited number of categories and lexical items. Deviations of this type show up among the morphological errors discussed in Donag-Kinrot (1978), although no classification is offered there. I assume that the deviant forms referred to in Davis (1976a/b, 1978, 1981), Nir (1977, 1981) and Rabin (1981) are of the Nonstandard type, though these authors fail to specify the kind of distinctions I have found relevant.

Examples of Nonstandard deviations in this study are the following:

(i) Collapsing *?*-final roots with *y*-final roots, e.g. *giléti* for standard *giliti* '(I) discovered', root *g-l-y* (compare *miléti* '(I) filled up', root *m-l-?*); *kafuy* for standard *kafu* 'frozen', root *q-p-?* (compare *afuy* 'baked', root *?-p-y*).

(ii) Standardizing roots ending in historical *H* (orthographic *Het* with roots ending in final *x* (orthographic *kaf*), e.g. *mucláxet* for standard *mucláxat* 'successful,Fm', root *s-l-H* (compare *musméxet* 'qualified,Fm', root *s-m-k*).

(iii) Subjecting exceptions to the general rule, e.g. *yoSénet* for standard *yeSena* '(she) is sleeping' (compare *yoSévet* '(she) is sitting').

(iv) Using the 3rd person future tense prefix *y-* for 1st person singular forms, e.g. *ani yiSmor* for standard *ani eSmor* 'I will-guard'.

(v) Adopting a single stop or spirant of the *bkp* class instead of alternating them, e.g. *viSálta* for standard *biSálta* '(you) cooked'.

Language Change Phenomena

These can be regarded as "deviations" only from the Normative point of view of the Hebrew Language Establishment; from the point of view of the native speaker, they are not deviations at all. These pheneomena occur across the board in the usage of all members of the speech community, children and adults alike, of all socio-economic backgrounds, except perhaps for the most self-consciously normativistic persons, members of the Language Establishment. Such "errors" point in the direction of a new standard that is arising in Modern Hebrew, especially in certain morphological categories which will be shown to constitute current "areas of instability."

The establishment of new standards in Contemporary Hebrew is discussed in Rosén (1952, 1953, 1956). Donag-Kinrot (1975, 1978) makes a distinction between *Norm* and *Standard*: A form is considered standard if used by at least 85% of the subjects. Several Normative forms were thus found to be Nonstandard! Schwarzwald (1981) points out that even university students deviate from the HLE prescriptions. Levy (1982) discusses the gradual loss of the feminine plural inflection as the standard grammatical marker of both genders (See also Bolozky 1982, Schwarzwald 1979, 1982a).

Examples of Language Change usage fall into two classes which roughly correspond to what Bar-Adon (1971) terms "essential or permanent creations" and "secondary creations." The first class includes forms that are already so well established that students learn that they are "incorrect" only when they reach formal grammar instruction in high school. These include, for example:

(i) Standardizing the stress pattern in 2nd person plural, past tense verbs to the penultimate stress pattern of the rest of that paradigm, which leads to non-reduction of the *a* in the first syllable in the *Pa'al* pattern, e.g. *baxártem* for Normative *bexartem* '(you,Pl.) chose' (compare *baxárnu* '(we) chose').

(ii) The standardization of past and present tense forms of *CaCeC* verbs, e.g. *yaSen/yaSan* 'sleeps/slept' respectively, where HLE requirements call for the same form *yaSen* in both tenses.

(iii) Failure to perform changes in bound forms of certain inflected nouns, especially in the *CiCCa* pattern, e.g. *miSxot* for Normative *meSaxot* 'salves' (singular *miSxa*).

Preliminary testing showed such changes to be indeed fully established, hence justifying Bar-Adon's classification of "permanence."[8] Accordingly, these occurrences were excluded from this discussion.

The second type of Language Change phenomena, Bar-Adon's "secondary creations," are of great interest from the point of view of the present study: the forms classified under this type of "deviations" are still regarded as errors by normativists, but I intend to show that many of them have in fact become the new Standard. Among them we find the following:

(i) Collapsing *y*-final and *?*-final roots—just the opposite of what is done in Nonstandard, e.g. *ripa* for Normative *ripe* 'cured', root *r-p-?* (compare *nisa* 'tried', root *n-s-y*).

(ii) Hypercorrecting *kaf*-final roots as though they were *Het*-final roots, again, the opposite of what is done in Nonstandard, e.g. *doráxat* for Normative *doréxet* '(she) steps', root *d-r-k* (compare *Soláxat* '(she) sends', root *S-l-H*).

(iii) Merging *n*-initial and glide-medial present-tense *Hif'il* verbs, e.g. *mepil* for Normative *mapil* 'is-dropping', root *n-p-l* (compare *merim* 'is-raising', root *r-w-m*).

(iv) Lack of agreement between subject and verb in non-SVO word order, e.g. *nigmar ha-hafsaka* 'ended,Masc the-break,Fm' for Normative *nigmera ha-hafsaka* 'ended,Fm the-break,Fm' (Berman 1980a, Ziv 1982).

The motivation and discussion of the nature and differences between these three kinds of departure from HLE stipulations constitute the central focus of this study.

Perspectives on Language Variation

Below I review the different linguistic aspects that serve as the background to this work and are relevant to the discussion of the phenomena presented above.

Spoken Hebrew

This study focuses on *spoken* rather than *written* Hebrew usage. Few studies are available on spoken Hebrew, and virtually none have been undertaken on a large scale: Hebrew scholars admit that "spoken Hebrew with its varieties has not been properly studied" (Ben-Hayyim 1985:22). This shortcoming stems from the attitude of the HLE towards the study of Modern Hebrew in general, and that of its spoken register in particular. Both Modern Hebrew itself and its scientific analysis came under attack in pre-state Israel and in the first decades of its existence (Rosén 1956). Scholars justified this reluctance to research Modern Hebrew in saying that it had not yet crystallized into its final form. For example, Rosén claims scholars were afraid to find out to what extent Modern Hebrew differed from its ancient ancestors (1956:122, and also see Wexler 1990:36-57 on the reluctance of the Hebrew revivalists to admit how much of Modern Hebrew is non-Semitic).

It was not until non-Israeli linguists had introduced the idea of analyzing Contemporary Hebrew that studies began to appear in Israel, advocating a synchronic-structural analysis of spoken Hebrew (Ben-Hayyim 1953, Blanc 1954, Goshen-Gottstein 1951, Harris 1952, Weiman 1950, and see also Morag 1959). The first major study of Contemporary (though not spoken) Hebrew as an autonomous system was Rosén's book (1956). This aroused a violent controversy: the very idea of applying general linguistic methods to the study of Modern Hebrew disjoined from its ancient sources was abhorrent to many Hebraists (Kutscher 1956, Zemach 1956), although there were scholars whose views concurred with those of Rosén (Bar-Adon 1963a/b, 1967, Goshen-Gottstein 1956).

The study of Modern Hebrew gathered momentum in the 1960s with legitimacy of such investigation now firmly established. Research focused on the phonetics and morphophonemics[9] of Contemporary Hebrew. Rather less was done on its syntax and semantics.[10] Almost none of these studies were based on spoken Hebrew data: most of them deal with what Rabin (1958) terms *Middle Hebrew*—the semi-formal usage typical of books, textbooks, newspapers and letters. Other, more recent studies have focused on sociolinguistic and psycholinguistic analysis, especially since the late 1970s. These were first concerned with a description of Hebrew slang (Ben Yehuda & Ben Amotz 1973, Berlowitch 1964, Sappan 1963, 1964, 1969, Shalev 1974). Later works deal with socio-cultural aspects of spoken and written Hebrew (Ben Tolila 1984, Cais 1981, Schwarzwald 1981, Stahl 1977, Vidislavsky 1984). A considerable part of our knowledge of spoken Hebrew, especially spoken child language, comes from the works of Berman (e.g. 1978a, 1980a, 1980b, 1981a, 1987c, 1989, 1990a/b, 1992, 1993, Berman & Ravid 1986, Berman & Sagi 1981, Berman & Clark 1989, Clark & Berman 1984, 1987, Dromi & Berman 1986). Yet to date, there has not been any large-scale, multi-generational analysis of the spoken usage of both educated and uneducated monolingual speakers of Modern Hebrew, such as this study provides.

Principles and Strategies in Language Acquisition and Language Processing

Another thrust of this study is psycholinguistic in nature. Both the child acquiring a language, and the adult facing opaque language input, must rely on broad principles that guide the speaker in the choice of strategies for language learning and processing (Anderson 1983, Anderson, Kline & Lewis 1977, Cromer 1976, Flores D'Arcais 1975, Fromkin 1980, Ravid & Shlesinger 1987a). One set of strategies is developmental in nature (MacWhinney 1985, Nelson 1973). Deriving from a set of procedures for the construction of language which have been termed *Predispositions* or *Operating Principles* (hence OPs), they guide the learner in the perception, storage, analysis and retrieval of linguistic information (Clark 1980, 1981, Clark & Berman 1984, Clark & Clark 1979, MacWhinney 1975, 1978, 1985, Slobin 1973, 1982). Slobin (1985a) has termed the collection of these acquisitional principles *The Language-Making Capacity*—the genetic program that constructs the child's inner representation of language at its initial phases.

In the course of acquisition, OPs interact with incoming language input and with growing cognitive, pragmatic and social knowledge, as well as with each other. The child is predisposed to seek regularities and rule-bound behavior in the specific linguistic input by leaning on these universal OPs, and the nature of this interaction between OPs and input is discussed in this study. For example, the notion of "regularity" is not clear at all: on the one hand, children overregularize towards the major paradigm, but on the other hand they may overextend a minor rule. Consider a child, who at the age of 3;4 produced the erroneous form *moréxet* for adult *moráxat* 'is-spreading, Fm', root *m-r-H* (compare *doréxet* 'is-stepping, Fm', root *d-r-k*). The child evidently regularized from the marked low *H* that requires a low *a* to the unmarked *x* taking the regular middle *e*. At the age of 4;0, the same child produced the form *sbonim* '(bars of) soap' for adult *sabonim*. He performed *a*-deletion in an unstressed syllable, which has been shown to be less frequent in children (Berman 1981c, Ravid & Shlesinger 1987a).

It is by no means clear how far these principles are due to general cognitive abilities rather than being geared specifically to the acquisition of language: research has shown that learning strategies become more structurally oriented with the rise in age, focusing on linguistic rather than pragmatic cues as the child grows older (Berman 1986c, Karmiloff-Smith

1986b). Thus for example a child of 4;3 interpreted the sentence *ha-arye nical biydey ha-axbar* 'the-lion was saved by the-mouse' as 'the lion saved the mouse'. Evidently, she took her cue from the state of affairs in the world and the basic SVO word order, rather than from linguistic elements such as the passive *Nif'al* pattern and the preposition *biydey* 'by'. By contrast, at the age of 7;5 a child produced the erroneous form *mizronot* for *mizronim* 'mattresses'.[11] He was evidently overgeneralizing the minor rule that attaches the feminine suffix *-ot* to masculine nouns ending in *-on*, e.g. *vilon-ot* 'curtain-s', *efron-ot* 'pencil-s'. This was a late mistake, contrasted with an earlier overregularization made by the same child (3;9) of an *-on* noun to the general masculine *-im* form: *xalonim* for adult *xalonot* 'windows'.

Apart from *learning* strategies, this study analyzes strategies for *processing* and *monitoring* language by adults as endstate speakers (Anderson, Kline & Lewis 1977, Bybee & Slobin 1982, Cutler & Fay 1982, Fay & Cutler 1977, Fromkin 1980, Hurford 1981). Strategies for language acquisition interact with ontogenetic language development over time, accounting for error-free and for late acquisition in terms of successive reorganization of specific linguistic subsystems (Berman 1986c, Bowerman 1981, 1982b, Karmiloff-Smith 1986a, Platt & MacWhinney 1983). However, adults fall back on similar strategies because of opacity and ambiguity of data encountered in ongoing discourse. In many cases, the difference is the *degree* of reliance on similar strategies: while children use them across the board, adults may resort to such use only in certain instances.

Take, for example, the process of *backformation* (Ravid 1990, to appear), in which a string is reanalyzed into a stem and an affix. Researchers and caregivers note many examples of backformation in preschool and even school-age children, e.g. *xanuya* for adult *xanut* 'store' from plural *xanuyot* (2;4), and *rak* for adult *rax* 'soft' from plural *rakim* (6;11). The same strategy preserving the given base form (Clark 1980) has been observed in adults, e.g. *gic* for Normative *gec* 'spark' from plural *gicim*. Of course adults do not backform everywhere; this strategy, like others, is adopted for certain morphological classes and is subject to competition with other strategies.

Language Variation and Language Change

A third central theme taken up in this study has to do with the causes, nature and promulgation of language change. A living language is an ever-changing organism, whose sub-systems are in a constant process of change (Bloomfield 1933, Jespersen 1922, Sapir 1921). The Saussurean tradition established the analysis of language structures as either *synchronic,* and thus relating only to a particular state of the language at some point in time, or *diachronic,* treating its development through time (de Saussure 1955). From this point of view, Modern Israeli Hebrew is far too young to allow the time-depth perspective necessary for an investigation of changes that are taking place in it. And the generative model of an idealized homogeneous community of speakers, each of whom knows the language perfectly, focuses interest on abstract linguistic competence, leaving no room for the study of performance issues such as variation and error (Chomsky 1965). The Chomskyan model seeks to account for the human language faculty as a biological phenomenon, properly studied only indirectly, by developing abstract systems of rules (Chomsky 1980). The language behavior of actual people is considered completely inappropriate as a source of data for theory construction, since "no individual speaks a well-defined language. . . . In fact, each individual employs a number of linguistic systems in speaking. How can one describe such an amalgam?" (Chomsky 1979:54).

I adopt a different position here, one that runs counter to both the synchronic/diachronic dichotomy and to the homogeneous speech community hypothesis. I espouse the approach that claims that linguistic change has its source in synchronic variation in the speech community. According to this, variation is the normal situation of a speech community, which displays inherent heterogeneity in the wide range of variants, styles, registers, dialects, idiolects, sociolects and languages used by its members (Weinreich, Labov & Herzog 1968). This variation reflects ongoing processes of linguistic change constantly being initiated, promulgated and completed in the various sociological groups that make up the speech community. It is thus impossible to divorce synchronic diversity from diachronic processes of language change, since one is a reflection of the other.

The concept of inherent variation as a linguistic universal has been taken up by researchers from fields of study as diverse as historical linguistics, sociolinguistics, the study of pidgins and creoles, and developmental psycholinguistics. These together have laid the foundations for the contemporary study of language change. Bailey (1973) suggests that the study of patterned synchronic variation must take into consideration the function of time, while a native speaker's grammatical knowledge must also incorporate the ability to vary the use of grammar when necessary. In fact, Bailey recommends that the omnipresence of ongoing change be built into linguistic description. Blount & Sanches (1977) likewise regard language as inherently variable. They claim that variation exists at all levels of language, and is related to sociocultural background, so that language change operates within socially significant dimensions such as stratification and group membership. Milroy (1992) suggests that "it is the 'normal' state of language to exhibit structured variation" (p.62). The nature of these social variables and their relation to mechanisms of linguistic change were investigated by Labov in a series of works (e.g. 1966, 1969, 1970, 1971, 1972a/b, 1980, 1981, 1982). Labov regards a heterogeneous language system as the natural state of affairs. A homogeneous system would be dysfunctional due to the variety of factors involved in any one speech community, such as sex, age, class, education and ethnic group; if language is to function at all efficiently, it must be inherently variable. Labov claims that the factors governing linguistic diversity are interpretable as uniformity at a higher, more abstract level, since they form a body of processes and relations that govern historical derivation. Thus, a search for changes that fail to occur in language corresponds to the study of language universals in synchronic analysis. In fact, what appears to be change along the diachronic axis is manifested as variation in synchronic analysis (Wang 1969).

The study of Modern Hebrew provides a unique instance for determining the factors that govern language change, since the multiple sources of its variation give rise to accelerated change along the time axis. Moreover, children, adolescents and adults of different socio-economic backgrounds all face the morphophonological system of Contemporary Hebrew, responding to the same problematic area with the distinct solutions which stem from their respective linguistic capacities. One of my aims here is to investigate the contribution of these sources of variation to the three types of deviations discussed above, and especially to relate language change to psycholinguistic variables along the lines suggested in Slobin (1977, 1985c). According to Slobin, prototypical event categories represent semantic "high points" which are salient to children and which languages tend to grammaticize in their history. These would be found to operate in both child language and language diachrony. In much the same way, OPs that seek clarity of expression on the one hand and condensation of information of the other are likely to be called into play in child language, in the spoken usage of adults, and at different points of a language's history, resulting in parallel structures in childhood and diachrony (Baron 1977, Hooper 1979, King 1969, Slobin 1985c, Schwarzwald 1980c).

My concern is with the two foci where language change is initiated and promoted: the *language system* itself—underlying principles and inherent properties of the language structure that lead to change, and the *speaker* or the *speech community*—nonlinguistic factors such as age, education and socioeconomic background which govern the implementation of change (Milroy 1992).

Theorists of language change perceive two opposing trends within languages: one is a tendency towards *simplification* of complex paradigms and idiosyncratic exceptions by leveling off distinctions to minimize irregularity on the surface (so meeting Slobin's 1977 charges of "being clear" and "being processible"). This natural tendency towards semantic *transparency* is regarded by many as a general principle governing the direction of change (Bach & Harms 1972, Kiparsky 1982, Kuno 1974, Labov 1982, Lightfoot 1979, 1981, 1982, Manczak 1980, Thomason 1976). But language change does not involve only simplification. An opposing force erodes the tendency to simplify by demanding that language be maximally expressive, with the result of increasing the surface density of the message and the degree of complexity of grammatical nuances (Slobin 1977). This represents a tendency towards *markedness* and *elaboration* or *polarization*, introducing innovations and greater complexity by rule addition rather than by rule simplification, and following another natural tendency to-wards *saliency,* the property of being different from one's environment (Andersen 1973, Labov 1981, 1982, Naro & Lemle 1976). Moreover, in many cases the simplification of one subsystem in the grammar leads to elaboration and redundancy in another (Kiparsky 1982, Lightfoot 1982). Most current research agrees that the two opposing tendencies towards *simplification* and *elaboration* naturally co-exist in language, both exerting their influence on the system so that it is always in flux (Bailey 1973, Baron 1977, Halle 1962, Phillips 1984, Closs 1965, Wang 1969).

These two opposing trends in language change are related to extra-linguistic factors such as *age* and *socioeconomic status* (henceforth SES). Children as well as adults of all educational backgrounds have been shown to participate in the initiation and propagation of language change. The role of children in language change has been traditionally regarded as that of *simplification* (Bolinger 1975, Halle 1962, Hooper 1979, Kiparsky 1982:65, 204, Jespersen 1949, Tanz 1974): As a result of imperfect learn-ing, natural tendencies towards the simplest grammar possible, or a set of innate predispositions that lead the child to certain choices, children are assumed to initiate changes at "points of break" in the language structure. However, these changes are always minor, so they do not disrupt the flow of information or linguistic continuity between the two generations. Moreover, these changes do not violate universal laws governing the struc-ture and function of language. Rather, children, seeking maximal *regularity* and *transparency* in linguistic structures, make errors. Some of these devia-tions persist and result in general language change, e.g. the regularization of the past tense verb *dive* to *dived* instead of irregular *dove* in English (Bynon 1977). One goal of this work is to examine the nature of those childish errors that disappear early in childhood and do not lead to varia-tion in endstate language (classified as *transient* above) as compared with those that also occur in the usage of adults and hence lead to general language change.

Age is not the only factor in initiating and implementing language change. Change might also be rooted in the language system of adults. Studies reveal that in many cases uneducated lower-class adult speakers treat opaque structures in much the same way as do children, in the at-tempt to establish a more transparent relationship between surface and underlying structure (Baron 1977, Berman 1981b, Gal 1978, Hale 1973, Naro & Lemle 1976, Poplack 1980, Schwarzwald 1978, 1981). Other studies point out that change may start among higher-class speakers, who seek to add rules and thus cause elaboration in the linguistic system (Hooper 1976, Kroch & Small 1978, Labov 1972a, 1982). I wish to ascertain which type of change is more likely to be caused by literate adults or by uneducated speakers, respectively, and whether there is any affinity between deviant phenomena on the part of children and those produced by uneducated adults.

A field of study of importance here is that of *pidgins* and *creoles,* as providing insight into the emergence of new languages. The process of creolization is relevant to study of language change for several reasons. First, in many cases a creole may undergo a massive structural change, so that variation is to a great degree an inherent part of its linguistic system (Bickerton 1981, Bickerton & Givón 1976, Decamp 1971, Labov 1971, Naro 1978). Out of such great variation there emerges a *koiné*, a standard that entails some stabilization and an awareness of standard. As such, creoles are a natural laboratory for the study of variation, emerging norms, and language change. Then, too, the paucity of input to the creole due to its pidgin origins forces the creole-makers, children and adults, to come up with solutions for linguistic puzzles that follow innate predispositions and are not checked by existing solutions in the language. This makes it possible to observe closely what strategies speakers employ and whether social considerations such as age, education, socio-economic status, and prestige entail the use of different strategies in the evolution of creoles (Bickerton 1981, Householder 1983, Slobin 1977).

Contemporary Hebrew certainly did not derive from a pidgin, but it did establish itself as a spoken language within as little as two generations in a situation where no previous spoken model was in existence. In the process, it underwent considerable structural change, especially in syntax, with a major relexification of its vocabulary. Moreover, the adults who first spoke and taught Hebrew were all native speakers of other languages, and this certainly had an effect on Modern Hebrew. Finally, it was indeed the task of children, a first generation of native speakers, to make Hebrew a living natural tongue, again quite similar to a creole situation. From this point of view, Contemporary Hebrew presents a unique opportunity to study "an emergent language" (Izre'el 1986).

2

The Study

2.1. THE EXPERIMENT

Research Instruments

To test the hypotheses underlying this study, an experimental design was applied in the form of a structured test (see Appendix A) specifically devised for this purpose. The decision to construct a test aimed at production rather than comprehension of linguistic forms was dictated by the nature of the materials to be investigated—active knowledge of rules of inflectional morphology, e.g. Normative/Standard *nikíti* vs. Nonstandard *nikéti* '(I) cleaned'. The input test items directed respondents towards a limited range of possible output forms; the final choice depended on an array of structural, developmental, sociolinguistic and psycholinguistic factors that constitute the subject matter of this study.

However, a test situation is bound to be artificial and induced, even under the most favorable circumstances. And it lacks the extralinguistic and discourse clues normally available in language use providing children with contextual aids to comprehension and scaffolding their production in natural language usage (R. Clark 1977). As Romaine puts it: A test situation constitutes "a special type of ecological context, (while) findings which emerge from experimental settings have no privileged status as context-free or objective" (Romaine 1984:15).

In view of these reservations, the non-contextualized data-elicitation procedures of the structured test were supplemented with data derived from other sources as follows:

27

1. *Longitudinal records* of my two children: Sivan (female), from 0;7 to 9;0 years of age; and Assaf (male), from 0;9 to 8;0 years of age. Two types of data collection were used: (i) *Written diaries* were kept during their infancy, up to the ages of 2;6 and 1;5 respectively, and written records once or twice a month later on; and (ii) starting from their second year, *audio tape recordings* of conversations between the two children on an average of once or twice a month.

2. *Free speech samples*: Occasional tape-recordings of the same children and adults who took part in the structured test. These materials were collected in the subjects' natural settings, in kindergarten or at school, in their homes, or at social gatherings such as PTA meetings.

3. *Observational data* in the form of notes and records based on the free speech usage of adolescent and adult speakers of Hebrew. These were collected in the course of my work as a language tutor in Israeli high-school and college classrooms over eight years or so.

These three additional sources provided supplementary materials as backup for the central research tool of the present study, the cross-sectional test.

Population

188 subjects participated in the cross-sectional study. For all of them, Hebrew was their only mother tongue,[12] and they were all (except for some of the adults) second-generation native speakers of Hebrew. This population was divided into six age-groups, with the oldest group, the adults, further subdivided into two groups of *younger* and *older* adults. Every second group consisted of two subgroups, each of a different SES, yielding a total of ten test groups (Table 1).

The major independent variable in this study was *age,* which has been shown to be a developmentally critical factor in connection with different subsystems of linguistic structure (e.g. Berman 1984a, Brown 1973, Bowerman 1978, 1982b, Romaine 1984, Schwarzwald 1981), as well as in developmental psychology (Flavell 1985, Piaget & Inhelder 1968), and it is recognized as such by those combining an interest in general cognitive and linguistic development (Karmiloff-Smith 1979).

The six age groups that comprised my study started at age 3, the youngest age at which children are able to handle experimental language tasks (Clark & Sengul 1978, Derwing & Baker 1986, Schmidt & Sydow 1981). By the end of their third year children have already acquired the rudiments of their native grammar, including noun and verb inflections, and basic semantic and grammatical relations (Berman 1985, Slobin 1982). By this age, Israeli children are already in the process of socialization engendered by their attending nursery school, usually from age two or even earlier.

Table 1. Breakdown of test population into 10 groups by age, level of schooling and SES

Group ID	Age in yrs;ms Range	Mean	Level of Schooling	SES	N
3-year-olds	3;0–3;11	3;4	Nursery School	Middle/High	23
5-year-olds a	5;0–6;6	5;7	Kindergarten	Middle/High	21
5-year-olds b	5;1–6;2	5;7	Kindergarten	Low	20
8-year-olds	8;0–9;7	8;11	Third Grade	Middle/High	24
12-year-olds a	12;3–13;4	12;10	Seventh Grade	Middle/High	21
12-year-olds b	12;6–14;2	13;2	Seventh Grade	Low	21
16-year-olds	15;11–17;11	16;10	Eleventh Grade	Middle/High	20
Young Adults a	22–35	29		Middle/High	11
Older Adults a	49–61	55		Middle/High	10
Adults b	19–50	32		Low	17
Total					188

The second age group is the 5-year-olds. By age 5, a major part of language acquisition has taken place in the young learner: sentence-level knowledge (Berman 1985, 1986a, Berko 1958, Karmiloff-Smith 1979, Maratsos & Chalkey 1980, Strohmer & Nelson 1974). This age group also represents the phase immediately preceding the start of formal school studies and the acquisition of literacy.

Grade school is represented by the 8-year-olds, who are in possession of general cognitive and language-specific knowledge that goes beyond the fundamental constructs of early childhood. Their memory, as well as their ability to make abstractions, to perform classification, and to comprehend conversation all take their final shape in these years (Ehri 1979, Ferreiro 1982, Tolchinsky-Landsmann 1986). These children are already able to discard immature linguistic strategies such as the Minimal Distance Principle, have a more than basic grasp of discourse, and are undergoing internal processes of linguistic "repair" that are not immediately obvious (Berman 1988, C. Chomsky 1969, Karmiloff-Smith 1986). They are able to read and write fluently, and are quite familiar with Hebrew orthography. Three years of schooling have introduced them to a variety of usage and distinctions of registers, including some familiarity with Biblical Hebrew.

The 12-year-olds serve as a link in the chain of language knowledge and language use leading from childhood to adulthood. Cognitively, linguistically and communicatively these young speakers are breaking away from the concrete and the context-bound, and are now able to perceive language as one more domain where formal problem-solving is required. This development is fostered by seven years of formal schooling: Israeli seventh graders, entering junior high school, are already well-versed in first language instruction, adept at reading non-vocalized texts, and have had 4 years of English teaching.

High schoolers constitute the new generation of speakers: while having a well-established grammar as well as required norms, and being able to analyze and deploy abstract linguistic and non-linguistic clues in a communicative situation, they represent current use of Modern Hebrew at its most turbulent and unbuttoned (Donag-Kinrot 1978, Rabin 1986, Romaine 1984). On the other hand, their metalinguistic awareness is augmented by the school-leaving Hebrew grammar examination taken in the 10th grade.

The oldest adult group consisted of two subgroups: (i) younger adults (19–35) and (ii) older adults (40–61). This was done in order to ascertain whether the speech of the older group, born in mandatory Palestine, would differ significantly from that of younger people born after the establishment of the state of Israel with Hebrew their sole colloquial and official language. Moreover, the younger adult speakers grew up in a differently structured speech community: with the mass immigration of African and Asian-born Jews in the early 1950s, the demographic balance, which had previously been heavily in favor of Jews of Eastern European descent, shifted in favor of Mideastern Jewry (Schmelz & Bachi 1973, Bar-Adon 1975).

Every second age-group was further subdivided according to the second independent variable of this study, *socio-economic status* (SES). Two types of population were selected: well-educated, middle-class speakers, compared with disadvantaged subjects. In determining the latter, I adopted the criteria established by the Israeli Ministry of Education to specify what constitutes a disadvantaged population:[13] A low level of income, a high average number of children per family, and a low level of parental schooling, which characterize Jewish population of Mideastern and North African extraction. However, studies have shown that the difference between middle/high SES and low SES is related not so much to amount of income, as to size of family, level of education and type and status of occupation (Algrabli 1975, Smilansky & Yam 1969, Samocha & Peres 1974).

For example, despite a steady rise in the number of high-school students of Mideastern and African descent in the last 15 years, they constituted only about 40% of the academic-trend high-school population in 1982, while constituting 56% of ages 14–17 in the general population. In the universities, Oriental[14] students were only 24% of the general student body in 1985 (Shprinzak & Bar 1987). Recently, Israel has been shaken by press reports on the low success rate in school-leaving exams in disadvantaged populations in outlying areas. The crucial difference between groups, then, is that of formal education and level of literacy. This parameter is often linked to ethnic origins of the subject population, with Israelis of Oriental origin coming from a more "oral" tradition, compared with those of European and North American descent who are said to have received a more literate background from early on (Feitelson & Krown 1968, Stahl 1977).

The Language Domains

The focal language domain of this study is Hebrew inflectional morphology, regarded as the most characteristic "problem area" in spoken Hebrew today (Berman 1992a). Most work to date has dealt with the development of inflectional morphology at preschool age (e.g. Bybee & Slobin 1982). The current study carries this investigation further to middle childhood, adolescence and beyond.

General Morphological Development

The development of morphological structure and rules in children has been the focus of numerous studies, both naturalistic observational ones and experimental. That preschool children have productive morphological rules was demonstrated in Berko's famous (1958) experiment, which was followed by a number of similar studies, all indicating rule-governed knowledge in English-speaking children (Anisfeld & Tucker 1968, Bryant & Anisfeld 1969, Ervin 1984, M. Smith 1978, Solomon 1972). Other studies have shown that such morphological knowledge relies heavily on awareness of form-class membership and on morpheme recognition (Derwing 1976, Derwing & Baker 1977, 1986, Maratsos 1982, Maratsos & Kuczaj 1979). The early development of morphological competence was studied extensively for English in the works of Brown and his associates, establishing an order of acquisition for 14 grammatical morphemes (Brown 1973, Brown, Cazden & Bellugi-Klima 1968, Brown & Fraser 1963, Cazden 1968, 1972). Similar developmental ordering was found in other studies (Menyuk 1969, deVilliers & deVilliers 1973, 1978).

Once the major order of acquisition for English was established, researchers turned to formulating a general model that would account for the acquisition of languages of different genetic origins and typological traits. To this aim, cross-linguistic studies were carried out in the 1970s and 1980s in a wide variety of languages of different genetic families, including English, French, Hebrew, Japanese, Kaluli, Polish, Russian and Turkish. This research sought to determine the relationship between the types of innate linguistic abilities that children possess, and the role of typologically diverse input. Two important models of language acquisition based on such research are those proposed by MacWhinney (1978, 1985) and Slobin (1973, 1985a). These models provide insight into the nature of the language-making capacities that make up the child's language-learning device, and the type of learning strategies employed by children which derive from these capacities. MacWhinney's studies explore the interaction between rote-learning and combinatorial devices in language acquisition, while Slobin's model establishes a set of innate principles that guide children in language perception, storage, organization and analysis. These ideas are developed in the present study.

Of particular interest is the interaction of the specific typological features of a language with the innate acquisitional apparatus established by the cross-linguistic studies. This interaction has been shown to result in different rates of acquisition of particular domains of grammar in different languages. The typological traits of a language account for alternative uses of strategies for dealing with the specific ways information is grammatically marked in the language being acquired. Thus, for instance, children are shown to become attuned to inflec:ional categories such as number, case and tense, and to develop early sensitivity to formal properties of syntactic categories in highly inflected languages such as Russian, Latvian, Italian and French (Karmiloff-Smith 1978, Pizzuto & Caselli 1992, Popova 1973, Ruke-Drarina 1973, Slobin 1966). The learning of inflections is influenced by both the semantics of the lexical item and the syntactic structures in which it appears (Antinucci & Miller 1976, Bloom, Miller & Hood 1975, Bybee & Slobin 1982, Kucjai 1977).

This study is particularly concerned with the role of structural organization in the acquisition of morphology. Studies have shown formal complexity in the grammar to be a delaying factor in the acquisition of languages as diverse as Egyptian Arabic, French, German, Russian and Spanish, and to lead to a high frequency of overregularization (Clark 1985, Mills 1985, Omar 1973, Park 1978, Smoczynska 1985). By contrast, the extreme regularity of the Turkish morphological system and of Japanese case-particles both facilitates and hastens their acquisition (Clancy 1985, Aksu-Koc & Slobin 1985).

Acquisition of Hebrew Morphology

Hebrew-speaking children, like every child learning a mother tongue, must pay attention to the typological features that characterize Hebrew morphology. The most salient property of this system is its highly bound nature, which forces the learner to focus on word-internal structure and on conditioned alternations occurring in the paradigm (Berman 1981a, 1982a). The synthetic nature of Hebrew morphology has two facets: one, a specifically Semitic one, is the notion of the consonantal root and affixal patterns. Another, which at least superficially resembles non-Semitic languages, is the array of agglutinating and fusional devices that encode most of the grammatical meanings and functions. Once Hebrew-speaking children are past the initial stage of learning unanalyzed amalgams by rote, they must come to terms with this bound nature of their language in order to handle its morphology productively (Borokovsky 1984).

All Hebrew verbs are formed out of a combination of a consonantal root and an affixal verb pattern. Verb patterns (*binyanim*) encode syntactico-semantic functions such as Voice, Transitivity, Causativity, Reciprocity, Incohativity and Reflexivity (Ariel 1971, Berman 1975b). Many, though not all, nouns and adjectives consist of root and pattern; noun patterns carry a variety of nominal meanings such as Agent, Location, Instrument, Collective and Abstract Noun. These meanings are alternatively denoted by a set of derivational affixes such as Agentive *-an* (as in *taklitan* 'disc jockey') or Abstract -*ut* (e.g. *batlanut* 'idleness') (Berman 1987c, Bolozky 1991, Bolozky & Schwarzwald 1992, Ravid 1978, 1990).

Studies of the development of word-formation capacities in Hebrew reveal that by the age of four, children have developed a typological bias towards vowel alternation within the same consonantal skeleton, and the various changes in meaning that follow. As early as the 1930s, it was noted that children were able to manipulate roots, coining innovations like *menumas* 'dissolved' from *names* 'dissolve',[15] or *hictafléax* 'eluded' from *clofax* 'eel' (Avineri 1946, Barles 1937, Dolzhansky 1937). More recent studies describe the route Hebrew-speaking children take in learning to recognize root radicals and manipulate them productively: from initial alternations of familiar items like *li-Son* 'to-sleep' and *yaSánti* '(I) slept', through increasing awareness of consonant-vowel relationship in actually occurring words, to abstract perception of root and pattern, as exemplified by the girl aged 4;8 who created the innovation *kacar* 'shortener' by making use of root *k-c-r*, extracted from *kacar* 'short', and agentive pattern *CaCaC*, as in *zamar* 'singer' (Bar Adon 1959, Berman 1982a, 1983, 1990b, Berman & Sagi 1981, Clark & Berman 1984, Walden 1982). These studies confirm that children construe verbs, nouns and adjectives as sharing a basic semantic and formal core in a single consonantal sequence, and that the Semitic root is thus crucial in describing and explaining processes and strategies of morphological acquisition (Bentur 1978).

Another important facet of the synthetic character of Hebrew morphology is the numerous bound affixes that denote a variety of grammatical meanings and functions. Nouns are obligatorily marked for gender and number,[16] and these features spread both within the NP to the adjective and across to the VP, e.g. *SaloS rakdaniy-ot muxSar-ot yoSv-ot al ha-bama* 'three,Fm dancer-s,Fm talented,Pl.Fm are-sitting,Fm on the-stage'. Feminine gender is marked on nouns and adjectives by the following suffixes: -*a* (as in *tmuna* 'picture'), -*it* (as in *mapit* 'napkin'), -*ut* (e.g. *samxut* 'authority') and -*éCet* or -*óCet* (*magévet* 'towel' and *bikóret* 'criticism' respectively). The masculine plural suffix is -*im* (as in *gvarim* 'men') while feminine plurals are marked by -*ot*, e.g. *tmunot* 'pictures'. The system abounds with exceptions and irregularities: for example, *eS* 'fire' is feminine although it lacks any external feminine markers, *kirot* 'walls' are masculine and *beycim* 'eggs' are feminine although they take opposite markers.

It has been shown in a number of studies that the gender/number system is acquired very early in Hebrew nouns, before the age of 2;6, while adjective agreement takes place later, and full mastery of less common or more complex plural forms is not achieved before school age (Berman 1981c, Levy 1980, 1982).

Hebrew verbs are inflected for tense, gender, number and person, in addition to being comprised of the consonantal root and a verb pattern. Verb inflection is both synthetic (tense) and analytic (gender, number, person), and is often fusional. Consider, for example, the verb *titlabSi* '(you,Fm) will-get-dressed', root *l-b-S*, the *Hitpa'el* pattern.

Table 2 depicts the "portmanteau" nature of Hebrew morphology: The root radicals, separated by the *binyan* vowels and sometimes preceded by a *binyan* prefix, carry the core meaning, and most of the segments that make up the verb have a plurifunctional nature. For example, future tense is expressed by the prefix *tit-* which also expresses 2nd person while serving as part of the *Hitpa'el* pattern as well.

Clearly, then, Hebrew words have a complex fusional structure, extending over both derivational and inflectional domains. The acquisition of this complex system has been described in a number of studies. Bar Adon (1959) devoted his pioneering work to the development of the verb system in children 3 to 12. Kaplan (1983) found that verb inflections were among the first formal markers to be acquired in early childhood. An interesting note is provided by Rabinowitch (1985), who reports that monolingual Hebrew speakers have better proficiency than Hebrew/English bilinguals in language-specific domains peculiar to Hebrew such as gender, number and verb patterns, while no such differences were observed in elements shared across languages.

Bound morphology is not confined to the major lexical categories: it is also exhibited in oblique (case-marked) pronouns. Hebrew pronouns occur in their free form only in subject position. In all other cases they appear as inflections on prepositions, often fused together, e.g. *al* 'on' inflected for the 3rd person singular feminine becomes *aléyha* 'on-her' while a similar inflection changes *im* 'with' into *ita* 'with-her'. Basic case-marked pronouns are acquired by age 4, but mistakes in less common and more complex forms persist into grade-school age (Berman 1981a, 1985, Kaplan 1983, Rom & Dgani 1985).

Typologically, then, Hebrew is a synthetic rather than isolating language, with a rich array of morphological structures displaying both fusional and agglutinating devices. This is a typological characteristic that children acquiring the language cannot disregard. From early on, Hebrew-speaking children become attuned to the structural options available in their native tongue, a knowledge which sets up predispositions governing the acquisition of its grammar (Berman 1984a, 1986b, Slobin 1982, 1985a, and see Dromi, Leonard & Shteiman 1993 for the implications for language disorders). This tendency is strengthened by the obligatory nature of inflectional rules: the young Hebrew learner has no choice but to

Table 2. Meanings and functions in the Hebrew verb 'You, Fm. will dress yourself'

	Hitpa'el	verb	pattern,	reflexive	function
	‖	‖	‖	‖	
Future Tense, 2nd Pr. ══ t	i	t	l	a	b	S	i ══ Fm.Sg.
		‖		‖	‖	
		root		r a d i c a l s	
				'wear'	

come to terms with obligatory markings such as tense, person, number, gender and case marking—all of which are expressed through bound morphology. And indeed, Hebrew-speaking children have been shown to acquire the main features of these systems by their fourth year (Berman 1985, Levy 1982, Rom & Dgani 1985). For instance, tensed forms appear early in Hebrew (Berman & Dromi 1984, Kaplan 1983).

Although Hebrew-speaking preschoolers acquire the overall systems of inflectional marking quite rapidly, these same phenomena serve as a source of many errors in child language, some of which persist into adult usage (Berman 1981b, Clark & Berman 1987, Ravid & Shlesinger 1987a, Schwarzwald 1981). Leveling of phonemes and opacity of roots and patterns constitute impediments to the child's eventual mastery of the morphophonological system. This explains why most current processes of Hebrew language change, occurring in both child language and the Nonstandard sociolect, contrast sharply with the prescriptivistic demand for linguistic purity advocated by the HLE. Most such criticism and most attempts at correction are directed at morphological categories of the kind that concerns us here, rather than to syntactic phenomena (Bendavid & Shay 1974, Kremer 1980, Manzur 1962).

My main concern here is crucially with the morphological aspects of the grammar, which constitute part of the speakers' obligatory core of language knowledge, shared by mature speakers irrespective of individual lexical repertoire, personal style, level of education, or SES. Inflectional morphology is located between often rote-learned lexical expression, conserving idiosyncracies, and rule-bound syntactic expression, thus being a natural domain for change as the result of a clash between the forces of polarization and regularization (Bybee 1985, Kiparsky 1982, Thomason 1980). Indeed, the areas where change seems to be taking place in current Hebrew are primarily inflectional. Unlike many lexical processes, inflectional affixation operates on whole stems and words, rather than on roots, causing stem-changes that affect both consonants and vowels. The morpho phonological framework of Modern Hebrew is particularly unstable, due to a lack of phonetic frame of reference during the period of its revival. As a result, inflectional processes do not always produce the stem-changes required by normative stipulations. For example, the colloquial singular form of *SmaSot* 'panes' is *SmaSa,* instead of normative *SimSa.* It is in morphophonological alternations motivated by inflectional processes that historical leveling most critically leads to surface opacity of form.

Historical Neutralizations

Nearly one third of the items constituting the experimental study[17] were chosen to represent morphophonological "areas of instability" resulting from neutralization of historically distinct elements. Many of these distinctions have long since disappeared from the main dialect of Contemporary Hebrew, usually termed General Israeli Hebrew (Medan 1953). Yet they continue to underlie differences in surface forms and in formal alternations between items which are phonetically identical in certain contexts (Blanc 1957, Ornan 1973, Rosén 1956).

CONSONANTS

Biblical Hebrew had two sets of consonants peculiar to Semitic languages: the low so-called "guttural" or "pharyngeal" obstruents (traditionally known as *groniyot*)—*?, h, H, y*; and the *emphatic* consonants *ṣ, q, T* (Blau 1981a/c, Laufer & Condax 1981, Ornan 1983, Weinberg 1966). In addition, Classical Hebrew had a set of *stops—p, b, t, d, k, g*—traditionally termed the *béged-kéfet* group, which regularly alternated with a corresponding set of fricatives—*f, v, Θ, δ, x, R* under set conditions (Schwarzwald 1976). Erosion of distinctions between consonants has led to the quite general loss of the *groniyot* in the main dialect of Contemporary Hebrew (Ben Hayyim 1955, Chayen 1972, Rabin 1940), and to the total disappearance of the *emphatics*. Partial loss of the *béged-kéfet* alternants has led to a consequent loss of the phonological motivation of the stop/spirant alternation.

Another set of historical segments which have undergone leveling is the glides or semi-vowels (called "weak letters" in Gesenius 1910). Classical Hebrew had two glides: the back *w* and the front *y*. These two semi-vowels alternated with the corresponding back and front vowels *u,o* and *i,e* respectively, e.g. *yiSev/noSav* 'settled/was settled', root *y-s-b*; *la-gur/le-hitgorer* 'to-live', root *g-w-r*; *re'i/reiya* 'mirror/sight', root *r-?-y*. In Modern Hebrew there is only one glide—*y*—while the other semi-vowel *w* has become a full-fledged consonant *v*, merging with the spirant alternant of *b, v* (Bar-Adon 1975).

A number of consonants in Hebrew have thus merged phonetically (Table 3), while still retaining their distinct characters in the orthography, and in underlying morphophonological structure. This causes problems in spelling, but more significantly, it is a direct source of opacity in Hebrew morphology, as demonstrated in the following: *saxar/yiskor* 'hired/will hire', root *s-k-r*; *saxar/yisxar* 'traded/will trade', root *s-H-r*; and *sakar/yiskor* 'surveyed/will survey', root *s-q-r* (Bolozky, to appear).

VOWELS

Table 4 details the neutralization of vowels in Modern Hebrew. Note that the historical form of these vowels is a broad approximation encompassing the vast period of time during which these vowels underwent many changes.

The Biblical vowel system derives from a double Proto-Semitic system of short and long *i,u,a*. The precise nature of Biblical and Mishnaic Hebrew vowels is controversial: While Masoretic vocalization makes only qualitative distinctions between vowels (e.g. *segol* represents a lower *e* than *ṣerey*), it is clear that pre-Masoretic Hebrew made quantitative distinctions as well (e.g. long *u* was denoted by *Suruq*, short *u* by *qibbuṣ* (Blau 1981b, Gesenius 1910). Modern Hebrew does not retain any phonematic quan-

Table 3.

álef א	?	? ~ 0
áyin ע	y	? ~ 0
he ה	h	? ~ 0
Het ח	H	x
xaf (= kaf) כ	x (~k)	x
qof ק	q	k
kaf כ	k (~x)	k
Tet ט	T	t
tav ת	t	t
waw ו	w	v
vet (= bet) ב	v (~b)	v

Table 4. Leveling of historically distinct vowels in Modern Hebrew

Orthographic Form	Historical Form	Modern Hebrew
Hiriq	*i*	*i*
Suruq/qibbus	*u*	*u*
serey	long *e*[18]	*e*
segol	short *ε*	*e*
Holam	*o*	*o*
qamas	long *a*	*a*
pattaH	short	*a*

titative distinctions, and makes 5 qualitative distinctions: High front *i*, high back *i*, mid front *e*, mid back *o*, and low back *a*. This holds true across the board in Modern Hebrew pronunciation.

Modern Hebrew thus has only 5 vowels, while the vocalization system (the *nikud*) has 2 to 4 orthographic symbols for each vowel[19] (Blau 1981c). *Nikud* is no longer part of the Hebrew grammar school curriculum (TAL 1980), and so apparently has no bearing on language knowledge, however it is a powerful explanatory device in motivating morphophonological alternation, e.g. the operation of the vowel deletion rule in *matos/metosim* 'plane/s' (historically long *a* deletes) vs. *masok/masokim* 'helicopter/s' (historically short *a* does not undergo deletion) (Ravid & Shlesinger 1987a).

Research Categories

The 61 items constituting the 10 research categories (see Appendix B) are all common, everyday words occurring in the speech of both children and adults from different socio-economic backgrounds. They represent properties typical of Modern Hebrew morphophonology and morphosyntax in areas manifesting numerous deviations from the educated norm. Pilot testing screened out items where the Standard was too distant from the norm (e.g. Normative *dvaSot* vs. Standard *davSot* 'pedals') so that for these items, Normative actually equals Standard. Below, I discuss the ten research areas that make up this study. For the input items and the actual form of the test see Appendices A and B.

Weak Final Syllable

The items making up this morphophonological domain involve the three gutturals "muted" in the main dialect of Contemporary Hebrew— ?, *h(=y)*,[20], *y* , and the historical voiceless pharyngeal fricative *H*. Two of the roots of these items end with the voiceless pharyngeal fricative *H* typically incurring vowel lowering in its vicinity, (e.g. *?órex* 'length', root *?-r-k* vs. *róxav* 'width', root *r-H-b*). However, *H* does not have a unique realization in the mainstream dialect of Hebrew (Blanc 1957, Chayen 1972, Fischler 1979, Morag 1973). For some speakers of Oriental Hebrew *H* has phonetic realization, but its distribution is either a sociolinguistic variable or else is random (Ben-Tolila 1984). On the whole, it is rare for a single speaker of Oriental Hebrew to have both *y* and *H* (Dagan 1973). The first three items in this category were selected to demonstrate the neutralization of distinctions between phonetic *x* deriving from either *H* or *k* which leads to problems in two major areas: vowel lowering (compare *novéax* 'barking', root *n-b-H*, to *noSex*, root *n-S-k*) and stop/spirant alternation (compare *kiven/yexaven* 'directed/will direct', root *k-v-n*[21] to *xiber/yexaber* 'joined/will join', root *H-b-r*) (Bolozky, to appear) (Table 5).

The remaining seven items represent the phenomenon termed "Final Open Syllable" by Bar-Adon (1959, 1971). These are words ending in an open syllable representing the now non-differentiated ?, *y* , *y*. This neutralization leads to surface ambiguity in many cases. For example, the string *kara* may derive from any one of the following roots: *q-r-?* 'read', *q-r-y* 'happen', *q-r- y* 'tear', *k-r-y* 'mine' and *k-r- y* 'kneel'. When conjugated in different verb-forms, the underlying nature of each final radical yields a different output (Table 6).

The native speaker needs to "know" the underlying roots of each *kara* surface form in order to produce correctly conjugated forms. Knowledge of such "defective" radical elements is part of knowing the lexical properties of any word, but in cases of partial knowledge of morphophonemic alternation errors are likely to happen, e.g. a 5-year-old kibbutz child said *liknóa* for adult *liknot* 'to-buy', root *k-n-y* (compare *liSmóa* 'to-hear', root *S-m- y*). The last item on the list— *taklit* 'record'—does not end with an open syllable, however its final syllable resembles the suffix *-it* with the underlying final root radical *-y* as in *tavnit* 'cakepan', plural form *tavniyot*.

Table 5. Weak Final Syllable Items

Input item	Responses Normative	Nonstandard	Gloss	Historical Root
niftax	*niftáxat*	*niftéxet*	opened,Int/opening,Fm	*p-t-H*
dorex	*doréxet*	*doráxat*	stepping/Fm	*d-r-k*
kadax	*kodéax*	*kodex*	drilled/drilling	*q-d-H*
Sata	*Satíti*	*Satáti*	drank/(I) drank	*S-t-y*
mevi	*hevéti*	*hevíti*	bringing/(I) brought	*b-w-?*
menaka	*nikíti*	*nikéti*	cleaning,Fm/(I) cleaned	*n-q-y*
soxe	*soxa*	*soxétet*	swimming/Fm	*s-H-y*
mexake	*xika*	*xike*	waiting/waited	*H-k-y*
kine	*kin'a*	*kinta*	was jealous/Fm	*q-n-?*
taklit	*taklitim*	*takliyot*	record/s,N	*q-l-T*

Table 6. Conjugations of *kara* forms

Root	Gloss	Past Tense	Present Tense Masc.	Fm.	Inf.	Perfective
q-r-?	read,	*kara*	*kore*	*koret*	*likro*	*karu/y*[22]
q-r-y	happen	*kara*	*kore*	*kora/et*	*likrot*	
q-r- y	tear	*kara*	*koréa*	*koráat*	*likróa*	*karúa*
k-r-y	mine	*kara*	*kore*	*kora/et*	*lixróa*	*karuy*
k-r- y	kneel	*kara*	*koréa*	*korá'at*	*lixróa*	

Stop/Spirant Alternation

This is another major area of instability, where a rule, or a set of rules, is undergoing a process of collapse, described from a variety of points of view in Ben Asher 1969, Barkai 1972, Ben-Horin & Bolozky 1972, Ephratt 1980, Faber 1986, Fischler 1975, Morag 1960, Ornan 1973, Ravid 1978, in press, Rosén 1956, Schwarzwald 1976, 1980b, Tur-Sinai 1954).

This language domain involves six segments—the three stops *p,b,k,* and the three corresponding fricatives *f,v,x,* which alternate according to phonologically, morphologically, and lexically determined factors, some of which have no psychological reality for the native speaker. *batax* 'trusted', for example, and *yivtax* 'will trust' both derive from the root *b-T-H.* Similarly, the root *k-b-s* yields both *kibes* 'laundered' and *mexabes* 'launders', while the root *p-t-H* is used for both the passive participle *patúax* 'open' and the noun *maftéax* 'key'. This group of obstruents is a remnant of the class of obstruents *pb, td, kg, fv,* Θδ, xr, traditionally known as the *béged kéfet* group, which were subject to phonologically determined alternation in Biblical Hebrew: spirantization after a vowel (Garbel 1959, Tur-Sinai 1954).

Today, as a result of phonological neutralizations stop/spirant alternation is no longer a natural rule. This results in constant violations of stop/spirant alternation in Contemporary Hebrew. For example, a child of 3;1 produced the form *lixSor* for adult *likSor* 'to-tie', root *q-S-r*, where the *q*-derived *k* does not alternate with *x;* the root *t-p-r* 'sew' may yield in adult speech both the colloquial infinitive *litfor* and the Normative infinitive *litpor,* more or less in free alternation (Barkai 1972, Rosén 1956); and the Standard/Normative form *bikaSt* '(you, Fm) asked' is often produced as *vikaSt* by lower-class adults as well as children.

Table 7 enumerates the stop/spirant test items.

Stem Change

Nouns and adjectives in Hebrew are associated with a wide range of different morphological subclasses, which affect how words alternate under linear inflection and derivation (Ravid 1978, to appear). For example, the particular form taken by a stem may change in the presence of a plural suffix (e.g. *daf/dapim* 'page/s'), or before a derivational suffix (e.g. *máyim/meymi* 'water/watery').

Hebrew Stems fall roughly into six classes: (i) those that do not change in linear suffixation, e.g. *sal/salim* 'basket/s', *buba/bubot* 'doll/s'; (ii) stems that undergo vowel deletion, for example *pakid/pkida* 'clerk/Fm'; (iii) stems undergoing vowel change, e.g. *xec/xici* 'arrow/my arrow'; (iv) stems that undergo stop/spirant alternation, e.g. *kaf/kapit* 'spoon/teaspoon'; (v) stems undergoing final consonant deletion, for instance *taglit/tagliyot* 'discovery/s'; and (vi) stems that undergo complete structural change, e.g. *séfer/sifriya* 'book/library'.

Stem change has independently been shown to be hard for language learners in a number of unrelated languages (MacWhinney 1978, Clark & Berman 1984). The same difficulties arise in Hebrew, where the problem is exacerbated by morphophonological leveling, as noted above: words that appear identical in their basic or unmarked free form may undergo changes that may seem both semantically unmotivated and structurally opaque. Compare, for example, *karov/krova* 'relative/Fm', *kaxol/kxula* 'blue/Fm',

Table 7. Stop/Spirant Alternation Items

Input item	Responses		Gloss	Historical Root
	Normative	Nonstandard		
safar	*sofer*	*soper*	counted/counting	*s-p-r*
hikpía	*kafu*	*kapuy*	froze,Tr,Fm/frozen	*q-p-?*
mefazéret	*pizra*	*fizra*	scattering,Fm/ed,Fm	*p-z-r*
Savar	*Savur*	*Sabur*	broke,Tr/broken	*S-b-r*
cahov	*cehubim*	*cehuvim*	yellow/Pl	*ṣ-h-b*
li-rkav[23]	*roxev*	*rokev*	to-ride/riding	*r-k-b*
rax	*raka*	*raxa*	soft/Fm	*r-k-k*

paot/paota 'toddler/Fm'. Conversely, a single derived surface form may derive from different types of free forms, e.g. the form *CCuCim* derives from two different sources in *matun/metunim* 'mild/Pl' and *matok/metukim*[24] 'sweet/Pl'. Such apparently unmotivated or arbitrary form-class membership associations impose a heavy learning burden on the Hebrew speaker. The three items selected (Table 8) each represent morphological classes with a large membership, and they all undergo radical stem changes in plural inflection.

Hif'il *Vowel Alternation*

The so-called "full," i.e. regular, root yields a structurally predictable output when associated with any verb pattern. Thus for any full root the present form of *Hif'il* is *maCCiC*, e.g. *mavhil* 'terrifying', root *b-h-l*. However, there are also "defective" or irregular roots, whose historical/orthographic radicals are partially inaccessible since they do not surface in all inflectionally derived forms of the verb (Table 9).

While defective roots with initial *n-* or a medial glide start with an open syllable *mV* (either *ma-* or *me-*) the full verb has an additional consonant (*mastir*). The similar *mVCiC* structure of initial *n-* and glide-medial roots in present tense of *Hif'il* does not provide the native speaker with any phonetic cues as to the historical or underlying root; choice of stem-initial vowel seems to be arbitrary and results in numerous deviations from HLE norms not only on the part of children and less-educated adults, but also in the speech of high SES adults (Schwarzwald 1981). Colloquial *mekir* and *ma'ir* are commonly heard in Standard speech along with Normative *makir* 'knows', root *n-k-r* and *me'ir* 'waking', root *y-w-r*.

The failure of Hebrew speakers to make the Normative distinction between these two types of defective roots, and their subsequent tendency to fluctuate between *mecic* and *macic* despite special attention accorded to this

Table 8. Stem Change Items

Normative	Nonstandard	Gloss	Pattern
iparon/efronot	*iparon/iparonim*	pencil/s	*CiCaCon*
éven/avanim	*éven/évenim*	stone/s	*CéCeC*
adom/adumim	*adom/adomim*	red/s	*CaCoC*

Table 9. Conjugation of roots in present-tense *Hif'il*

Historical Root	Root Type	Verb Form	Gloss
s-t-r	regular	*mastir*	hides
n-g-S	irregular, initial *n*	*magiS*	serves
s-w-r	irregular, medial *w*	*mesir*	removes
b-y-n	irregular, medial *y*	*mevin*	understands

subject in school causes much consternation among purists and proponents of normativism. The four verbs chosen to represent this category are
given in Table 10.

Verb Tense

Systems of tense, mood and aspect have been discussed in a variety of
recent studies in general linguistics (e.g. Anderson 1982, Comrie 1976,
1985, Dahl 1985, Dowty 1972, Hornstein 1977, Traugott 1978). Different aspects of how children acquire temporality marking have also been
studied for several languages (summed up in Weist 1986, and see Berman
& Dromi 1984, for Hebrew).

Hebrew does not mark verbs for aspectual distinctions and thus tense is
the major semantic category encoded in inflectionally-marked verbs[25] that
Hebrew-speaking children must command (Berman 1983, 1985). Verb
paradigms in Hebrew do not have an unmarked base-form, such as '*go*' and
'*take*' in English, since every finite verb is inflected for tense, number and
gender, and past and future tense verbs for person as well. A choice must
be made for all four categories just about every time a finite verb is used.
The Hebrew learner must thus take account of temporal distinctions and
other obligatory verb inflections from early on. And indeed, Hebrew-
speaking children from as young as age two have been observed to use a
variety of different verb-forms including all three tenses, even though
genuine acquisition of the semantics of time may only be attributed to
older children (Berman & Dromi 1984, Kaplan 1983). Very young
Hebrew speakers made wide use of the infinitive form (e.g. *le-haklit* 'to-
record'), which is morphologically (as well as semantically) more basic
since it is unmarked for any of the four verb inflections mentioned above;
then they move into use of the imperatives and present and past tense, with
future tense forms lagging far behind (Berman 1978b, Kaplan 1983).
Against this background, I chose to analyze two features of how children
formally construct tense-inflected verbs: redundant tense-marking and first
person marking on future-tense verbs (Table 11).

   (i) *Redundant tense-marking*: Out of the five *binyan* patterns used in
   childhood (excluding the two passive conjugations), three mark
   the present tense with an *mV-* prefix. In *Nif'al* and in a certain
   conjugation of *Pa'al* present and past tense forms are identical:
   niS'an 'leaned/is leaning', *Sar* 'sang/is singing'. Young Hebrew
   learners up to around three years or so add a *mV-* prefix to present
   tense verbs, where there is no formal difference between past and
   present forms. This yields juvenile forms like *mikanes* 'enters' for
   nixnas 'enters/entered', root *k-n-s* in *Nif'al,* and *maSir* 'sings', for
   Sar 'sings/sang', root *S-y-r,* in *Pa'al*. Another, less widespread
   strategy is to add a redundant *hi-* prefix to mark past tense, as in
   childish *hiSavárti* for adult *Savárti* '(I) broke' in the *Pi'el* conjugation.

Table 10. *Hif'il* Vowel Alternation Items

Input Item	Normative	Nonstandard	Gloss	Historical Root
higía	*magía*	*megía*	arrived/arrives	*n-g-y*
hipil	*mapil*	*mepil*	dropped/drops	*n-p-l*
herímu	*merimim*	*marimim*	lifted/lift, Pl	*r-w-m*
heríax	*meríax*	*maríax*	smelled/smells, Tr	*r-y-H*

Table 11. Present and past tense forms of verbs in the nonpassive verb patterns

Verb Pattern	Present Tense	Past Tense	Gloss
Pa'al	*poked*	*pakad*	give an order
Pa'al glide-medial	*kam*	*kam*	get up
Nif'al	*niftax*	*niftax*	open, Int
Pi'el	*mekabel*	*kibel*	receive
Hif'il	*mafxid*	*hifxid*	frighten
Hitpa'el	*mitlabeS*	*hitlabeS*	get dressed

(ii) *1st person marking on future tense verbs.* For historical reasons, Hebrew has an asymmetric system of tense-marking, whereby the category of person is marked by suffixes in past tense, and by prefixes in future tense—compare past tense *dibár-ta* '(you) talked' with future tense *te-daber*. The 1st person singular prefixal marker is further asymmetrical in future tense, since it alone derives from a historical glottal stop, which is ordinarily no longer pronounced in today's Hebrew (Rabin 1940). Nonetheless, it still entails vowel lowering, so that the vowel in this prefix may differ from that in all other persons (Table 12).

In less monitored speech the distinction between 1st person singular and 3rd person singular is neutralized, and the dominant vowel across the person system is adopted, e.g. *ani yesader* for *ani asader* 'I will arrange'. This may have been initially due to phonetic assimilation of the off-glide *y-* at the end of *ani* 'I' to the initial vowel of the verb prefix, however many such cases occur today in environments other than following the 1st person pronoun *ani* (Bolozky 1982) (Table 13).

Lexical Exceptions

The rich bound morphology of Hebrew is reflected in the way nouns, adjectives and verbs fall into a variety of categories and subcategories that determine their surface shape. Rules governing classes with a broad semantic and/or formal basis, such as those marking plural or feminine forms, are acquired by and large during the third year of life (Berman 1981c, Dromi

Table 12. Future-tense marking in 1st person singular

Root	Gloss	Verb Pattern	1st Sg	3rd Sg	1st Pl
S-m-r	guard	*Pa'al*	*e-Smor*	*yi-Smor*	*ni-Smor*
y -z-b	leave	*Pa'al*	*e-ezov*	*ya-azov*	*na-azov*
d-b-r	talk	*Pi'el*	*a-daber*	*ye-daber*	*ne-daber*
l-k-d	unite	*Hitpa'el*	*et-laked*	*yit-laked*	*nit-laked*

Table 13. Verb Tense Items

Input Item	Normative	Nonstandard	Gloss
Sáru	*Sarim*	*masirim*	sang/sing,Pl
rávu	*ravim*	*marivim*	fought/fight,Pl
nizhar	*nizhar*	*mizaher*	was/is being careful
nixnesu	*nixnasim*	*mikansim*	entered/enter,Pl
mesaxek	*sixákti*	*hisaxákti*	plays/(I) played
kotev	*extov*	*yixtov*	writes/(I) will-write
lamdu	*elmad*	*yilmad*	studied/(l) will-study

& Berman 1982, Levy 1980, Kaplan 1983). There are, however, many irregular items which have to be learned as lexical exceptions. Some of these are present in very early child language, and are learned by rote as unanalyzed amalgams (MacWhinney 1978), since the young learner acquires each item on a word-by-word basis, and his or her early lexicon may contain only one form of a lexeme (e.g. singular *pe* 'mouth' and plural *naaláyim* 'shoes') (Borokovsky 1984).

At a later age, the child may appear to regress into making overregularizations, e.g. *máxat* 'needle' yields childish plural *máxot* (for adult *mexatim*) (Levy 1980). This is due to a more advanced stage of linguistic acquisition, where a partial knowledge of rules leads to inappropriate regularization (Bowerman 1982b).

By school age, the remaining overregularizations belong to two major classes: Genuine unprincipled lexical exceptions and items belonging to minor, rare or opaque paradigms (Berman 1981a/b/c, Kaplan 1983). For the first case, consider *iSa/naSim* 'woman/women', where the stem undergoes an unpredictable change and takes the masculine plural suffix while being marked (by *-a*) for feminine gender. This is a case where the child eventually "has no choice but to learn by rote for each verb and noun which class it belongs to" (Brown 1973:324, and see also Bybee & Slobin 1982). Until he/she does so, overregularizations such as *iSot* are produced. However, apparently idiosyncratic words need not be strict exceptions, but may rather belong to minor paradigms which may be extremely marginal or structurally opaque, e.g. *lev/levavi* 'heart/hearty' with an underlying "double" root *l-b-b* which surfaces in suffixation. Children, and sometimes less-educated adults, will produce nostem-change overregularizations here as well since they are unaware of the historical root. Similarly, *gdi* 'kid' is historically related to the *segolate* penultimately stressed *CéCeC* pattern (e.g. *dérex/draxim* 'road/s', and thus takes the Normative plural form *gdayim* (Gesenius 1910); yet this connection is so occasional as to make *gdi* an exceptional form, so that it is overregularized to produce Nonstandard *gdiyim*.

Around school age, by a process of reorganization, aided by expanding linguistic experience and literacy, such irregular forms emerge "to acquire a new status: they are no longer isolates operating independently from their uninflected counterparts and from regular inflected forms: rather, they are integrated into a system, as exceptions to it" (Bowerman 1982b:321).

Stem-change items appear in Table 14.

Case-Marked Pronouns

In acquiring personal pronouns, children are confronted with a complex of semantic, syntactic and morphological distinctions, such as deixis (Clark 1977, Clark & Sengul 1978, Deutsch & Pechmann 1978, Tanz 1980, Wales 1986). Personal pronouns are crucial to conducting a conversation, since they encode conversational roles of speaker, addressee or nonpartici-pant in a speech event (Charney 1980). In order to express their function in the sentence, pronouns may be morphologically inflected for case, e.g. *I* for subject position, *me* for object position, *my* for the Genitive case (Chiat 1981, 1986, Fletcher 1985). Children use pronouns widely in their speech for a variety of purposes (Maratsos 1979), starting initially with deictic

Table 14. Lexical Exceptions Items

Input Form	Normative	Nonstandard	Gloss	Comparable Regular Forms
bat	*banot*	*batot*	girl/s	*kat/katot* butt/s
dli	*dlayim*	*dliyim*	pail/s	*si/siim* record/s
iSa	*naSim*	*iSot*	woman/Pl	*sika/sikot* pin/s
yaSna	*yeSena*	*yoSénet*	(she)slept/sleeps	*maxra/moxéret* (she) sold/sells
loveS	*yilbaS*	*yilboS*	wears/will-write	*kotev/yixtov* writes/will-write
yaxol	*yaxol*	*yaxal*	can/could	*soxev/saxav* drags/dragged
ába[26]	*avot*	*ábaim*	dad/dads	*sába/savim* grandad/s

reference to participants present in the speech situation, and only later moving into anaphoric use of 3rd person (Wales 1986). Most pronominal forms are acquired in various languages at approximately age 2;6-3;6 (Berman 1985, Brown 1973, Deutsch & Pechman 1978, Kaplan 1983, Huxley 1970, Rom & Dgani 1985, Waterman & Shatz 1982).

In Hebrew, the acquisition of the pronominal system interacts not only with syntactic and semantic development, but also with the acquisition of inflectional morphology, since all pronouns except those in subject position take the form of inflectional suffixes bound to a preposition which specifies the pronoun in question as Accusative, Dative, Genitive or many other kinds of Oblique, e.g. *l-o* 'to-him' (Bin-Nun 1983). The way in which pronouns are affixed to case-marking and other prepositions is illustrated below in Table 15.

Unlike many other morphologically bound forms, such as the genitive marker on nouns (e.g. *sifri/ha-séfer Seli* 'my book'), case-marked pronouns do not have any analytic counterparts: *axaréxa* 'after/behind-you' has no periphrastic alternative at any level of usage. Consequently, young learners of Hebrew must use case-marked pronouns to express their meaning, and indeed they start using them as early as age 2;0, and by 5;6 have command of the inflection of those expressing basic relations (Rom & Dgani 1985).

However, mastery of case-marked pronouns requires the speaker to know not only the meaning and use of both the preposition and the pronoun in each case, but also to combine them in the uniquely appropriate form and learn most of them by rote, including suppletive forms, e.g. *im/it-i* 'with/with-me'. This is because structural anomalies and irregularities make the system hard to learn: both the prepositional stem and the pronominal suffix may change form in inflection, see for example the changes in *mi-* 'from' (historical *min*). Pronominal suffixes depend on the historical class of preposition, and the difference is most pronounced in 2nd person feminine singular: "true" prepositions (such as Accusative *et*); prepositions which underwent categorial shift (e.g. *min* 'from'); and historically plural-stem prepositions (such as *al* 'on', historically plural *aley*).

Table 15. Pronoun suffixation[27] on prepositions

	Accusative *et*	*al* 'on'	*mi* 'from'
1st Sg	*ot-i*	*al-ay*	*mimén-i*
2nd Sg	*ot-xa*	*aléy-xa*	*mim-xa*
2nd Sg Fm	*ot-ax*	*aláy-ix*	*mim-ex*
3rd Sg	*ot-o*	*al-av*	*mimén-u*
3rd Sg Fm	*ot-a*	*aléy-ha*	*mimén-a*
1st Pl	*ot-ánu*	*aléy-nu*	*me-itánu*
2nd Pl	*ot-xem*[28]	*aley-xem*	*mi-kem* *mim-xem*[29]
3rd Pl	*ot-am*	*aley-hem*	*me-hem*[30]

The motivation for these distinctions is opaque to the contemporary speaker, so that case-marked pronouns take a great deal of rote learning, and there are many deviations from the norm at all levels of usage, e.g. Girl, aged 2;8 *mimén-ax* for *mim-ex* 'from you, Fm'; Nonstandard *it-ex* for Normative *it-ax* 'with you, Fm'; and colloquial *biSvil-ax* for Normative *biSvil-ex*, 'for you,Fm' common among all speakers. Table 16 enumerates the case-marked pronouns category.

Verb-Governed Prepositions

Many Hebraists as well as general linguists regard verb-governed prepositions as an integral part of the lexical entry of the verb (Ben-Asher 1974, Berman 1978a, Blau 1973, Chayen & Dror 1976, Goshen-Gottstein 1969, Kaddari 1976, Rabin & Radday 1976, Ring 1976, Sadka 1977). The study of governed prepositions is motivated in the linguistic literature by the desire to distinguish objects, on the one hand, from adverbials, on the other (Lerner 1976). Thus Azar (1972) and Rosén (1977) claim that (non-direct) objects follow verb-governed prepositions which (i) may not be either deleted or replaced by other prepositions, and (ii) need not be semantically well-motivated (Azar 1972:221, Ornan 1969). In the examples given below, all verbs in group (i) govern prepositions which fulfill both conditions, and they are compared with pure transitive verbs which take direct objects (group ii) (Table 17).

The lexical entry of preposition-governing verbs includes the governed preposition, implying that such verbs are stored in long-range memory together with the governed preposition that constitutes an inseparable part of their argument structure. The argument structure of such governing verbs would be something like: *NP(ex) V P(s) NP(in)*, where NP(ex) stands for an external argument, NP(in) for the internal argument, and the preposition is specified for each governing verb (Williams 1980).

Children would have to learn the whole matrix of the verb by *rote*, as governed prepositions are not semantically well-motivated. Since rote is an early developmental strategy, the governed preposition can be presumed to be part of the knowledge of young children (Berman 1978b, 1984a, Borokovsky 1984, Bowerman 1982b, R. Clark 1974, 1978, Dromi 1982, MacWhinney 1978, Peters 1983, Wong-Fillmore 1979).

Verb-Governed Prepositions items are presented in Table 18.

Table 16. Case-Marked Pronouns Items

| Free Form | Inflected Form | | Gloss |
	Normative	Nonstandard	
et	*ot-ax*	*ot-ex*	Accusative, you, Fm Sg
mi-	*mim-xa*	*me-ata*	from-you
al	*al-av*	*al-o*	on-him
kmo	*kamó-xa*	*kmo ata*	like-you
bli	*biladáy-ix*	*bli at*	without-you, Fm

Table 17 Governing verbs

1.   (i) *dan hirbic le-rina*
      Dan hit to-Rina
             'Dan hit Rina'

     (ii) *dan hika et Rina*
      Dan hit Acc Rina

2.   (i) *dan baz la-mimsad*
      Dan loathed to-the-establishment
          'Dan loathed the establishment'

     (ii) *dan te'ev et ha-mimsad*
      Dan loathed Acc the-establishment

3.   (i) *dan paxad me-ha-xok*
      Dan feared from-the-law
            'Dan feared the law'

     (ii) *dan yare et ha-xok*
      Dan feared Acc the-law

Table 18. Verb-Governed Prepositions Items

Normative	Nonstandard[31]
tiStameS be- 'use in'	*tiStameS im-* 'use with'
tesaxek be- 'play in'	*tesaxek im-* 'play with'
tetapel be- 'treat in'	*tetapel be-* 'treat in'
al tarbic le- 'don't hit to-'	*al tarbic le-* 'don't hit to-'
al tefaxed me- 'don't be afraid of'	*al tefaxed me-* 'don't be afraid of'
al tix'as al 'don't be angry on'	*al tix'as al* 'don't be angry on'
tistakel be- 'look in'	*tistakel al-* 'look on'

Subject-Verb Concord

According to Hebrew scholars, the basic word order in Modern Hebrew is SVO (Berman 1978a, 1980a, Givón 1976, 1977, Glinert 1989, Ravid 1977, and as implied by Rosén 1977). Verbs (and predicating adjectives) manifest obligatory agreement with the subject NP in number and gender, and in past and future tense verbs—in person as well (Tables 19–20).

Subject-predicate concord poses no special problem to Hebrew speakers, apart from a number of exceptions (e.g. *eS* 'fire, Fm' unmarked for feminine gender). However, instances of concord violations are quite common among all speakers when the word order is V-first.

Such constructions mainly manifest existential or "presentative" types of predicates, which regularly precede the subject in discourse (Berman 1980a, Givón 1976, 1977, Ziv 1976).

Table 19. Nonverbal predicates

(i)	*ha-nos'im* The-topics	*hayu* were	*meanyenim* interesting,Pl
(ii)	*ha-sixa* The-talk,Fm	*(hi)* (is,Fm)	*meanyénet* interesting,Fm
(iii)	*ha-hesber* The-explanation	*yihye* will-be	*meanyen* interesting

Table 20. Verbal predicates

Past and present tense

(i)	*ha-menahélet* The-manager,Fm	*hizmína* invited,Fm	*et* Acc	*ha-cévet* the-team	*le-diyun* to-(a)-discussion
(ii)	*atem* You,Pl	*tivxanu* will-test,Pl	*et* Acc	*dan* Dan	*beyáxad* together

Present tense

(i)	*ani* I,Fm	*mexaka* (am) waiting,Fm
(ii)	*hi* She	*mexaka* (is) waiting,Fm

Thus both constructions (i) and (ii) in Table 21 are common in what Givón (1976) terms "Street Hebrew."

This phenomenon has ancient roots in Biblical Hebrew (Gesenius 1910, Kaddari 1976, Meyuchas 1928). In Arabic, a related Semitic language, the verb does not agree in number (nor, sometimes, in gender) with the ensuing subject in a VS construction (Meyuchas 1928).

Subject-Verb Concord items are presented in Table 22.

Backformation

The ability to analyze a surface form into two or more elements of which it is composed is a necessary linguistic skill which underlies all but the most elementary language knowledge. Normally, morphological analysis of a linguistic structure involves the addition of segments to simpler bases, most typically adding affixes as in English *boy/boyhood*, Hebrew *nagar/ nagarut* 'carpenter/carpentry'.

A special kind of analysis, or rather, re-analysis, is found in cases of what is termed *Backformation*, where speakers derive a simpler form from a more complex one, e.g. English *self-destruct* from *self-destruction*, despite the existence of *destroy*, and the Hebrew creation of *ayara* 'town' from plural *ayarot*, originally deriving from singular *ir* 'city' (cf. modern *ir/arim* 'city/s) (Adams 1973, Aronoff 1976, Bauer 1983, Ravid 1990, to appear, Roeper

Table 21. Concord in VS constructions

1.	(i)	*hayu*	*Sam*	*makot*
		were	there	blows
				'People were fighting there'
	(ii)	*haya*	*Sam*	*makot*
		was	there	blows
2.	(i)	*nigmera*		*ha-hafsaka*
		was-finished,Fm		the-break,Fm
				'The break is over'
	(ii)	*nigmar*		*ha-hafsaka*
		was-finished		the-break,Fm

Table 22. Subject-Verb Concord Items

Normative	Nonstandard
hayu yeladim 'Were children'	*haya yeladim* 'Was children'
koévet ha-béten 'hurting,Fm the-stomach,Fm'	*ko'ev ha-béten* 'hurting,Masc the-stomach,Fm'
niSbera ha-caláxat 'broke,Fm the-dish,Fm'	*niSbar ha-caláxat* 'broke, the-dish,Fm'
niSaru botnim 'remain,Pl peanuts'	*niS'ar botnim* 'remains peanuts'
ze tmuna 'this is (a) picture,Fm'	*zot tmuna* 'this is,Fm (a) picture,Fm

& Siegel 1978, Pennanen 1975, Selkirk 1982). Backformation is a gap-filler, a process which fills in empty lexical slots missing in a small vocabulary.

Such a vocabulary is typical of children, on the one hand, who produce what Clark (1981) terms *illegitimate innovations,* and of nonliterate adults, on the other, who may not be aware of the precise structure of the complex base form.

Today, backformation is a productive process in Contemporary Hebrew in the sense that it is commonly found in ordinary speech, especially in that of speakers with less awareness of formal structure. In the examples below (Table 23), the first seven items occur in everyday adult speech, while the last two are childish productions.

Table 24 enumerates the Backformation items.

Summary

The test items (Appendix B) were randomized and rearranged by "Task Type," which refers to the type of operation subjects were required to perform. Table 25 below summarizes the test categories, the items and the tasks presented to the subjects.

Table 23. Backformation in Modern Hebrew

| | Backformed Form | | |
Plural Base	Normative	Nonstandard	Gloss
anav-im	*enav*	*anav*	grapes/grape
klay-ot	*kilya*	*klaya*	kidneys/kidney
gic-im	*gec*	*gic*	sparks/spark
karciy-ot	*karcit*	*karciya*	ticks/tick
karsuláy-im	*karsol*	*karsul*	ankles/ankle
ugiy-ot	*ugit*	*ugiya*	cookies/cookie
maca-im	*maca*	*mac*	beddings/bedding
rak-im	*rax*	*rak*	soft,Pl/soft

Table 24. Backformation Items

Inflected Base	Normative	Nonstandard	Gloss
cdaf-im	*cédef*	*cdaf*	shells/shell
acam-ot	*écem*	*acama*	bones/bone
dma-ot	*dim'a*	*dma'a*	tears/tear
kivs-a	*kéves*	*kivs*	sheep/ram
par-a	*par*	*para*	cow/bull
tarnegól-et	*tarnegol*	*tarnególet*	hen/rooster

As shown in Table 26, the Alpha test of Reliability (internal consistency) indicated that the 61 test items constituted one major domain, a single dimension. The test as a primary tool was varied enough and each category sufficiently well-represented thanks to the extensive piloting. At the same time, it was short enough to be used with preschool children from as young as age 3.

Procedures

The test was administered to each subject individually in familiar surroundings. Sessions lasted an average of 15 minutes, ranging from 10 minutes with the high-SES adults to 30 minutes with the nursery-schoolers. Two kinds of ancillary materials were used for elicitation: picture-cards, and two types of dolls—big floppy cloth dolls, and small Lego figures. These aids were considered necessary for children prior to the stage of Piagetian formal operations, to provide them with concrete objects to refer to. The pilot test showed that the picture cards were also, and unexpectedly, necessary in the case of low-SES adults who, lacking experience in formal test-like situations, coped better with the required tasks when these were backed up by pictures.

The test was conducted as follows: the younger children were told they were going to play a game with the interviewer. Older subjects and adults

Table 25. Summary of test categories and items

Test Category	# of Items	Subclasses	Task Type
Weak Syllable	10	9 verbs, 1 noun	Masc to Fm
		3 final *x*,	Past to Pres
		6 final vowel,	3rd to 1st Pr
		1 final -*it*	Sg to Pl
Stop/Spirant Alternation	7	5 verbs,	Past to Pres
		2 adjectives,	Pres to Past
		3 *p~f*,	Inf to Pres
		2 *b~v*, 2 *k~x*	Sg to Pl
			Act to Pas
			Masc to Fm
			Fm to Masc
Stem Change	3	2 nouns, 1 adjective	Sg to Pl
Hif'il Vowel Alternation	4	4 *Hif'il* verbs	Past to Pres
		2 *n*-initial roots	
		2 glide-medial roots	
Verb tense	7	7 verbs	Past to Pres
			Pres to Past
			Pres and Past to
			Future, 1st Pr
Lexical Exceptions	7	4 nouns, 3 verbs	Sg to Pl
			Past to Pres
			Pres to Past
			Pres to Future
Case-Marked Pronouns	5	5 prepositions	Prep to Prep
			marked for:
			2nd Pr Fm
			2nd Pr Masc Sg
			3rd Pr Masc Sg
Verb-Governed Prepositions	7	7 verbs	Verb to
			Verb + Prep
Subject-Verb Concord	5	4 verbs,	Pres to Past
		1 demonstrative Pro	Inf to Pres
			Inf to Past, Pl
			Masc to Fm
Backformation		3 plural nouns	Pl to Sg
		3 feminine nouns	Fm to Masc
Total	61	61 items	

were told that they were participating in a study concerning grammatical categories in Modern Hebrew (despite the interviewer's protests, some subjects nonetheless regarded the interview as some sort of test in prescriptive Hebrew grammar!). The interviewer then introduced the test items with or without ancillary materials, and the subject had to change them grammatically according to given verbal cues. For example, to elicit a change from singular to plural, numerals or quantifiers were used, e.g. *híne*

Table 26. Reliability indices of test categories

Test Category	# of Items	α
Weak Syllable	10	0.85
Stop/Spirant Alternation	7	0.85
Stem Change	3	0.66
Hif'il Vowel Alternation	4	0.58[32]
Verb Tense	7	0.84
Lexical Exceptions	7	0.83
Case-Marked Pronouns	5	0.78
Verb-Governed Prepositions	7	0.76
Subject-Verb Concord	5	0.65
Backformation	6	0.82
Entire Test	61	0.97

dli, ve-kan yeS Snáyim. éle Sney . . . 'Here (is a) bucket, and-here there (are) *two*. These are two'[33] . . .

Coding

All responses were analyzed into two major response types: Appropriate and Inappropriate, where Inappropriate responses were irrelevant, or where subjects did not give an answer at all.

Appropriate responses were subdivided further into three classes, constituting the focal variables of this study: (i) *Normative,* the response an educated adult would give to an input item, and as close as possible to the norms set by the Hebrew Language Academy; (ii) *Expected,* which is the most common deviation from the norm,[34] indicating full understanding of the nature of the task involved and of the test item, e.g. *mikódem ha-yéled lo higía la-délet, ve-gam axSav hu lo* . . . 'Before the-boy (did) not reach to-the-door, and-also now he (does) not . . .' where the response is *megía* rather than the Normative *magía* 'reaches'; (iii) Other-Appropriate, a third possibility, neither Normative nor Expected, yet suitable to the task, e.g. when asking for the plural form of *dli* 'bucket', the Normative response is *dlayim,* the Expected Nonstandard form is *dliyim,* and other (incorrect but plausible) options are *dlilim* or *dlalot.*

Test-Related Hypotheses

The hypotheses presented below relate actively to the two independent variables of the experimental design: *Age* and *SES* (1–7), and to the dependent variables—the research categories (8–10).

1. The number of Appropriate responses on the test items will increase with age for all subjects, due to general cognitive and specifically linguistic developmental factors.
2. The number of Normative responses will increase with age due to the onset and development of literacy.

3. Subjects with a low SES background will have lower Normative scores than higher-class subjects owing to a lesser sensitivity to literate norms.
4. An interaction will be found between age and SES.
5. Young children will use strategies differently from adults. They will rely heavily on strategies deriving from pragmatic factors, and from frequency and familiarity of usage. At a later age, they will make use of strategies that promote transparency and saliency. Adults will be more sensitive to formal linguistic cues.
6. There will be a certain amount of similarity between language strategies employed by children and low-SES adults.
7. Certain deviations will characterize subsets of the test population. Deviations typical of children's usage will occur in the adult population less frequently than those which prior research has determined to characterize adults as well. There will be deviations that will occur more frequently in the uneducated population.
8. A hierarchy of stability will be reflected in the Normative scores of each test category. The categories lowest on the hierarchy will be the most unstable, in the process of change.
9. The changes involved will not be radical, so as not to disrupt the transmission of language within the framework of time and the speech community (Halle 1962, Labov 1982).
10. Instability will be observed at those points in the language structure characterized by idiosyncracy and opacity.

Statistical Methods

Test hypotheses relating to maturation were tested using One-Way Analysis of Variance (ANOVA). The Scheffé Procedure was applied to determine the significance of differences in the mean scores of all pairs of groups, all and only to Normative responses, since this response type was considered to be the most significant in both developmental and sociolinguistic terms. Test hypotheses concerning both differences in socioeconomic background *and* age were also tested by means of Analysis of Variance techniques, applied to all and only the six groups subdivided by both age and SES. The significance of the relationship between these two variables and the 10 research categories was tested by means of the Multivariate Test of significance (Wilks' Lambda). Where an overall significance was attested, the ten category scores were further analyzed by a Two-Way Analysis of Variance to determine interaction as well as main effect.

2.2. RESULTS

The Normative (conforming to the educated standard in Contemporary Israeli Hebrew) responses given on the structured test were analyzed using the statistical measures described in 2.1 above. The following is a short summary of the results.[35] Overall results on the test for each of the ten groups are laid out in Table 27 and in Figure 1.

There is clearly a steady increase in the number of Normative responses in all groups except for the last, the low SES Adults b. There is also a clear

Table 27. Mean percentages of the Normative responses on the test as a whole, given by each group.

Group ID	N	School Level	SES	% Normative	SD
3 year olds	23	Nursery School	high	27.4	14.4
5 year olds a	21	Kindergarten	high	51.1	11.6
5 year olds b	20	Kindergarten	low	33.8	8.7
8 year olds	24	Grade School	high	72.5	10.8
12 year olds a	21	Junior High	high	87.2	5.2
12 year olds b	21	Junior High	low	69.6	8.6
16 year olds	20	High School	high	86.5	5.0
Young Adults a	11		high	88.7	5.3
Older Adults a	10		high	86.6	5.2
Adults b	17		low	55.9	13.4
T o t a l	188			63.5	

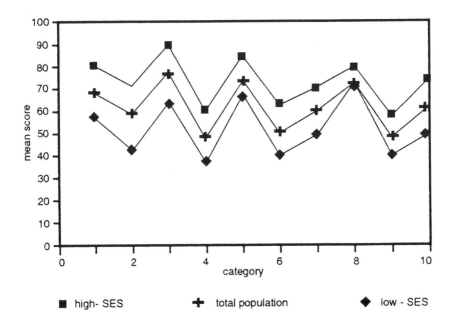

Figure 1.

difference between SES groups of the same age, the gap increasing with age. Normative responses rise also for the low SES population, but the Adults b score less than the low SES 12 year olds. The low SES groups thus seem to lag one chronological step in proportion of Normative responses behind the high SES groups, and this lag is found in every single one of the test categories. Standard deviation scores reflect the relative homogeneity of all but the extreme groups in the test population as a whole: The most variety is displayed by the youngest children, reflecting different rates of development, and by the low SES Adults b, reflecting a variety of educational and social backgrounds.

Since a One-Way Analysis of Variance revealed significant differences between groups, the Multiple Range Test (Scheffé Procedure) was performed on the same Normative scores, arranging pairs of groups differing significantly ($p < .05$). The results are depicted in Table 28, where shaded cells indicate groups differing at the $p < .05$ level.

The patterns revealed in Tables 27–28 form three pairs that score alike and are statistically homogeneous: the high-SES 3 year olds with the low-SES 5 year olds; the high-SES 8 year olds with the low-SES 12 year olds; the high-SES 5 year olds and the low-SES adults. Then there is a block of all the older high-SES groups, with no significant difference between older and younger high-SES groups. This suggests a normative plateau achieved by age 12 in the high-SES groups.

The same pattern of language knowledge in four major population blocks is revealed in all ten research categories; however, the rate and degree of mastery of each category varies according to its status in Contemporary Hebrew morphology. In some categories, there is a clear developmental rise, while in others scores start low and stay low, and yet in others children start off with a comparatively high Normative score. The scores of

Table 28. Statistically significant differences in amount of Normative responses on the test as a whole between groups of subjects, by age and SES. Groups are ranked horizontally in ascending order of age; vertically, the test groups are arranged in ascending order of Normative responses, from lowest to the highest.

Group ID	3	5a	5b	8	12a	12b	16	Young Ada	Old Ada	Adb
3 year olds		X		X	X	X	X	X	X	X
5 year olds b		X		X	X	X	X	X	X	X
5 year olds a	X		X	X	X	X	X	X	X	
Adults b	X		X	X	X	X	X	X	X	
12 year olds b	X	X	X		X		X	X	X	
8 year olds	X	X	X		X		X	X		
16 year olds	X	X	X	X		X				X
Older Adults a	X	X	X			X				X
12 year olds	X	X	X	X		X				X
Young Adults a	X	X	X	X		X				X

each group in each category are presented in Tables 29, 30 and 31 below, while the factors that govern the acquisition and mastery of my research categories are discussed in the next chapters.

The findings presented in 27–29 show a clear rise in Normative scores with the rise in age and SES, with a discrepancy between groups of the same age with a different socioeconomic background. But despite this maturational and socioeconomic variation between test groups, each study category has a distinct character owing to its rate of acquisition and degree of mastery by the various groups. In some categories acquisition is fast and the degree of mastery is high. These morphological areas are not undergoing change in Modern Hebrew. Others, however, display poor success rates by all groups, and these are the unstable morphological domains currently undergoing change in Hebrew. These aspects of the test results are depicted below in Tables 30 and 31, and in Figure 2.

Table 30 shows that both age and SES make a highly significant contribution to the total score and to each test category separately. Moreover, the interaction between them is significant for the total score, and for five out of the ten research categories. These three parameters—age, SES and the interaction between them—explain 80% of the amount of variation in the test as a whole, and more than two thirds of the variation in six out of the ten test categories (R^2). The two categories where age and SES make the least contribution to explaining variation are *Hif'il Vowel Alternation,* the least stable category undergoing massive change in the population as a whole, and *Verb-Governed Prepositions,* a very stable category where mastery is achieved very early on.

On the whole, *age* was found to be a better predictor of Normative scores than SES, and this is also true for eight out of the ten test categories. *SES* was found to be equally more important in predicting Normative scores in two categories only: *Vowel Alternation* (I believe for the reason discussed above) and *Weak Final Syllable,* as will be discussed below. Table 31 ranks the test categories in order of stability, from lowest to highest.

The Current Status of Study Domains

The major trends found in the Normative responses indicate the following current situation in the morphophonological domains studied in spoken Hebrew:

Stable Areas

Two very stable categories are Stem Change and Verb-Governed Prepositions. Children as young as 3 already have almost 50% Normative scores, and by age 8 almost all groups have more than 80% Normative scores. For example, 74% (!) of the three-year-olds give *adumim* 'red,Pl' for *adom* 'red', while 88% of them come up with Normative *tarbic le-* 'hit to'. In both categories the gap between younger ages and low-SES groups, on the

Table 29. Mean percentage of Normative responses on the test categories for each group, by age and SES. Percentages are rounded to the nearest point to facilitate reading.

Group Id Age SES	Weak Syllable	Stop/Spirant Alternation	Stem Change	*Hif'il* Vowel Alternation	Verb Tense
3 high SES	35	21	46	23	34
5a high SES	68	40	73	44	67
5b low SES	35	23	40	26	59
8 high SES	78	67	88	53	86
12a high SES	91	91	98	69	95
12b low SES	73	62	84	43	84
16 high SES	92	89	98	64	91
Young Adults a high SES	93	95	100	66	99
Older Adults a high SES	94	86	100	58	96
Adults b low SES	57	42	78	37	70
Total	69	58	78	47	76

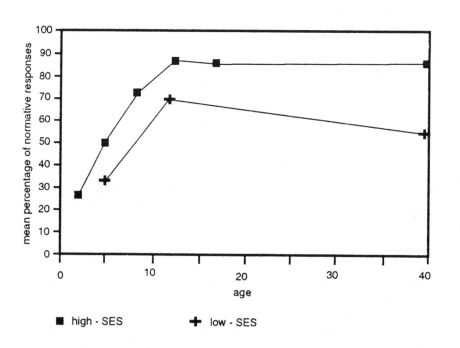

Figure 2.

Lexical Exceptions	Case-Marked Pronouns	Governed Prepositions	Subject-Verb Concord	Backformation
12	15	46	21	23
26	34	72	39	48
14	19	69	23	22
58	71	84	60	76
74	95	88	78	90
57	67	85	63	71
78	91	84	83	91
88	95	86	62	94
89	90	86	64	92
49	64	73	32	58
50	61	76	52	63

Table 30. Significance of the Normative responses given on the test as a whole and on each of the ten test categories by members of the double-SES groups (5s a/b, 12s a/b, Adults a/b) [N = 121]; results of a 2-way ANOVA

Test Category	F (age)	F (SES)	(age × SES)	R^2 [37]	Age	SES
Weak Final Syllable	67.8**	119.7**	4.7*	.7	.6	.6
Stop/Spirant Alternation	88.3**	110.5**	9.1**	.7	.7	.5
Stem Change	70.7**	72.8**	4.2*	.6	.7	.5
Hif'il Vowel Alternation	9.3**	31.8**	.4	.3	.3	.4
Verb Tense	51.1**	40.8**	6.7**	.5	.6	.4
Lexical Exceptions	178.9**	88.4**	12.1**	.8	.8	.4
Case-Marked Pronouns	106.8**	49.0*	1.7	.7	.8	.4
Verb-Governed Preps	18.0**	7.7*	1.7	.3	.5	.2
Subject-Verb Concord	34.3**	26.6*	1.6	.4	.6	.4
Backformation	98.7**	83.4*	2.5	.7	.7	.5
Total Test Score	182.4**	173.9**	7.9*	.8	.7	.5

(The "F" header spans F (age), F (SES), and (age × SES); the "B weights[36]" header spans R^2 [37], Age, and SES.)

*p<.05
**p<.01

Table 31. Mean percentages of Normative responses on the 10 test categories ranked in ascending order of achievement for the population as a whole, and for high-SES compared with low-SES (double groups only) subjects

| Test Category | Mean percentages of Normative Responses | | |
	Total population N = 188	High SES N = 63	Low SES N = 58
Vowel Alternation	46.8	58.3	35.3
Lexical Exceptions	50.2	62.6	39.4
Subject-Verb Concord	51.5	60.0	40.0
Stop/Spirant Alternation	58.4	73.9	42.6
Case-Marked Pronouns	60.5	74.0	49.3
Backformation	63.4	77.0	50.0
Weak Final Syllable	68.7	82.5	55.3
Verb Tense	75.5	86.2	71.2
Verb-Governed Prepositions	76.2	82.1	75.9
Stem Change	78.4	90.5	67.2
T o t a l	63.5	75.3	53.2

one hand, and older, more literate subjects, on the other hand, is rather small.[38]

In Verb-tense, acquisition of this essential inflectional feature is fast, so that all groups over 5 score 60% Normative and higher. Due to the fast acquisition rate, the regular low-SES 5s/high-SES 3s block is prevented. For example, 48% of the 3-year-olds gave Normative *Sarim* rather than *maSirim* 'are singing' as the present-tense form of *Sáru* '(they) sang', with all the rest of the groups scoring more than 90%! When asked to form future-tense verbs, especially in the first person, an area undergoing language change, as in *lamdu/elmad* '(they) studied/(I) will-study', the scores are much lower, which is why this category is not the most stable.

Middle Categories

The medial categories of Table 31 are those strongly governed by developmental or SES components, with overall maximum scores under 70% due to maturational and literacy factors. Case-marked Pronouns and Backformation Normative scores start under 25%, and gradually work up to over 90% in the older literate population; however, they stay between 60 and 70% in the older low-SES groups. For example, *kmo-* 'like' yields less than 20% Normative *kamóxa* (Nonstandard *kmo ata*) 'like-you' under age 8, but all older high-SES groups score more than 95%, while the low-SES 12s give 50% Normative and the low-SES adults 65%. Normative *dim'a* (Nonstandard *dma'a*) 'tear' from plural *dma'ot* has quite similar scores.

The Weak Syllable category is a good example for the steady progression of maturation: the youngest subjects start off with more than one third Normative responses, and by puberty high-SES subjects have already mastered the alternations involved in stem-final low consonants and semi-vowels; while subjects from a low-SES background reach a peak of less than 3/4 Normative at 12, and adults score little over half Normative. For example, for the input item *menaka* 'cleaning,Fm', 3-year-olds start off with around one fifth Normative responses *nikíti* 'I cleaned', while another one fifth give the expected Nonstandard *nikéti*. By age 12, more than 90% of the high-SES population give the Standard *nikíti* form, however only 29% and 18% (!) of the adolescent and adult low-SES population do so.

Areas of Instability

Two very unstable categories with low start-off scores and very low literate adult scores are *Hif'il* Vowel Alternation and Subject-Verb Concord, both high in instability (Table 31). The gap between young/low-SES subjects and older/high-SES subjects is not very large, since most Normative scores for all groups are under 70% and much less. For example, only 9% of the youngest children give *meríax* 'smelling' as the present form of past-tense *heríax,* with the Normative score climbing to 54% in the 8s, 71% in the high-SES 12s and peaking in 86% in the high-SES adults, the only group that passes three-quarters.[39]

In the two other unstable categories, SES and age are responsible for a changing standard. Lexical Exceptions comes out as very unstable due to the make-up of its items. Certainly, both the maturational and SES factors govern acquisition in such a way that even the low-SES 12s achieve under 60% Normative scores, but Item Analysis shows that the language-change item *yaxol* 'is able' is responsible for much of the lower scores. In other items, such as *Isa* 'woman', children start off with only Nonstandard responses, however by age 8 they already produce 75% Normative responses, reaching a perfect score in all the older high-SES groups.

In Stop/Spirant Alternation, the interplay between developmental and Literacy factors dictates the great gap between the scores of young/low-SES groups and others. For example, for the item *mefazéret* 'scattering,Fm' *none* of the high-SES 3-year-olds and low-SES 5-year-olds, and only 5% of the high-SES 5-year-olds gave the Normative form *pizra* 'she scattered', while 50% or more of them gave the Nonstandard form with an initial fricative *fizra*. The low-SES scores for this item stay very low (between 20 and 30% in the adolescent and adult low-SES groups) while those of the older high-SES population are very high, between 95 and 100%. These results differ markedly from those of Schwarzwald (1981), where low-SES adults perform better than low-SES adolescents, and in one domain (first radical of the root) the low-SES population perform as well as the high-SES subjects. My interpretation of this difference, as well as the socio- and psycho-linguistic factors responsible for the picture revealed in this study, is discussed below in Chapter 6.

To complete the picture, I present in Table 32 the amount of Appropriate (that is, Non-Normative but test-task-appropriate) responses out of

Table 32. Percentage of Appropriate and Non-normative responses given on the test as a whole, by age and SES

Group ID	% of Non-Normative Responses out of all Test Responses	% of Appropriate Responses out of Non-Normative Responses
3 year olds	72.6	38.3
5 year olds a	48.9	70.0
5 year olds b	66.2	52.7
8 year olds	27.5	76.3
12 year olds a	12.8	72.0
12 year olds b	30.4	75.4
16 year olds	13.5	85.4
Young Adults a	11.3	74.4
Older Adults a	13.4	70.2
Adults b	44.1	64.4
Total	36.5	67.3

the total non-Normative score. These scores are significant as well, since they indicate the ability on the part of the test subjects to carry out the grammatical operations required of them. The interested reader can find a detailed test-category analysis in Ravid 1988.

Summary of Findings

Analysis of the Normative as well as of the Appropriate responses on the test as a whole and on each of the test categories confirmed most of the study hypotheses. The findings are summed below.

1. The rise in the amount of Appropriate and especially of Normative responses is a direct result of increasing age and of higher literacy and socio-economic status.
2. Age and SES were found to interact. Specifically, older low-SES groups performed on the same Normative level as younger high-SES groups.
3. Some of the test categories and individual items (Appendix C) were found to be more unstable than others: Hif'il Vowel Alternation, Subject-Verb Concord, Lexical Exceptions and Stop/Spirant Alternation. The particularly unstable items were the following: Weak Syllable *kine* 'envied'; Stop/Spirant Alternation *hikpía* 'she froze, Tr.' and *Savar* 'broke, Tr.' Lexical Exceptions *yaSna* '(she) slept' and *yaxol* 'is able'; Case-Marked Pronouns *bli* 'without'; Verb-Governed Prepositions *tistakel* 'look' and Backformation item *cdafim* 'sea-shells'.
4. The acquisition of some categories and of specific items was clearly dependent on *developmental* factors. These were the categories of Weak Syllable, most particularly the items *Sata* 'drank', *soxe* 'swims' and *taklit* 'record'; the item *cahov* 'yellow' in Stop/Spirant Alterna-

tion; Stem Change, in particular the items *éven* 'stone' and *adom* 'red'; Verb-Tense, especially the items *Sáru* '(they) sang', *rávu*, '(they) fought' and *mesaxek* 'plays'; Case-Marked Pronouns, specifically *et* 'Accusative Marker' Verb-Governed Prepositions, with the exception of *tistakel* 'look' (see above); and the items *acamot* 'bones' and *tarnególet* 'chicken' in Backformation.

In categories and items whose acquisition was specifically governed by maturation, all or most items showed a clear rise in Normative responses with age, while the low-SES 12-year-olds, and sometimes even the less literate Adults b, had ceiling scores of the Normative type. This shows that acquisition of these domains proceeds regardless of SES. For example, the item *acamot* 'bones' had Normative scores of 90% and over from age 5 onwards, and this included all groups except for the youngest low-SES group of the 5-year-olds. In addition, beta weights in these domains indicated that age, markedly more than SES, was a significant predictor of success in giving Normative responses.

5. Some categories and specific items were more affected by socioeconomic factors. These were the items *niftax* 'opens,Int.' *dorex* 'stepping' *menaka* 'cleaning,Fm' and *mexake* 'waiting' in Weak Syllable; Stop/Spirant Alternation, and specifically the items *mefazéret* 'scatters,Fm', *lirkav* 'to-ride' and *rax* 'soft'; Lexical Exceptions, especially the items *dli* 'bucket', *yaSna* 'slept,Fm' and *loveS* 'wearing'; the items *kmo* 'like' and *bli* 'without' in Case-Marked Pronouns; and the items *cdafim* 'shells' and *dma'ot* 'tears' and *para* 'cow' in Backformation.

Where SES was the leading factor, there was a marked disparity between the amount of Normative responses given by the older high-SES groups, especially the school-going 12- and 16-year-olds, and those given by the older low-SES groups, especially the school-going 12-year-olds, where other findings indicate Normative responses reach a plateau and level off. Thus for instance SES *mexake* 'waiting' scored 100% Normative with *xikíti* '(I) waited' in all older high-SES groups, but only 67% and 47% in the low-SES 12s-b and Adults b respectively.

6. Finally, some of the test categories were especially *stable* and conformed to Normative requirements. These were Stem-Change, Verb-Tense and Governed Prepositions.

3

Analysis of Results: The Effects of Literacy and Maturation

The following chapters discuss the results of the structured elicitation task described in Chapter 2, supplemented by findings from three sources of spontaneous data:

1. Longitudinal diary studies of two children, Sivan (a girl) and Assaf (a boy), based on written diaries and recorded sessions, henceforth *DIA*;
2. Recorded free speech samples of the same subjects that took part in the structured test (*SAM*);
3. Observational data of the free speech usage of children, adolescents and adult speakers, collected in the course of seven years (*OBS*).
   These are used in formulating an explanatory model relating language acquisition, linguistic variation and language change.[40]

This chapter evaluates the test hypotheses underlying the structured test against the results described in 2.2 above. In general, I hypothesized that the amount of both Appropriate and Normative responses should rise with age; that there would nonetheless be a disparity between the amount of Normative responses given by high-SES and low-SES speakers of the same age; that certain deviations should characterize specific sections of the population; and that children would approach the task differently than adults, but that their strategies would be somewhat similar to those employed by older low-SES subjects.

3.1. APPROPRIATE RESPONSES:
THE FACTOR OF MATURATION

Maturation was indeed found to have the expected effect on the test subjects: The number of Appropriate responses on each of the test categories as well as on each item rises with age, although not in a linear fashion. There is a particularly sharp rise between the ages of three to five, whereas after age five there are no significant differences between groups, except for the 16-year-olds. These findings express the difference between young preschool children, still in the process of acquisition of the morphological system, and the rest of the population. Since acquisition of the major components of Hebrew morphology takes place between the ages of two and five (Berman 1985, 1986a, Kaplan 1983, Levy 1980, Rabinowitz 1985, Rom & Dgani 1985), it is not Normative (educated adult) responses that should be considered at this age-span, but rather actual performance on the task, indicating that the child is able to carry out operations that change grammatical features of cue-items such as tense in verbs, or number in nouns. Making these changes yields an Appropriate response-type, a function of age-related development.

This is confirmed by the many child language studies showing that acquisition of grammatical inflections of person, number, case, tense and aspect as well as pronominal forms, takes place mainly during preschool years (Brown 1973, Bloom, Lifter & Hafitz 1980, Cazden 1968, Derwing & Baker 1986, Deutsch & Pechmann 1978, deVilliers & deVilliers 1978, Kuczaj 1977, MacWhinney 1978, Maratsos 1982, Menyuk 1969, 1977, M. Smith 1978).

In my free-speech data, too, children frequently produce non-Normative forms which nonetheless include the necessary grammatical changes, e.g. plural *iSim* for *anaSim* 'people', from *iS* 'man' [3;7,SAM]; or *régelot* for *ragláyim* 'feet' from singular *régel* [2;7,OBS]. There were fewer examples of inappropriate forms where the grammatical operation was not carried out at all, e.g. *harbe kos* 'many glass' for *kosot* 'glasses' [3;7,SAM]. This is in contrast to the number of such Inappropriate responses given on the test, especially by young children and low-SES adults. The difference lies in the nature of the experimental situation: While the free-speech data were recorded or collected in a natural context of use, the structured test demanded non-contextualized responses elicited in a relatively formal situation. This has been shown to hamper performance compared to more contextualized situations (Karmiloff-Smith 1979). The experimental design and the supplementary data from the free speech samples thus tap two different types of linguistic knowledge: A structured test forces the subject to concentrate directly on the linguistic task as a problem to be solved, involving conscious application to the task as a goal in itself. This might block access to knowledge that could be available when implicitly used as a means to another goal. The free speech samples, in contrast, are taken from on-line conversation, a language activity serving as a means towards a non-linguistic end, so providing a different sort of access to linguistic knowledge (Karmiloff-Smith 1986b).

In line with these arguments, giving Appropriate responses depended on the difficulty presented by the linguistic category as well as by the experimental task. Developmental factors determined the ability of subjects to give more Appropriate responses in some categories rather than others. And the grammatical operations that had to be performed on specific items in the same category also presented various degrees of complexity. For example, Open Syllable items such as *hevi* 'brought', *soxe* 'swims' and *taklit* '(a) record' had to be changed into 1st person past tense, feminine, and plural forms respectively. Some of these operations may have been more difficult for young children than others (Edwards 1975). For instance, changing verbs into future tense proved more difficult than into past and present, accounting for the low percentage of Appropriate responses on the Verb-Tense cue-items *kotev* 'writes' and *lamdu* '(they) studied', and on the Lexical Exception cue-item *loveS* 'wears', especially in the 3s and the low-SES adults (Similar results were found by Kaplan 1983).

My diary study presents similar instances, e.g. of a child saying *naxon eyn lahem maxar máyim ve-hem novlim?* 'Isn't it true that they don't have water tomorrow and they wilt,Pl?' instead of *lo yihyu lahem máyim ve-hem yiblu* 'they won't have water and they will wilt' [3;1,DIA]. Or, *aval axár-kax ani lo yaxol lehagía* 'but later I cannot reach', instead of *ani lo uxal* 'I won't be able' [3;4,DIA]. Future-tense forms occur in the speech of children much less frequently than past and present-tense forms (Berman & Dromi 1984), while Schwarzwald (1981) found more errors in future-tense forms than in others. These difficulties may be conceptual, and not purely formal, as shown by data on future tense acquired in other languages (Bloom, Lifter & Hafitz 1980, Bronchart & Sinclair 1973, Clark 1977, Lewis 1971).

Difficulties with the task itself were enhanced among less literate subjects by lack of experience with test situations. The high number of Appropriate responses given by the 16-year-olds compared with other groups can be explained by their familiarity with what is expected and how to behave on a test. They were the most oriented towards school-type testing and "right answer" so typical of scholastic settings. They were adept at strategies for interpreting and using language in ways that work best at a school situation (Romaine 1984). Demuth, Faraclas & Marchese (1986) found similar differences between spontaneous and experimental studies in their study of gender and number concord in Niger-Congo languages. Nouns presented out of context made the task of noun class assignment much more difficult, and they conclude that "It is in less normal contexts, as that provided in language tasks . . . where the productivity of such a system comes into jeopardy" (1986:467). On the other hand, experiments reported in Bybee & Moder (1983) and Bybee & Slobin (1982) revealed productive rules not otherwise perceptible in spontaneous speech.

In sum, developmental factors account for the number of Appropriate responses on each of the test categories. This explains the high number of Appropriate responses on both Stem-Change and Lexical Exceptions, even though the two rated very differently on Normative responses. Both involved much the same task across their items, to inflect for plural and for feminine gender, basic processes acquired early on (Levy 1980, Kaplan 1983). This proved easier for children and for non-tutored adults than, say, changing the tense on verbs.[41]

3.2. NORMATIVE RESPONSES: THE FACTOR OF LITERACY

I hypothesized that the number of Normative responses would rise with age, due to effects of maturation and literacy, and that low-SES speakers would nonetheless give fewer Normative responses than high-SES speakers. This indeed proved to be the case: the number of Normative responses does rise with age, but reaches ceiling only among high-SES speakers. In the higher-class population, 5-year-olds have an overall Normative score of 50%, and this rises sharply with the onset of literacy at school. From age 12 onwards there is no significant difference between high-SES groups. The lower-class groups present a different picture: they, too, show a rise in Normative scores with age, especially conspicuous between 5 and 12, but low-SES subjects consistently score less than their high-SES peers, and there is also a sharp decline in Normative responses in adulthood. The spontaneous data-base contains numerous examples of non-normative forms typically produced by low-SES speakers. For example, *zikénu* '(we) refunded', *niséti* '(I) tried', for Normative *zikínu* and *nisíti* [31,SAM]; *limSóax* 'to-pull' with vowel epenthesis typical of *H*-final stems for *limSox* (root *m-S-x*), [55,SAM]; *niftéxet* 'opens,Fm' for *niftáxat* (root *p-t-H*), [12;6,Rec]; *ani yavo kmo oréax* 'I will-come,3rd like (a) guest' instead of *ani avo* 'I will-come,1st', [30,SAM]; *hayíti yoSénet* 'I was-sleeping' for *hayíti yeSena*[42] [24, SAM]; *fSa'im* 'crimes' for *pSa'im*, [12;3,SAM]; *fixádeti* '(I) was-scared' for Normative *paxádeti* [15,SAM].[43]

This discrepancy between the Normative scores of the two populations can be explained by two properties of low-SES speakers, involving both a communicative and a structural facet: Their relative lack of access to normative usage, and their reliance on simplified rules. Together, this means that the low-SES members of the speech community have a slightly different sociolect from the high-SES speakers. This non-normative (and in some cases, as we shall see, Nonstandard) sociolect is not as distinct from Standard Modern Hebrew as, say, the Black English dialect described by Labov (1969, 1972b) is from Standard English. The differences are mainly morphophonological rather than syntactic, and are often present, though to a lesser degree, in the usage of more educated speakers as well.

One reason that low-SES speakers produce fewer normative forms is because they are not fully literate. Only the fully literate have access to all possible registers and levels of linguistic usage (See Berman 1987b for Hebrew; Harrel 1957, O'Donnell, Griffin & Norris 1967, and Ruddell 1978, for English). Thus Southworth (1971) reports that forms used by less educated speakers of Marathi were consistently further from the literary standard. Martin (1983) claims that children's major linguistic achievement over the school years is a better ability to distinguish differences in register; and academic language has been shown to enlarge vocabulary and semantic terrain (Corson 1983, Smith 1978). But such language usage is also more conservative in the sense that it employs fewer colloquial and Nonstandard forms (Chafe 1985, Perera 1986, Shlesinger 1985). For example, the number of Nonstandard constructions is much lower in the written usage of older compared with younger students as a result of more years of schooling (Cheshire 1982).

For speakers of Modern Hebrew, being literate means being more sensitive to norms set by the Hebrew Language Establishment, which are taught at school as part of the Hebrew grammar curriculum. Low-SES speakers, having less access to higher-register language, to books and textbooks, poetry, newspapers, periodicals and drama, are less exposed to the more normative varieties of Hebrew, and as a result produce more deviations of the Nonstandard type. Similar findings and observations were reported by Cais (1981), Davis (1976b, 1981), Donag-Kinrot (1978), Kemp (1984), Nir (1977), Schwarzwald (1981) and Vidislavsky (1984). Low-SES junior high schoolers (7th grade) had higher Normative scores on this test than pre-literate low-SES 5-year-olds, on the one hand, and non-literate adults, on the other. This is due to the effect of seven years of exposure to textbook norms and school-type language.

One effect of literacy is to enhance awareness of abstract underlying morphophonological structure: Andersen (1973) notes that educated English speakers are able to reconstruct the phoneme /x/ which is absent in their language in foreign words, especially proper nouns. Such sensitivity to underlying representation checks the tendency towards rule simplification which would otherwise be perfectly natural, following Slobin's (1973, 1977) injunction of "being clear," that is, of maintaining a minimal distance between underlying form and surface realization, and avoiding exceptions. This is especially important in Hebrew where awareness of underlying gutturals and pharyngeals, and of historical roots in general, motivates surface alternations that otherwise appear idiosyncratic, so that irregular forms become more transparent and direct the literate respondent to the historical, or Normative, form.

Without these guidelines, speakers are inclined to simplify rules. This is especially true of children, who seek the simplest grammars (Halle 1962, Kiparsky 1982); but it also commonly occurs among less literate adult speakers, in varieties of informal speech, and was observed both in pidgins (Ferguson 1971) and in historical trends. For example, Mishnaic Hebrew had forms such as *yacta* '(she) went-out', for *yac'a,* root *y-ṣ-?* (Schwarzwald 1980c), analogous to the test Expected (Nonstandard) response *kinta* '(she) was-jealous' (Normative *kin'a*, root *q-n-?*) given by speakers and low-SES adults, and attested too in my longitudinal data. In both cases, speakers extended the internal *-t-* typical of *y-* final roots in past tense singular feminine to *?*-final forms. This could be expected in Standard speech as well, if not for the retarding influence of literacy: The knowledge of the two different underlying elements, represented by two letters in the orthography (ה *he* and א *álef* respectively), prevents such rule collapse in the more monitored speech of educated speakers.

Likewise, Poplack (1980) found that s-deletion was common only in uneducated Puerto Rican Spanish; and Samuels (1972) claims the written language has a strong influence on preservation of formal variants in a given language. Givón (1985) goes on further to claim that it is literacy and education alone that preserve irregular sub-systems of morphology. According to him, children "won't stand for" the high degree of code-irregularity in morphology if not for education.

Literacy had another kind of effect on high-SES subjects: they occasionally "falsified" normativity by giving responses which differed from what I had judged to be their usual standard, knowing (and sometimes saying so explicitly) that these forms were "more correct." This attitude characterized both high-SES adolescents and adults in the controlled experiment. Unlike the children and the low-SES sub-population, who might have been intimidated by the test situation, the high-SES subjects, and especially the school-goers, thrived on it. They thus avoided structures which they knew to be non-Normative. For example, a 59-year-old woman gave the response of *Savur* 'broken' to the cue *ha-tinok Savar et ha-bakbuk, ve-axSav ha-bakbuk Selo* . . . 'the baby broke the bottle, and now its bottle is . . .'. As she did so, she laughed and said: "Did you expect me to say *Sabur*? I know it's wrong". But later, on another part of the test, when attending to noun-verb agreement rather than to spirantization, she said *ha-caláxat Sbura* 'the-plate (is) broken' for Normative *Svura*.

My records contain numerous instances of high-SES speakers producing forms that they avoided giving on the test, e.g. Case-Marked Pronouns such as *alex, otex, itex, elex* for *aláyix* 'on-you,Fm', *otax* 'Acc-you,Fm', *itax* 'with-you,Fm' and *eláyix* 'to-you,Fm' respectively [32,SAM]; Open-Syllable forms like *le-malot* and *somáxat* for Normative *le-male* 'to-fill', root *m-l-?*, and *somáxet* '(she) relies', root *s-m-k*, respectively [35,SAM]; or Stop/Spirant forms such as *tiSfot* and *Sabra* for *tiSpot* '(you) will-judge' and *Savra* '(she) broke' respectively [39,SAM], *nisvélet* and *liktov* for *nisbélet* 'bear-able,Fm' and *li-xtov* 'to write' [22,SAM]. I believe that the high-SES adults, conscious of accepted norms and of the school-type experimental situation, were able to monitor the kind of forms they produced on the test, in a way low-SES subjects could not. Speakers of the Standard sociolect are aware of language norms, but will adhere to them only in monitored speech. These norms, many of which are no longer identifiable with Householder's (1983) kyriolexia (established norms), belong more to comprehension than to production, to the formal 'elaborated' code than to the colloquial, restricted one. The high-SES subjects were able to 'falsify' normativity since they knew what the normative usage was; the low-SES subjects could not, since their scope of language usage did not include those norms. And indeed, Labov (1972) emphasizes the significance of monitored speech in language change: Speakers of the lower middle class displayed hypercorrect behavior, stemming from a high degree of sensitivity to sociolinguistic elements, leading to one type of change; while on the other hand speakers with a greater degree of control and linguistic feedback mechanisms may block change if directed towards stigmatized forms.

Low-SES usage thus has two relevant characteristics: Less exposure to more formal or scholarly varieties of Modern Hebrew, and hence regularization of morphological subsystems where surface forms and abstract structure diverge considerably. These two features combine in a distinct sociolect, no less structured than the standard one, yet which contains slightly different versions of the same morphological rules. The Nonstandard phenomena typical of this sociolect are most prevalent in child speech and in the low-SES adults. The low-SES 12s are closer to their high-SES counterparts than the adults, demonstrating the effects of schooling and the consolidation of Hebrew in its third generation of native speakers, at a time when 88% of Jewish Israelis aged over 15 have Hebrew as their sole or major mother tongue (Stern 1987).[44]

3.3. INTERACTION BETWEEN AGE AND SES: THE LOCUS OF LANGUAGE CHANGE

The fourth hypothesis predicted some interaction between the two independent variables of age and SES. A statistical relation of this kind was found for the test as a whole, but only for half of the test categories. Significant interaction was not found in Case-Marked Pronouns and Back-formation and in the stable Verb-Governed Prepositions category, as well as in the two most unstable categories of Vowel Alternation and Subject-Verb Concord (Tables 30 and 31).

Interaction indicates a disparity between the two types of population; lack thereof indicates they share certain traits. The least stable categories are where language change is in progress in both subpopulations; in the other three categories where statistical interaction is lacking, age had a major effect (Table 30). Thus lack of statistical interaction between subpopulations reflects either ongoing, across-the-board change, or similar developmental trends in both populations.

The fifth hypothesis predicted that children would apply different strategies than adults to linguistic operations. This was shown to be correct, but the notion of "strategies" needs to be refined. Two types of strategies were detected: (i) Tactical Measures elicited by the task at hand, directly relating to the linguistic operation and treating the test item in isolation—less typical of normal ongoing conversation (R. Clark 1982, Karmiloff-Smith 1979, 1986b, Romaine 1984), described directly below; and (ii) General Developmental Strategies in language acquisition and language process-ing, which derive from inherent general cognitive and specifically linguistic Predispositions or Principles which are employed by children and adults in both experimental and natural language use.

Employing Tactical Measures

The youngest groups—the 3-year-olds, and also the low-SES 5-year-olds—were most distinct in the strategies that they applied. They made wide use of non-structural, ad-hoc tactics, especially (i) repetition and (ii) suppletion of five types: A general term for a specific one, resultative state or cause of state, associated actions or states, use of "empty" words and ellipsis. These accounted for most of the Inappropriate responses given on the test.

Repetition

The most immature tactic found among the 3s is *repetition*—simply re-taining the cue form, e.g. *ha-délet niftax* 'the-door-Fm opened-Masc', in response to the stimulus *ha-xalon niftax* 'the window opened'; *Stey éven* 'two stone' in response to *éven axat* 'one stone'; *maxar ha-yéled loveS mix-nasáyim* 'tomorrow the-boy wears trousers' in response to *ha-yéled axSav loveS mixnasáyim* 'the-boy is-wearing trousers now'; and *exad acamot* 'one bones' in response to *harbe acamot* 'many bones'. There are a few such examples in my spontaneous-data records: *harbe kos* 'many glass' for *harbe kosot* 'many glasses' [3;7 SAM]; *bakbuk* 'bottle', instead of *bakbukim* 'bot-tles', said in response to Mother's question *hine od bakbuk, ve-beyáxad?* 'here (is) another bottle, and-together'? [2;4, DIA]; *ába arye ve-íma arye;* 'daddy lion and-mummy lion', and soon afterwards *arye-íma! arye-ába!* 'mummy lion! daddy lion!', for *arye* 'lion' and *levia* 'lioness' [3;6,DIA]; *ze makaron, lo, ze makaronim exad* 'it('s a) macaron, no, it('s) macaroni-one'[45] [2;11,OBS].

The scarcity of such examples in naturalistic child language of the same age-range testifies to the task-specificity of this immature tactic of repeti-tion. In employing this measure, in both experimental and free-speech situations, children compensate for the lack of the grammatical marker on the item itself by supplying a lexical marker carrying the necessary informa-tion in proximity to the non-inflected item, e.g. *harbe* 'many' for plural; *maxar* 'tomorrow' for future-tense; and *íma* 'mummy' for feminine gen-der.[46] The semantic information is thus present in the output so that communication is effective. This is a common device at a much earlier age, before the onset of grammatical acquisition. Borokovsky (1984) reports such examples for her daughter Efrat at 1;7 using base-forms (plural and singular) together with lexical markers to express plurality, e.g. *od exad klafim* 'one more cards', *harbe buba* 'many doll'. This is also what adults do sometimes to mark future intention: *maxar ani noséa le-xáyfa* = 'I go to Haifa tomorrow', as in English *The train leaves at 6 o'clock*. This type of compensation may occur in general language use as well, for instance where a language lacks a formal marking for aspect. In Modern Hebrew, for example, speakers quite commonly use adverbials such as *kvar* 'already' and *axSav* 'now' to denote perfective or progressive aspect, which have no explicit grammatical realization in Modern Hebrew, e.g. *kvar ra'ínu et ha-séret haze* 'We've already seen this film', *axSav hu higía* 'He's just arrived', and *ani axSav kotévet* 'I'm writing now' (Berman 1978a, Berman & Dromi 1984). In other words, the youngest subjects reverted to a juvenile tactic of presenting semantic information lexically rather than syntactically when pressed for a direct linguistic operation on that item (see Anisfeld & Tucker 1968 for similar observations on English, and Kaplan 1983, Yifát 1981 for Hebrew). This same strategy is common in pidgins and in second language acquisition. The result was grammatically inappropriate, but the device is firmly based on pragmatic grounds and is standard procedure in endstate usage (i) when the language provides no other way to convey the information and (ii) to express modalic intention.

This tactic was quite typical of the responses of the 3-year-olds, and was found less frequently among the low-SES 5s. They mostly repeated verbs, e.g. *ha-yéled hipil et ha-mexonit, ve-axSav ha-yéled gam* . . . 'the-boy dropped Acc the-car, and-now the-boy is also . . .' yielded repetition of the cue *hipil* 'dropped'. This means two things: One, that five-year-olds have a good enough command of the inflection of nouns (and adjectives) to handle them even under experimental circumstances; and two, that *axSav* 'now' is ambiguous between (at least) present and past tense.

An additional conclusion has to do with the nature of punctive verbs: a number of older subjects, including high-SES, responded in the same manner, which seems surprising, unless we consider the punctive nature of 'drop' with the anterior meaning of *axSav* 'now'. Responding with *hipil* cannot be considered repetition in the case of adults, but rather an interpretation of the act of dropping as punctual, carried out immediately prior to the time of speaking.

The high-SES 5s did produce a few examples of repetition as an ad-hoc strategy, typically lexical exceptions or future forms. This suggests that future forms are hard even at a later stage, and, together with lexical exceptions, still constitute a morphological stumbling block at school age.

Suppletion

The second tactical measure employed by children was suppletion, replacing one item by another, morphophonologically unrelated. *Suppletion* took several forms in responses to the test, as follows:

(i) *General term replacing a more specific one:* The 3s and the low-SES 5s often substituted a broader, more general term with the required morphological change for the test item provided, and so did the high-SES 5s occasionally. The 3s, for example, substituted *holéxet* '(she) walks' for *doréxet* '(she) steps'; *noséa* 'travels by vehicle' for *roxev* 'rides'; *raxact* '(you,Fm) washed' for *nikit* '(you, Fm) cleaned'; *dodim* 'uncles', a general term for grown-ups in Hebrew child language, replaced *avot* 'fathers' and *imahot* 'mothers'. The low-SES 5s gave *kufsa'ot* 'boxes' for *dlayim* 'buckets', *anaSim* 'people' for *avot* 'fathers', *imahot* 'mothers' for *naSim* 'women', *noséa be-ofanáyim* 'travels by bicycle' for *roxev* 'rides', and *ose xorim* 'makes holes' for *kodéax* 'drills'. Similar examples were encountered in the pilot study, where children asked to give the plural form of *pisga* 'summit' said *harim* 'mountains', or replaced *neSarim* 'eagles' by *ciporim* 'birds'. In doing so, the young subjects performed the required operation, while avoiding the need to find the precise term or the correct alternant where morphological motivation was unclear. This strategy reveals a hierarchical cognitive structure where the more general governs the more specific hyponym (Anderson 1983, Bourne, Dominowski & Loftus 1979).

In a sense children who resort to this tactical measure are reverting to an earlier developmental stage, where generic terms compensate for lack of adequate lexical specificity, also a characteristic of pidgins (Carey 1982, Clark 1973a, and see Kaplan 1983 on Hebrew. See also Klein 1986 on similar tactics in second language acquisition).

(ii) *Substituting a resultative state or cause of action* was a second *Suppletive* strategy. Here, the child either gave a word denoting the act or state semantically or pragmatically entailed by the cue item, or else a word denoting its cause. For example, the 3s gave *nisgéret* 'closes,Fm' for *niftáxat* 'opens,Fm'; *tiyel* 'took a walk' for *xika* 'waited'; *mazag* 'poured' for *Sata* 'drank', *mesadéret* '(she) is tidying up' for *pizra* '(she) scattered'; *lokéax* 'takes' and *oxel* 'eats' for *meríax* 'smells' (denoting an act preceding and following smelling food); *marim*[47] 'picks up' for *mapil* 'drops'; *yoc'im* 'go out,Pl' for *nixnasim* 'enter,Pl'; *yorid* 'will-take off' for *yilbaS* 'will-put on'; and *oxlim* 'eat,Pl' for *niSaru botnim* '(there are some) peanuts left'. The low-SES 5s had fewer examples of this tactic, e.g. *mezanéket* '(she) springs' for *soxa* '(she) swims'; *kilela* '(she) cursed' for *kin'a* '(she) was jealous'. The response children usually gave was a word in the required syntactic category, e.g. a verb in present tense or a noun in plural, but they failed to perform the necessary linguistic operation on the cue item. Especially difficult was the passive form, which is in general a late acquisition, problematic for children under school age (Berman 1985), and which presented problems even for the high-SES 5s. They replaced *kafu*[48] 'frozen' by verbs and adjectives such as *xam* 'hot', *kar* 'cold', *names* 'melted', *hitkarer* 'cooled', *mekulkal* 'spoiled' and *lavan* 'white'. Replacing the required item with a different, though semantically-related lexical item, is thus a task-related form of suppletion, relying on semantic and pragmatic rather than grammatical knowledge.

(iii) *Associated actions or states:* There were a host of responses triggered by the picture or by the verbal cue item, mostly in the required syntactic category. e.g. *mesudéret* 'neat,Fm' and *cvu'a* 'painted,Fm' for *raka* 'soft,Fm'; *niSarim* 'are-staying' for *Sarim* 'are-singing' (clearly triggered by the resemblance between these two words); *noténet artik* 'giving,Fm an ice-cream lollipop', *niSpax* 'spilled' and *menaka* 'cleaning,Fm' for *kafu* 'frozen' (all triggered by the picture of a woman and a refrigerator); *mesaxakim* 'are-playing' for *merimim* 'are-picking up'; *hem halxu* 'they went off' and *natnu* '(they) gave' for *hayu yeladim* '(there) were children'; and *ha-béten Smena* 'the-stomach (is) fat' for *ko'évet lo ha-béten* 'he has a stomach ache'. Such responses were even less "appropriate" than the previous types, since they were the product of free association, lacking any kind of semantic link to the task involved. It is not surprising that this strategy was confined to the 3-year-olds, and was totally absent in the 5s of both backgrounds. This is a tactic adopted only by young children faced with a formal situation where they are asked to perform meta-linguistically with pictures and words. Free association is of course a common device in children's games, when objects and verbal stimuli in the environment trigger off different paths in the child's output.

(iv) *Use of "empty" words or gestures,* e.g. *asa fu* 'made a hissing sound (denoting the action of putting out a candle)' for *zo uga* 'this,Fm (is a) cake,Fm';[49] *osa káxa* '(she) is-doing like this'—using body gestures to denote actions when asked to give various present-tense forms of verbs; *gam* 'too' for *hine ha-yéled mexake, ve-etmol hu gam . . . ?* 'here (is) the-boy waiting, and-yesterday he also . . . ?'; *yaase mixtav* 'will-make a letter' for *yixtov* 'will-write'; and *yaasu od pá'am* 'will-do,Pl once again' for *yilmedu* 'will-study,Pl'. Like the third tactic, the last two suppletive measures were limited only to the youngest group of 3-year-olds. This strategy is more juvenile than use of a more general term, since a semantically empty verb such as the general-purpose *asa* 'did, made' implies no knowledge of the specific content of the verb, except that it denotes action. Reliance on semantically empty terms has been described as a context-bound characteristic of the more "restricted" code, where deictic and other non-verbal cues supply the missing information, rather than verbal elabora-

tion (Bernstein 1960, 1964). Stahl (1977) cites numerous examples of disadvantaged usage that includes "filler" words, deictics
and gestures, similar to those noted here. In both cases, speakers
rely on extra-linguistic context to clarify their intention. But our
examples result from the exigencies of direct elicitation in a controlled experiment whereas those cited by Stahl usually occurred
in natural conversation or in class discussion.

(v) *Ellipsis*— omission of a part of a phrase, leaving one lexical item
intact, usually a noun, e.g. *yeladim* 'children', a truncated form of
hayu yeladim '(there) were children'; *ha-béten* 'the-stomach' for
ko'évet lo ha-béten 'his stomach hurts'; *botnim* 'peanuts' for *niSaru
botnim* '(some) peanuts were left'; *uga* 'cake' for *zo uga* 'this,Fm
(is a) cake'; *pérax* 'flower' instead of the sentence *hevéti pérax* '(I)
brought (a) flower'. This way, subjects avoided grammatical
changes of any sort, with the noun alone left to carry the meaning they wished to convey. This is reminiscent of children at the
single-word stage, who, restricted by absence of grammar and
lexicon, put all lexical content into a single word. The 3-year-old
subjects who used this strategy may have done so as another
means of circumventing the direct manipulation of the cue item
in the required task.

Table 33 summarizes the information given above, showing that the terms
Appropriate and Inappropriate in fact form a (phylogenetically or ontogenetically) developmental continuum, on which ideas are either given a
syntactically appropriate form (as in Normative and Other-Appropriate
responses) by more mature speakers, or progressively less grammatically
governed and more semantically or pragmatically oriented forms by younger, less linguistically able speakers (Givón 1985). In sum, having recourse
to a limited vocabulary, and still in the process of acquiring inflectional
morphology, preschoolers resorted to non-structural ad-hoc strategies elicited by the immediate isolated task at hand, rather than by general principles applying to language structure. Instead of relating to the form of the
cue-item, they related to its lexical content, replacing it by more general,
associated or "empty" terms. In doing so, children were dealing only with
full words instead of analyzing them into their component parts. This in
itself is a juvenile strategy that avoids the challenge of grammatical alternations. Three-year-old tactics are thus often semantically and pragmatically
governed, directed by the need for communication rather than by grammar. This is why the youngest groups yielded so many Inappropriate
responses. By age five, repetition of stem form and suppleting general
terms and causes/results were much rarer, with the last three types of
Suppletion absent, indicating greater reliance on structure than on content
and function. Most non-Normative responses at this age and over were
structurally deviant, making use of general principles operating in language
development and language processing.

Table 33. Task-Related Tactics

Syntactic Mode + Appropriate			Semantic/Pragmatic Mode − Appropriate	
Normative	Other	Suppletion	Repetition	
	Resultative Actions/States	Associated Actions/States	Empty Devices	Ellipsis	General Term

Language Strategies in Children and Low-SES Adults

The sixth hypothesis dealing with the independent variables predicted a certain amount of similarity between language strategies employed by children and by low-SES adults. This prediction was confirmed at two levels: On the one hand, low-SES adults tended to resort to childlike tactics when confronted with a test situation. These included repetition of cue item, e.g. *Sote* 'drinking' given as a response to *ha-yéled axSav Sote, ve-gam ani mikódem . . .* 'the-boy (is) now drinking, and-also I before . . .'. Like the children, these uneducated adults had problems in shifting into future-tense forms, and so repeated the cue-item unchanged in many such cases, e.g. *kotev* 'writes' in response to *ha-yéled axSav kotev. gam ani maxar . . .* 'the-boy (is) now writing. I, too, tomorrow . . .'. This group also employed suppletion of a general for a specific term, e.g. *banot* 'girls' for *naSim* 'women', and semantically related resultatives instead of inflected forms of cue-items, e.g. *xozer* 'returns' as a response to *yaxol la-vo* 'can (to-)come'. The low-SES adults did not produce as many repetitive and suppletive forms as the 3s and the 5s-b, but they did have relatively many Inappropriate responses. Their use of ad-hoc strategies, relying on semantic and pragmatic cues, can also be attributed to their lack of experience with experimental tasks. Unable to perform a decontextualized structural operation, some uneducated adults preferred a fuzzier, less grammaticized way of answering, by repeating or replacing a tricky item.

Lower-class adults likewise could be compared to young children in using simplified rules when faced with opaque structures, employing similar strategies leading them towards Nonstandard forms. This shows up in the low number of their Normative responses, where low-SES adults fall statistically together with high-SES 5-year-olds on most test categories.

To conclude, the first six predictions were confirmed: The number of Appropriate responses rises with age, and the extent of Normative responses is directly related to Maturation and Literacy. Interaction between these factors accounted for most of the variation in responses. Where this was not the case, Maturation alone proved to be a major determinant, or else language change was found to be underway across the population. Young children relied heavily on semantically and pragmatically motivated task-related measures, while older children and adults attended mainly to structural cues. Low-SES adults employed ad-hoc strategies to some extent similar to those used by the younger respondents.

The seventh hypothesis, which predicted the distribution of deviations in the test population, and the hypotheses concerning the dependent variables, were also confirmed, and are discussed in the coming chapters.

4

Structural Opacity

The discussion of the central role of structural opacity in processes of language change focuses on five constructions in Modern Hebrew that most clearly demonstrate different causes, manifestations, and results of opacity: *Weak Syllables, Stop/Spirant Alternation, Hif'il e/a Alternation, Case-Marked Pronouns* and *Junction*. Each represents a distinct instance of current instability in morphological structure, deriving from both diachronic sources and from the unique position of spoken Modern Hebrew as a revived language. And all five alike highlight the initiation of change in a linguistic community (Baron 1977).

4.1. OPACITY IN LANGUAGE CHANGE

Traditionally, according to the Neogrammarian view, there are two types of language change:[50] Sound change, purely phonetically conditioned, with grammar playing no role in it, absolutely regular, admitting no exception, altering gradually over time, by small increments too minute to observe (Bynon 1977, Hocket 1965, Martinet 1960); all other morphophonemic evolution was taken to operate through rules of analogy which leveled off grammatical distinctions (Hoenigswald 1963). More recently, Wang has shown that sound change is not exceptionless and that although it is phonetically gradual, it is lexically abrupt, that is, it affects all relevant words simultaneously (Chen & Wang 1975, Wang 1969, Wang & Cheng 1977). Labov (1981) suggests that there are two types of sound change:

Low-level output rules, which observe "Neogrammarian" regularity, and more abstract changes located within the word. I will argue that all the constructions shown to be undergoing change in this work belong to the latter type, and that even changes in single phonemes are governed by a complex of morphological, lexical, semantic, and syntactic factors (Barkai 1972, Bolozky 1978). I also claim that "analogy" is too vague a term to characterize the variety of processes that take place when change is implemented, and that it too is conditioned: Allomorphy reduction and pattern extension are not random "catch as catch can" phenomena, but are rather principled, rule-governed processes. A major factor that gives rise to variation and consequently change is *Opacity* in the sense of Kiparsky (1982), Lightfoot (1979, 1981, 1991).

Opaque structures violate the *Transparency Principle* (TP) proposed by Lightfoot (1979, 1991)—the requirement that a grammar be shallow, that is, that the distance between underlying representation and surface structure not be too great. Thus TP requires derivations to be minimally complex and initial, underlying structures to be 'close' to their respective surface structures (1979:121).

When a construction violates this principle, its surface structure is so far removed from its underlying representation that speakers are no longer able to perceive the relationship between them, or a motivation for the surface alternations (Bates & MacWhinney 1982). This is when the speaker will perform "therapeutic" reanalysis (parameter re-setting in the terminology of Lightfoot 1991), re-structuring the offending construction in such a way as to make it conform to TP. Such reanalyses constitute deviations from norms that eventually lead to change in a particular structure. Kiparsky (1982) also argues that reanalyses proceed from a non-abstract synchronic analysis, and notes that instability seems to show up mainly where the neutralized distinction is weakly embedded in the grammar. Such reanalyses result in rule loss when rules are hard to learn in the transmission of language from one generation to another, with rule opacity a major factor in making rules hard to learn. Kiparsky defines rule opacity as follows in Table 34.

Other researchers too agree that opaque rules are what causes re-structuring. Hankamer (1972) expresses a view close to that of Thomason (1976) that an inflectional system may undergo changes in reaction to a grammatical "weak" point like rule opacity, and that there is a diachronic tendency to eliminate opacity in unstable morphological structures. Linguists concur that it is during childhood that speakers react most strongly

Table 34. Rule Opacity (Kiparsky 1982:75)

A rule A $\longrightarrow$ B/C————D is opaque to the extent that there are surface representations of the form
(i)   A in environment C————D or
(ii) B in environment other than C————D

against structural opacity. Children are synchronic linguists par excellence: a child learns his or her mother tongue in complete ignorance of its history, and must work backwards to reconstruct a string so that its surface structure makes morphological sense and is constructable as a part of a rule-governed system. As a result, the classical Neogrammarian view is that child language is the most likely source of analytical change (Halle 1962, Kiparsky 1982), a view prevalent in the works of Baron (1977), Hooper (1979), and also Clark (1981) and Slobin (1977, 1985c). Clark notes the central role of ST, while two of Slobin's 1977 charges are also for a one-to-one mapping of form and meaning—"Be Clear" and ease of perception, "Be Processible." He shows how these charges are observed along four parameters: in child language, in diachronic evolution of languages, in language contact, and in emerging language (pidgins and creoles).

It makes sense to assume that children learning Modern Hebrew as their mother tongue should likewise react strongly to opaque structures. And in fact, my findings definitely point in that direction. The question still remains, however, whether opacity-eliminating procedures survive into adulthood.

Consider, first, *Hitpa'el* metathesis, a morphophonemic rule that exemplifies Transparency, and is thus an early acquisition, never re-analyzed by any section of the population nor revealing any deviant phenomena. The *Hitpa'el* construction consists of the *binyan* prefix *hit-* (*mit-* and *yit-* in present and future tense respectively), followed by the stem -*CaCeC*, e.g. *hitlaked* 'united', root *l-k-d; hitkadem* 'advanced', root *q-d-m*. When the first root radical is a strident, it changes places with the prefixal -*t,* as in Table 35.

This transparent rule fulfills only the first part of Kiparsky's requirements:

$$A \longrightarrow B \quad / C\text{------}D$$
$$t + str \longrightarrow str + t \ /[hi\text{------} aCeC]v, Hitpa'el$$

This is because Hebrew sibilants, unlike *bkp* segments and gutturals, retain their distinct character; The rule[51] takes place only in *Hitpa'el* and its derivatives with no exception, extending to borrowed affricates as well, e.g. *C* in the slang term *hiCtakmek* 'became untidy' (case i); Occurrences of a *t* + strident sequence in other contexts never undergo metathesis (case ii), whether or not across a morpheme boundary, e.g. *tSuka* 'desire', *tzuza* 'motion', *matsis* 'ferment', or *natSa* 'abandoned,Fm' (see Greenberg 1966b). The rule is thus restricted to a single morphophonological environment, with the metathesizing segments uniquely defined (Bolozky, to appear).

Table 35. Hitpa'el Metathesis Rule

/hitsader/	$\longrightarrow$	*histader* 'arranged itself', root *s-d-r*
/hitca'er/	$\longrightarrow$	*hicta'er*[52] 'was sorry', root *ṣ- y -r*

In contrast to the metathesis rule, the five constructions described below demonstrate various degrees of opacity and are consequently "hard to learn" in Kiparsky's sense. In the next sections I analyze these domains of instability and identify their respective sources of opacity.

4.2. DOMAINS OF INSTABILITY

Stop/Spirant Alternation

Spirantization is a central phenomenon in Hebrew morphophonology, since it relates word-structure to phonology, consonants to vowels, and classical to more recent periods of Hebrew. This process alternates *bkp* stops and *vxf* spirants, e.g. *avar* 'passed', *maabóret* 'ferry', root *y-b-r; kivun* 'direction', *haxvana* 'guidance', root *k-v-n; pésel* 'sculpture', *mefasel* 'sculpts', root *p-s-l*. Historically, this rule assimilated six stops—*pb td kg*—into fricatives—*fv* Θδ xr—after vowels. Compare, for example, the historical forms *sofer* 'counts' and *yispor* 'will count', root *s-p-r; hevin* 'understood' and *bina* 'understanding', root *b-y-n; kaΘav* 'wrote' and *mixtav* 'letter' root *k-t-b* (Gesenius 1910, Morag 1960, Schwarzwald 1981). This alternation was originally allophonic and unrelated to word structure (Barkai 1972, Ben-Horin & Bolozky 1972, Fischler 1975, Garbel 1959, Ornan 1973). In Modern Hebrew, spirantization is a typical example of an opaque rule, for the following reasons:

(i) *Collapse of a Natural Phonological Class:* Historically, all six stops spirantized after long vowels, so that they formed a distinct and coherent phonological sub-system: Two anterior, two coronal, and two velar stops, with a voiced and a voiceless stop in each pair. This was a symmetrical and natural phonological class, all of its members sharing the following features: Today, by contrast, there are only three stops that alternate with fricatives: *pbk/fvx*. Two bi-labial stops, and a velar one; or, two voiceless stops, and a voiced one. The rest were lost before the revival of Modern Hebrew (Faber 1986). Though these three still share the features depicted above, there is not a single feature that serves to set *pbk* apart from the rest of the class of stops that do not spirantize. Thus the stops that spirantize in Modern Hebrew do not form a natural phonological class, as do, say, the stridents. This makes it hard on the speaker to determine the nature of A undergoing spirantization (Table 36).

(ii) *Loss of the phonetic motivation of the spirantization rule:* Spirantization is no longer phonologically conditioned, since the phonetic environment that characterized it in Classical Hebrew has disappeared: stops spirantized after vowels, so the phonetic environment for spirantization was unique. In Modern Hebrew, stops

Table 36. Characteristics of the historical class of spirantizing stops in Hebrew

[+ cons]
[− voc]
[− cont]
[α voice]

may or may not spirantize after vowels. Compare *ibdu* 'lost, PL' with *avdu* 'were lost'; *yetapel* '(will) take-care' with *yitafel* '(will) pick on'; *sika* 'pin' with *sixa* 'oiling'. This is because stop/spirant alternation today reflects two historical phenomena: (i) the lenition of stops to spirants after (long) vowels and (ii) gemination of stops following a (usually) short vowel, with the historical geminate currently reflected as a stop rather than a fricative only in the *bkp* set, e.g. *sabal* 'porter', underlying form /*sabbal*/ (Tur-Sinai 1954). Gemination took place in a different phonetic environment than spirantization, after short vowels, yet both are reflected today in the same stop/spirant alternation. The result is a violation of transparency (see below). The speaker of Modern Hebrew thus receives conflicting phonological clues as to the environment for spirantization (Table 37):

(iii) *"Parasites" on the system:* Historical circumstances led to (1) the introduction of foreign segments into Hebrew and (2) to the merger of a number of segments. Borrowed words contain *p/f, b/v* and *k* that occur in positions violating spirantization. *p,b* and *k* fail to spirantize following vowels in *mikroskop* 'microscope', *Zlob* 'big ungainly person' and *bok* 'stupid' respectively (case i); and *f/v* occur anywhere, e.g. word-initially in *festival* 'festival' or in *vákum* 'vacuum' (case ii). Moreover, foreign *bkp* segments do not display stop/spirant alternation: Compare *fintez/mefantez* '(slang) fantasized/is fantasizing' with *pilpel/mefalpel* 'peppered/is peppering'.

Language-internally, segments have merged: The classical glide /*w*/, (orthographic *vav*) merged with the fricative allophone of /*b*/, to yield *v*; Historical emphatic /*q*/ (orthographic *qof*) merged with /*k*/ (orthographic *kaf*), surfacing as *k*; Guttural /*H*/ (orthographic *Het*) merged with the spirant allophone of /*k*/, both pronounced as *x*. As a result, opacity pervades the system: The "parasites" that have merged with the allophonic alternants of the original spirantizing class fail to observe stop/spirant alternation. On one hand, *k* deriving from *qof* never spirantizes, so we get both *soker* 'surveyor', root *s-q-r*, and *soxer* 'rents', root *s-k-r* in the same environment; and on the other hand, historical /*w*/ and /*H*/ never occur as stops in any environment: compare *bitúax*

Table 37. Violation of Transparency by the current phonetic environment of *bkp* segments

A $\longrightarrow$ B / C————D
stp   spr V————X

but

    i) A occurs in C————D

         stp   V————X,   e.g. *sapar* 'barber'

                                          kibel 'received'

                                          yetapes 'will-climb'

Table 38. Violation of Transparency by confusion with "parasites"

    (i) A occurs in   C————D

          stp   V   e.g. *mekapec* 'skips'

and

    (ii) B occurs in environment other than   C————D

          spr   V

e.g. in word-initial position: *filosófya* 'philosophy', *xaver* 'friend', *vilon* 'curtain'; or after a consonant: *hitxameS* 'armed' and *hitfaléax* '(slang) sneaked in'.

---

in the *CiCuC* noun-pattern; and *yiskor* 'will-rent', root *s-k-r*, with *yisxar* 'will-trade', root *s-H-r*, both in the *Pa'al* verb-pattern, as against *saxar* 'rented', root *s-k-r*, compared with *sakar* 'surveyed', root *s-q-r*.

    Spirantization operates only on "true" stop/fricative alternants, not on the "parasites," but what the native speaker observes is a seemingly sporadic behavior of *bkp/vxf* segments. Thus, both types of violation of Kiparsky's rule occur (Table 38):

(iv) *Morphologization of root segments*: New-word formation employs roots exclusively in the derivation of new verbs and verb-related nominals (Berman 1987c, Ravid 1978). In many cases, words are derived from words (Aronoff 1976), with the consonantal root relating base form and new derivation, e.g. the new secondary root *m-x-z-r* relates the new verb *mixzer* 'recycled' to its base-word *maxazor* 'cycle', root *H-z-r* 'return' (Ravid 1990). The new word typically retains the meaning and consonantal skeleton of its base form. To do so, a *bkp* alternant that occurs in the base word is adopted as a non-alternating root segment in the derived word (Fischler 1975). For example, *rixel* 'gossiped' instead of Normative *rikel*, from the noun *rexilut* 'gossip' (cf. *sikel* 'aborted') and *le-kaxev* 'to-star' instead of Normative *le-xakev*, from *koxav* 'star' (cf. *le-xaven* 'to-direct'). This, of course, contributes to rule opacity, since again stops and spirants occur in conflicting environments.

There are thus (at least) four sources of opacity in spirantization: Collapse of the phonological class, loss of phonetic environment, "parasites" on the system and morphologization of root segments. Such dense opacity must yield re-analysis and instability, and indeed the Stop/Spirant Alternation category ranked among the four lowest for normativity.

e/a Alternation in *Hif'il*

The normatively lowest-ranking category in this study was that of *Hif'il* present-tense forms such as *mepil* 'drops' (Normative *mapil*), root *n-p-l,* and *marim* 'picks up', (Normative *merim*) root *r-w-m*. There were numerous such examples in the free speech data as well, e.g. *megía* 'reaches', *mekir* 'knows', *mecía* 'suggests', *megiSa* 'serves,Fm' [35,OBS,hi-SES]; *mecig* 'introduces', *mebía* 'expresses', [52,OBS,hi-SES]; *metiS* 'exhausting', *maríax* 'smells' [40,SAM,hi-SES]; *mavi* 'brings', *maxin* 'prepares', *mecil* 'saves' [12;8,SAM,lo-SES]. Normatively, all these verbs should have the opposite initial vowel values: *e* for *a,* and *a* for *e*. In a little experiment I conduct in various university and college classes every year, native-speaking linguistics and even Hebrew Studies majors are unclear as to what the Normative form of an *e/a* verb is, offering both vowels, whereas with other categories they all agree on what constitutes the Normative form. This suggests that this category is undergoing change in all sections of the Hebrew-speaking population.

The basic problem here is to distinguish two types of underlying structures in present-tense: (i) *n*-initial roots, such as *n-p-l* 'fall', *n-k-r* 'know', *n-ṣ-l* 'save, use',[53] which Normatively surface as *maCiC* (e.g. *mapil* 'drops'); and (ii) glide-medial roots, such as *b-y-n* 'understand', *r-w-m* 'rise', and *q-w-m* 'get up', requiring *e* in present-tense, e.g. *mevin* 'understands'. In *n*-initial forms the initial radical *n-* may be deleted in a consonant cluster, e.g. *yita* 'will-plant', root *n-t-y* (compare *yilmad* 'will-study', root *l-m-d*), while the underlying medial glide generally fails to surface, or else is realized as a vowel, e.g. *kam/yakum/hitkomem* 'rise/will-rise/rise against', root *q-w-m*. Thus there is a clear distinction between *n*-initial and glide-medial roots across most of the verb system.

But in *Hif'il,* the weak root radical (*n* or glide) never surfaces in any of the five verb inflections: past, present, future, imperative and infinitive forms. Consider the regular root *m-S-k* 'go on' together with the roots *n-k-r* 'know' and *q-w-m* 'rise' in the form: *himSix/hikir/hekim, mamSix/ makir/mekim, yamSix/yakir/yakim, hamSex/haker/hakem, le-hamSix/le-hakir/ le-hakim*. The weak verbs have only two root radicals, while the full verb has three, and the missing root radical is not always accessible, since a verb in each *binyan* is a separate lexical entry, and the relationship between occurrences of the same root in different *binyan* forms is not always predictable or even recognizable (Ornan 1971), e.g. *nafal/hipil* 'fell/dropped', root *n-p-l,* but *hikir* 'knew, recognized' alternates with *hitnaker* 'alienated', root *n-k-r; sar/hesir* 'went away/removed', but *he'id* 'testify'—*hit'oded* 'cheer up', root *y-w-d.* In both root-types, then, a root radical is missing in *Hif'il* and is often difficult to reconstruct.

Then, too, the future, imperative and infinitive forms of both these two roots in the *Hif'il* pattern are identical. The only remaining difference is in past tense (*hikir* 'knew', root *n-k-r,* vs. *hekim* 'raised', root *q-w-m*) and present tense (*makir* vs. *mekim*). The syllable structure is *mVCiC* in both cases, and the difference is only in the quality of the vowel: *maCiC* (*n-* initial, e.g. Normative *magiS* 'serves', root *n-g-S*) or *meCiC* (glide-medial, e.g. *mesir* 'removes', root *s-w-r*). Opacity is a certain consequence, as the same environment (*mVCiC*) entails two alternative vowels with no possible access to the underlying roots which would supply the motivation for either. Choice of either vowel is entirely local, with no effect on other structures and with no semantic load associated with one vowel or the other. Given this, re-analysis of two minor structures into one is inevitable.

Weak Final Syllable

Roots ending with guttural *h,?,* pharyngeal *y* and *H,* and with the glide *y,* constitute a problem to both young learners and adult speakers of Modern Hebrew (Bolozky 1978). In the mainstream (non-Oriental) Israeli dialect, *h, ?* and *y* are not pronounced when syllable- or word-final, and in syllable-initial position they coalesce into either a glottal stop or again are deleted. Only when reading aloud will the distinctions between *h* and *?* be made, if in a stressed syllable, while the speaker of General Israeli Hebrew has to make a special effort to pronounce *y*. The voiceless pharyngeal fricative *H* always surfaces, but it has merged with the spirantized version of *k,* both occurring as surface *x*. Table 39 illustrates the distribution of final weak syllables in various contexts. Not only are *?, y* and *h* "silent" when word-final, they also merge word-initially (*h* disappears in fast speech). And though verbs with roots containing different gutturals have the same form in past-tense masculine singular, the underlying segments affect the form of the verb in other parts of the paradigm, so that in order to conjugate it one must know the underlying root. Moreover, when these roots occur in other *binyan* patterns, the underlying segments entail different vowels, e.g. *piníti* '(I) evacuated', *le-fanot* 'to-evacuate', root *p-n-y, xitéti* '(I) sterilized', *le-xate* 'to-sterilize', root *H-T-?,* both in the *Pi'el* verb-pattern. The opacity, then, is two-fold: (i) A root radical may or may not occur on the surface, and (ii) phonetic merger causes what appears to be the same weak segment to have different behaviors in the same environment, e.g. *-et, -áat, -a* in present-tense feminine singular, or *-o, -óa, -ot* in the infinitive (Table 39).

Table 39. Weak Final Syllable Roots in the *Pa'al* Verb-Pattern in General (non-Oriental) Israeli Hebrew

Root	Gloss	Past Tense	Past Tense Fm	Present Tense Fm	Infinitive
m-ṣ-?	find	*maca*	*mac'a*	*mocet*	*li-mco*
n-g-y	touch	*naga*	*nag'a*	*nogáat*	*li-ngóa*
q-n-y	buy	*kana*	*kanta*	*kona*	*li-knot*
?-r-H	be a guest	*arax*	*arxa*	*oráxat*	*le-eróax*
y -r-k	edit, set	*arax*	*arxa*	*oréxet*	*la-arox*
h-l-k	walk	*halax*	*halxa*	*holéxet*	*la-léxet*

Case-Marked Pronouns

A complex of rules and historical facts are responsible for synchronic opacity in structures formed of preposition + bound pronoun, e.g. *itax* 'with-you,Fm', *alav* 'on-him', *mikem* 'from-you,Pl'. Their historical motivation is not at all apparent to an untutored speaker, let alone a child. Compare, for instance, the different forms of the second person feminine singular with various prepositions: *ot-ax* 'Acc-you,Fm'; *mim-ex* 'from-you,Fm'; *al-áyix* 'on-you,Fm'. The different suffixed forms of the bound pronoun on the preposition are due to the following reasons:

(i) Present-day prepositions have two sources: *Original prepositions,* and those that have undergone *categorial shift,* usually from noun to preposition. Categorial shifts have been demonstrated in a number of cases in Hebrew, including the current formation of new prepositions from nouns and adverbs (Rubinstein 1975, Shlesinger 1985). In fact, it has been claimed that all Biblical prepositions were originally nouns, precisely because of their ability to take pronominal suffixes, like nouns. For example, compare *melax-éynu* 'our kings' with *al-éynu* 'on-us', where both the noun 'kings' and the preposition 'on' take the pronominal suffix denoting first person plural (Ben-Asher 1974, Blau 1976, Gesenius 1910, Rosén 1956). The distinction between primary and category-shifted prepositions is most conspicuous in the second person feminine singular pronominal suffix. Original prepositions take the suffix of *-ax,* e.g. *b-ax* 'in-you,Fm', from *b-* 'in'; *Sel-ax* 'of-you,Fm', from *Sel* 'of'; and *it-ax* 'with-you,Fm', from *im* 'with'. By contrast, category-shifted prepositions take the suffix *-ex,* as do nouns, e.g. *biSvil-ex* 'for-you,Fm', from the noun *Svil* 'path', or *ecl-ex* 'close to-you,Fm', from the noun *ecel* 'the place close by' (Gesenius 1910). And compare the nouns *sal-ex* 'your,Fm-basket', *tik-ex* 'your,Fm-bag'; and *Seelat-ex* 'your,Fm-question'. Thus, at least two mutually exclusive vowels show up in the second person feminine singular pronominal suffix on prepositions depending on its historical origin. This renders the case-marked pronoun opaque for native speakers, since there is no way they can reconstruct the historical form of the different suffixes.

(ii) Historically, some of the prepositions were inherently *plural*, while others had basic *singular* forms (Gesenius 1910). The plural prepositions ended with *-ey*, e.g. *meaxor-ey* 'behind', *lifn-ey* 'in front of', and *al-ey*, today *al* 'on'. Some pronominal suffixes take a different form in plural than in singular prepositions, especially in first person, second person feminine and third person singular: Compare first person singular *l-i* 'to-me', *Sel-i* 'of-me', and *ot-i* 'Acc-me', with originally plural *al-ay* 'on-me', *lefan-ay* 'before-me', and *taxt-ay* 'under-me'.

There are thus three possible types of pronominal endings on prepositions: Regular (e.g. *-ax*, as in *it-ax* 'with-you,Fm'); Shifted-category (e.g. *-ex* as in *mi-mex* 'from-you,Fm'); and Plural (e.g. *-áyix* as in *al-áyix* 'on-you,Fm)'. In this case, X,Y and Z occur in the same environment C————D, without the speaker being able to synchronically motivate the choice of either one.

(iii) Case-marking prepositions change not only the form of their pronominal suffixes, but also that of their *inflected stem*. For example, the bound form of the Accusative Marker *et* is *ot-* when inflected, e.g. *ot-xa* 'Acc-you', *ot-ánu* 'Acc-us'; the colloquial bound form of *im* 'with' is *it-*, as in *it-i* 'with-me' or *it-o* 'with-him'. In fact, almost every preposition undergoes stem changes when inflected, and these are not uniform across the paradigm, e.g. *mi-méni* 'from-me' and *mi-ménu* 'from-him', vs. *mi-mxa* 'from-you' and *me-itánu* 'from-us'.

For every form of a case-marked pronoun one needs to know the *free form* of both the preposition and the pronoun, and relate them to the various occurrences of their *bound forms* in the ten possible combinations of preposition + pronominal suffix. The native speaker cannot always predict which shape the suffixed pronoun will take, and there are many suppletive forms which have to be learnt by rote. Hence a complex of factors governs the acquisition and use of case-marked pronouns.

The multiply opaque system explains the remarkably low percentage of Normative responses in the young ages, supporting the findings of Kaplan (1983) and Rom & Dgani (1985). Deviations in Case-Marked Pronouns seem also to characterize the Nonstandard sociolect. Case-Marked Pronouns ranked middle in normativity, with marked sociolectal differences. These results are supported by my spontaneous speech data, where deviations like the following are restricted to children and low-SES speakers: *biglalax, leyadax, miménax* and *elex,* for Normative *biglalex*[54] 'because of you,Fm'; *leyadex* 'beside-you,Fm', *mimex* 'from-you,Fm', and *eláyix* 'to-you,Fm' respectively [3;0,SAM]; *otex* for *otax* 'Acc-you,Fm' [35,SAM]; and *itex, mimánu* for *itax* 'with-you,Fm', *meitánu* 'from-us' [17,OBS]; a single example that characterizes the established sociolect is *biSvilax* for Normative *biSvilex* 'for-you,Fm' [40,OBS].

Junction

A morphological domain where speakers are particularly likely to perform "therapeutic" re-analysis is in the area of Junction, where a number of distinct morphological classes coalesce into a single plural stem CCaC-(CCaC-im or CCaC-ot), so that the singular form of a given item could be any of twelve different patterns. This is illustrated in Table 40 below. It shows that seven canonical noun-patterns, almost all branching out into phonologically conditioned allopatterns (see notes for elaboration), coalesce in the plural form to yield the stem CCaC-. The variant CaCaCim/CaCaCot (e.g. *xacavim* 'squills'/*xaradot* 'anxieties'), which is due to root gutturals, led me to add two other noun patterns, namely CaC(C)aC and CaC(C)aCa. Their surface similarity to patterns such as CaCaC and Ca-CaCa contributes to the general reduction in semantic weight of patterns with *a*, for which there is independent evidence (Ravid 1990, Ravid & Shlesinger 1987a). In this instance, the result is further opacity with two additional patterns joining the seven canonical ones with a single plural form.

The bound plural form CCaC- can thus derive from as many as twenty dissimilar singular forms, and so is extremely opaque. Opacity is perhaps reduced by speakers relating masculine patterns such as CéCeC and CCaC to the masculine plural suffix -*im* (e.g. *klaf/klafim* 'card/s'), and the feminine patterns such as CiCCa/CaCCa/CCaCa to the feminine plural suffix -*ot* (e.g. *simla/smalot* 'dress/es'). But the bound plural CCaC-, which is the main problem, remains the same in both. Also, gender exceptions abound in the system, as shown in the some of the examples above (cf. masculine *nahar/neharot* 'river/s,Fm'). Part of endstate knowledge of Hebrew gender is that such exceptions exist (Levy 1980), and thus speakers do not always expect to adhere to the feminine suffix even in the case of a feminine pattern, and vice versa. For three out of seven major noun patterns, the shift from singular to plural is rather simple: For CCaC and CCaCa, just attach the correct gender suffix (e.g. *klal/klal-im* 'rule/s', *klala/klal-ot* 'curse/s'). CaCaC entails *a*-reduction as well (e.g. *zanav/znavot* 'tail/s'). In these cases, shift from singular to plural form and back is straightforward, given knowledge of gender. Not so with the other four patterns (CéCeC/CóCeC and CiCCa/CaCCa) and their related allopatterns, which involve a morphological shift from one pattern to another, e.g. CiCCa/CCaC-ot. Finally, none of the large number of patterns with plural Junction structure CCaC-carries any specific semantic load which may help in inflection and in backformation (Ravid 1990, to appear).

I have presented five areas of Modern Hebrew morphophonology that manifest opacity in various degrees. Chapter 5 below discusses the principles and strategies speakers adopt to alleviate opacity.

Table 40. Morphological patterns with the *CCaC-* plural form

Canonical Pattern	Conditioned Allopatterns	Singular	Gloss	Plural *CCac* Stem
1. *CéCeC*		*séxer*	dam	*sxar-im*
		SémeS	sun	*SmaS-ot*
		xéder	room	*xadar-im*[55]
	CéCaC[56]	*pérax*	flower	*prax-im*
		céla	rib	*cla'-ot*
	CáCaC	*ráal*	poison	*re'al-im*[57]
	CéCi[58]	*péti*	simpleton	*pta'-im*
	CCi	*ɡdi*	kid	*ɡday-im*
	CáyiC[59]	*táyiS*	he-goat	*tyaS-im*
		ɡáyis	corps	*ɡyas-ot*
2. *CóCeC*		*kómer*	priest	*kmar-im*
	CóCaC	*ɡóva*[60]	height	*ɡvah-im*
	CóCi	*kóSi*	difficulty	*kSay-im*
3. *CiCCa*		*sidra*	series	*sdar-ot*
		kivsa	sheep	*kvas-im*
	CeCCa	*xevra*	firm	*xavar-ot*
4. *CaCCa*		*yalda*	small girl	*yelad-ot*
	CaCaCa	*naara*	girl	*near-ot*
5. *CaCaC*		*barak*	lightning	*brak-im*
		nahar	river	*nehar-ot*
		xatan	groom	*xatan-im*
6. *CCaC*		*kfar*	village	*kfar-im*
		nyar	paper	*nyar-ot*
	CaCaC	*xacav*	squill	*xacav-im*
7. *CCaCa*		*brax-a*	blessing	*brax-ot*
		nemal-a	ant	*nemal-im*
	CaCaCa	*xarada*	anxiety	*xarad-ot*
		adaSa	lentil	*adaS-im*
8. *CaC(C)aC*[61]		*balaS*	detective	*balaS-im*
9. *CaC(Ca)Ca*		*katava*	report	*katav-ot*

5

Principles and Strategies in Language Acquisition and Language Processing

In discussing the task-specific tactical measures in Chapter 4 above we saw that children used such ad-hoc strategies differently from adults, and that there were certain similarities between the measures of children and of low-SES adults. Young children typically used context-dependent strategies, relying on semantic and pragmatic cues rather than on structural ones. These findings are compatible with early strategies demonstrated by various researchers (e.g. Clark 1973a, Cromer 1976, Wilcox & Palermo 1974/5), as based on broad cognitive principles that are not necessarily linguistic in nature, e.g. the Probable Event Strategy (Strohmer & Nelson 1974) or the Appropriate/Inappropriate Contexts Strategy (Dewart 1975).

In contrast to the younger subjects, older children, adolescents and adults usually performed the necessary structural operations required in the test, so that most of their responses were Appropriate. But this does not mean they were also Normative: faced with opacity in various areas, speakers were guided by linguistic principles indicating possible solutions in the face of too great a distance between underlying and surface structure. These seek to recognize regularity in the system, and to resolve irregularities in such a way that their removal does not create problems elsewhere in the system. The application of strategies deriving from these principles often resulted in errors, or linguistic variation along the Normative/Non-normative axis, and sometimes linguistic change.

I assume that children are equipped from birth with a set of procedures that guide them in the perception, storage, and analysis of language. These constitute a Basic Child Grammar (Bowerman 1985, Slobin 1985a), a fundamental system, a sort of "ideal human language" along the lines of which they map their intentions onto linguistic structures (Bickerton 1981). These Mapping Preferences, Operational Principles or Predispositions (Bowerman 1985, MacWhinney 1978, 1985, Slobin 1973, 1982, 1985a) make up a blueprint of Language, and they are mainly used by those who are not adequately familiar with the specific ways their language grammaticizes particular notions. Such linguistically naive speakers include children, and, to a certain extent, uneducated adults; and in some cases, members of creole-speaking communities (Slobin 1977). In an established language, relying on innate Predispositions may lead to re-analysis of structures and hence to what purists would term "errors." When these deviations result in more regular, more coherent, optimally transparent structures, they may become established in the speech community. But more often than not, Operating Principles compete with each other, and preferring one over the other may lead to better results in terms of a larger subsystem.

Moreover, *Literacy* constitutes a strong counterbalance to the regularizing force of Mapping Preferences as the restraining force of the established, consolidated language, geared to preserving irregularities, opacities and idiosyncracies. The competition between the two forces governing language acquisition and language preservation is often determined by the criterion of *Cost* which evaluates the local benefit achieved by re-analysis in terms of other significant factors in language acquisition and in language processing (Bates & MacWhinney 1982, Givón 1979a, Haiman 1983, Kiparsky 1982, Ravid 1994). A change that is not "costly," that is, does not cause greater loss elsewhere, is promoted to spread among the population.

This principle operates at the morphophonological level and is subject to grammatical and psycholinguistic constraints, unlike Martinet's (1955) Economy Principle which is "la synthése des besoins et de l'inertie" (1955:97), maintaining a status quo between feature reduction and feature marking at the purely phonetic level. Obviously, Transient errors disappear because they are too "costly," impose too great a change on the language system, while Fossilized Phenomena indicates an inevitable result of opacity involving only a local re-analysis, and which is compatible with the operation of the other Operating Principles.

The more educated and mature the speaker, the less he or she is given to reliance on natural Predispositions and more to preservation of idiosyncratic structures. But special circumstances in the history of a language, as in Modern Hebrew where neutralizations and mergers prevent a straightforward association of the underlying representation with surface structure, may lead educated adults too to adopt linguistic strategies deriving from natural Operating Principles, e.g. *Hif'il e/a Alternation*.

Below I discuss such strategies for analysis of linguistic material, especially of the type labeled "the pattern makers" by Slobin (1985a). The principles that underlie them were discussed in Clark (1981, 1982), Mac-Whinney (1978, 1985) and Slobin (1973, 1977, 1982, 1985a). I show how speakers employ these strategies in order to treat specific problems in Modern Hebrew morphophonology, including the cases of opacity discussed in the previous section; and I discuss the interaction of these strategies with other linguistic notions, structures, and entities.

5.1. ROTE

Rote-memorization has been observed as a basic juvenile strategy used by children in the initial stages of language acquisition, or by older speakers with impaired language (Berman 1986a, Karmiloff-Smith 1986b, Mac-Whinney 1975, 1978). This notion is refined below by distinguishing between Primary Rote, an early strategy later replaced by creative rule-combination; and Secondary Rote, a more mature strategy that pre-empts the use of rules in cases where idiosyncracies must be memorized. The developmental path in the use of Rote is presented in Table 41.

These claims are illustrated with examples from *Verb-Governed Prepositions, Lexical Exceptions, Case-Marked Pronouns,* and *Backformation.*

The domain of *Verb-Governed Prepositions* has been shown as one of the most stable categories of this study. Even the youngest subjects start out with fairly high Normative scores of nearly half; while the low-SES subjects come very close to speakers of Standard Hebrew. This is due to the interaction of Primary Rote with transitivity and the thematic role of object, or Theme. The high Normative scores in Verb-Governed Prepositions constitute an instance of a rote-learned amalgam which is not re-analyzed at a later age. Usually, a form acquired early as an unanalyzed amalgam is later re-analyzed into its components, existent or assumed, which may result in error.[62] But *Verb-Governed Prepositions,* being devoid of semantic content, represent obligatory Government rather than Case, and are thus inseparable from the verb itself, remaining an unanalyzed amalgam together. These prepositions are hence part of the content of the lexical matrix of the verb, and are learned by rote when the verb itself is learned (Jackendoff 1975, 1983), so that knowing a verb entails knowledge of the preposition(s) governed by that verb, hence the early mastery of such prepositions.

There are indeed few examples of such deviations in my spontaneous data, too, only at early ages, e.g. *hu daxaf li* 'he pushed to-me' instead of *hu daxaf oti* 'he pushed Acc-me' [3;7,DIA]. This concurs with Kaplan's (1983) findings. Yet, the different Normative scores on each preposition

Table 41. Use of Rote learning in language maturation

Primary Rote ⟶ Rule-bound strategies ⟶ Secondary Rote pre-empts rules

(Appendix C) indicate that Rote interacts with additional factors, and this is directly reflected in speaker usage both on the test and in conversation. The relevant factor interacting here with rote-learning was transitivity.

Transitivity

The lexical entry of a verb specifies its valency, or argument structure (Bresnan 1982, Maranz 1984, Pinker 1989). This study focused on transitive constructions with governed objects, which differ from direct objects in being preceded by a preposition, unlike direct objects, which take the special Accusative marker *et* when definite and can be passivized (See Berman 1978a for further distinctions).

Thematically, both types of objects are themes manipulated by the agent (Gruber 1976, Slobin 1985d, van Valin 1990). Transitivity can be represented on a continuum of animacy and control, with highest transitivity represented attaching to a verb taking a human initiator (Comrie 1981, Hopper & Thompson 1980). The higher the transitivity of the verb, the more obligatory its valency, and the lower the semantic load assigned to the governing preposition, hence rendering it more subject to rote-learning. The prototypical transitive construction is one where a NP high on animacy and control physically manipulates a direct object (Bates & MacWhinney 1982, Slobin 1981, Slobin & Bever 1982). These indeed were the types of verbs that received the highest Normative scores on Verb-Governed Prepositions. By age 8, the test subjects completed the cue sentence by referring to the verb's argument structure, e.g. *tetapel ba-buba* 'take-care in-the doll'. But the responses of the 3-year-olds reflected the relative degree of transitivity of the verb, since they completed the cue sentence appropriately only when transitivity was high enough to force them to do so, or else produce an ungrammatical string. In cases of low transitivity, they interpreted the verb as non-object-taking, complementing it with a clause e.g. *al tefaxed, hu lo ose klum* 'don't (be) afraid, it/he (does)n't do anything' (see similar discussion of *kowai* 'fearful' in Japanese in Sugamoto 1982).

The verbs that were highest on animacy and control, hence on transitivity, were *tetapel* 'take-care', *tarbic* 'hit', *tiStameS* 'use', and *tesaxek* 'play', in that order. *tetapel be-* 'take-care in' (=of)' is high on transitivity and obligatorily governs an object via the semantically vacuous *be-* 'in'. There is no possibility of omitting the governed object, so **dan tipel* 'Dan took-care' is ungrammatical. Table 42 presents the test verbs with their governed prepositions in terms of animacy and control of the agent, and semantic role and focus of the object.

The high transitivity of *tetapel* 'take care' partly derives from the high animacy and control of the subject, since it's people who usually take care of things (Comrie 1981). It is also one of the few governing verbs that can passivize in Hebrew, e.g. *ha-inyan tupal* 'the-matter was-taken-care (of)', another criterion for transitivity. The high transitivity of *tetapel*

Table 42. Degrees and Features of Transitive Constructions

Verb	Gloss	Degree of Trans.	Agent Argument Animacy	Control	Patient Argument Semantic Role	Focus
tetapel	take care	1	human	high	animate/inanimate	+
al tarbic	don't hit	2	human	high	animate	+/−
tiStameS	use	3	human	high	inanimate	+
al tefaxed	don't be afraid	4	animate	low	animate/inanimate	−
tesader	play	5	animate	middle	animate/inanimate	+/−
al tix'as	don't be angry	6	animate	low	animate/inanimate	−
tistakel	look	7	animate	middle	animate/inanimate	−

'take-care' is directly reflected in the ceiling Normative score of the 3-year-olds.

Next is the dynamic verb *al tarbic* 'don't hit',[63] which takes a human initiator subject who is in control of one's object. I would intuitively assign a higher degree of grammaticality to negative objectless *al tarbic* 'don't hit' than to positive objectless *tarbic* 'hit', since negatives have lower control, making the object less specified. Nonetheless Normative scores are very high for all groups. Also high on transitivity is *tiStameS* 'use' that obligatorily requires an object governed either by Normative *be-* 'in' or colloquial *im* 'with' (already noted in Dolzhansky 1937). This achieves ceiling scores in most groups, including the 3-year-olds. The subject NP of *tiStameS* is high on animacy and control, though its verb cannot be passivized. *tesaxek* 'play' had lower Normative scores, partly because of the slightly lower degree of the subject's manipulation of the object.

However, the amount of Appropriate responses (*im* 'with' instead of *be-* 'in') reaches ceiling in all groups, indicating that it is the nature of the object that dictated these results. Lowest on transitivity are the affective verbs *al tefaxed* 'don't (be) afraid' and *al tix'as* 'don't (be) angry'. These are fairly high on animacy, though not necessarily human; but they are low on control, since the subject is an experiencer. The younger and low-SES subjects interpreted them as denoting inner emotions rather than directed at some external object; therefore they were often complemented by adverbial clauses, e.g. *al tix'as, hu lo aSem* 'don't be angry, (because) it's not his fault'.

Learning about the argument structure of the verb (Pinker 1989), when it is not obligatory (see Carrier-Duncan 1985), is shown in this study to be a maturational process that is completed by age five. The more obligatory the preposition, the better and earlier it is learned by rote. The less transitive the construction, the less binding the valency of the verb, offering more options of complementation. Often children react by selecting a less transitive construction with an adjunct clause enabling them to give their own personal interpretation of the cue item within the context-bound situation.

The second facet of transitivity at work which sometimes overrides the simple mechanism of rote is the semantic role of the object. In many languages, a highly transitive construction is one where the patient is lower on animacy and definiteness than the agent. In our test items, whenever the language offers the speaker a choice between animate or inanimate object, the amount of Normative scores diminishes. This happens in *tiStameS* 'use' and *tesaxek* 'play', where the object may be inanimate, e.g. a fork or a doll. Both require the governed preposition *be-* 'in', also Normative for the instrumental case. The object need not be inanimate with *be-*, but a higher degree of control on the part of the agent is assumed, as in *tipel be-* 'took-care of'. These verbs can also take an animate object, functioning as another agent with the comitative *im* 'with', e.g. *dan sikex ba-kélev ca'acúa* 'Dan played in-the-toy dog' (inanimate object) vs. *dan sixek im ha-kélev* 'Dan played with-the-dog' (animate co-agent object). These two semantic roles of the governed object are semantically related, as are the noun classes of agent and instrument (Clark & Berman 1984). They thus constitute two parallel options, a potential source of confusion. Hence the dip in the amount of Normative responses in the high-SES five-year-olds on the verbs *tiStameS* 'use' and *tesaxek* 'play': it seems that *be-* 'in' is rote-learned with these two verbs for the semantic roles of inanimate patient and comitative co-agent, hence the high Normative results in the three-year-olds. But by age five, high-SES children have a better understanding of these two different semantic roles, leading them to re-analyze the rote-learned *be-* 'in' as *im* 'with', representing the co-agent. Paradoxically, it is the low-SES 5s that continue getting higher Normative scores precisely because they do not follow this path of analysis. Kaplan (1983) found a similar dip in her older (3;6) compared to younger (2;3) Subjects: The latter demonstrated 90% successful use of governed prepositions, as against only 80% in the older ones, indicating rote-learning by the younger subjects and the beginning of analysis by the older ones (compare Karmiloff-Smith 1986b). *tiStameS* 'use', which always requires an inanimate tool, is compatible with the prototypical scene of a human agent in control, manipulating an inanimate object, hence the high Normative results from age eight onwards. But *tesaxek* 'play', which in many cases requires a co-player, continues fluctuating between *be* 'in' and *im* 'with' far into adolescence, where a strengthened sense of self, a gradual loosening of the ties to a particular play-situation, and knowledge of the Normative form, all reinforce Normative *be-*.

The overall scores of the young subjects on verb-governed prepositions were extremely high, reflecting rote-learning. The single exception is the item *tistakel* 'look', where Normative scores are usually below 20%. Here, a new standard is clearly being formed, shifting from Normative *be-* to colloquial *al* 'on', shared by all subjects across ages and backgrounds (see Appendix C). This suggests yet another parameter of transitivity relevant to the object: focus. I propose that direct focus on the object also determines the degree of transitivity of a syntactic construction. For instance, the objects of *tiStameS* 'use' and *tetapel* 'take-care' are both high in focus because the action involves direct manipulation of the object. By contrast, emotives like *tefaxed* '(be) afraid', *tix'as* '(be) angry' may be directed outside with no specific focus. Nor does *tesaxek* 'play' require an object in focus, since it may describe a generally oriented activity. The negative form of *al tarbic* 'don't hit' gives it the general meaning of 'don't display agressive behavior' without a focused theme, as opposed to positive *tarbic*, implying a focused theme. Hence the differences in grammaticality judgments described above. Thus *tistakel* is low on transitivity not only because of the type of subject it takes, lower on control than, say, *tetapel* 'take-care', but also because it lacks a focused object, indicating a generally directed look at one's surroundings, e.g. *tistakel! mi ze ha-iS ha-ze?* 'Look! who is that man?' The object of *tistakel* also lacks specification as to animacy. *tistakel* is thus often interpreted as intransitive, often followed by a (non-argument) clause. Another option is the use of optional *al* 'on' over obligatory *be-*. There is independent evidence that *al* is in the process of turning into a general all-purpose preposition in lower-transitivity constructions, especially in Nonstandard usage (Afek & Kahanman 1985). For example, *al* is unusually common in slang expressions, e.g. *hu avad al-ay* 'he worked on me' = 'he cheated me'; *hu gamar al-av* 'he finished on-him' = 'he defeated him completely'. Other instances from my Spontaneous Speech data are *hem la'agu al-ay* 'they made-fun on-me' = 'they laughed at me' [5;3, SAM]; *ha-nahag kirtes al-av* 'the-driver ticketed on-him' = 'the-driver punched his ticket', and *Amnon Silem al-ay* 'Amnon paid on-me' = 'Amnon paid for me' [13,OBS]; *David meSaker al-av* 'David is-lying on-him' = 'David is lying to him' [16,SAM]. And Dolzhansky (1937) notes *al* as a popular preposition in the Hebrew child language of fifty years ago. According to Afek & Kahanman (1985), *al* enhances the degree of transitivity of the construction by increasing the amount of control by the agent and the impact of the object. Governed prepositions are thus learned by rote, yet this path may be facilitated or hindered by the degree of transitivity of the governing verb and semantic properties of its arguments.

Primary and Secondary Rote

Early rote-learning, as illustrated by memorization of verb-governed prepositions, is a juvenile strategy, since it does not involve any kind of analysis. The output of early or Primary Rote, the unanalyzed amalgam, is subsequently subject to analysis and modification (Berman 1984a, MacWhinney 1978, 1985). But there is another kind of rote-learning, too, late or Secondary Rote, the result of literacy and of the disposition of the older, more sophisticated speaker's preference for the marked form. In Secondary as in Primary Rote, the speaker memorizes a complete form; however early Rote learning is a pre-grammatical maturational stage in which the child is not yet aware of structure, while Secondary Rote is a strategy that the speaker employs knowing full well that words are complex rule-bound entities. Late Rote is employed precisely with morphological exceptions, which are hence only partially motivated, if at all (Aronoff 1976, Bates & MacWhinney 1982). These are stored and retrieved as idiosyncratic members of a list, yet nevertheless activated by related morphological structures (Bybee 1988, Halle 1973, Stemberger & MacWhinney 1985, 1986). Consider the examples in Table 43:

The main difference between the two types of Rote, then, is that the first is employed *without* awareness of structure, while the second is employed *despite* awareness of structure. Children begin by learning both simple and inflected forms separately by Primary Rote (Ai), and then they proceed to analysis and rule-combination (MacWhinney 1978), so that irregular forms come out as mistakes (Aii, Bi), e.g. **iSim* for *anaSim* and back-formed **anaS* and **otiya*; later on Secondary Rote steps in to retrieve the idiosyncratic form (Bii). My spontaneous speech data confirm several such examples of non-grammatical rule-activated forms all in the speech of very young or non-literate speakers, e.g. *harbe yomim* 'many days' from singular *yom*, cf. Normative *yamim* [4;0,DIA]; or *kvas* for Normative *kéves* 'sheep' from plural *kvasim* 4;3 [DIA].

Secondary Rote may apply to items which are true exceptions, e.g. future *yi-lbaS* 'will-wear' (cf. **yi-lboS*,Ft. Most of the time, however, it occurs with historically but not synchronically motivated classes, or with minor, less productive rules. Take for example English *bad/worse:* While the linguistically naive speaker might seek regularity following Formal Simplicity (see below), to yield the ungrammatical **badder*, the linguistically sophisticated speaker will employ Secondary Rote to retrieve *worse* from the lexicon. But a lexical exception need not be devoid of structural relationship to other items (Bybee 1988): The literate speaker may seek partial relationships, as with the superlative form *worst*. Thus a large vocabulary can help in assigning some sort of regularity even to lexical exceptions. An example in this study is *dli/dlayim* 'pail/s', rendered *dliyim* in the Nonstandard sociolect. Historically, *dli* 'pail' belonged to the *CéCeC* pattern, which

Table 43. Primary and Secondary Rote

A. *Primary Rote*

(i)	Rote-learned amalgam⟶	(ii)	Analyzing the amalgam into its components: rule-activated form
	kubiya, kubiyot 'block, blocks'		*kubiya* 'block'
	ot, otiyot 'letter, letters'		**otiya* 'letter'
	iS, anaSim 'man, men'		**anaS, *iSim* 'man, men'

B. *Secondary Rote*

(i)	Rule-activated form⟶	(ii)	Rote-learned form, partially motivated
	otiyot/*otiya 'letters/letter'		*ot* 'letter'
	iS/*Isim 'man/men'		*anaSim* 'men'
	anaSim/*anaS 'men/man'		*iS* 'man'

---

explains the *CCaC-im* Junction plural form, but there is no synchronic cue for the speaker, so the plural appears to be a lexical exception, and hence even half of the 8-year-olds still give the non-Normative form *dliyim*.

A property of lexical exceptions which may actually aid Secondary Rote is suppletion, where one item bears little or no structural relationship to another in the paradigm. Being uniquely marked, it is salient and easy to learn by rote like the suppletive English *bad/worse*, and Hebrew *bat/banot* 'girl/s', or *iSa/naSim* 'woman/women' on the test. These are not true suppletives like *go/went*, but they differ enough from the base form to be specially marked and easy to learn. Since they are highly frequent in both singular and plural, they are able to resist regularization (Bates & Mac-Whinney 1982, Bybee 1985, 1988, Hooper 1976). Hence by age three almost half of the subjects gave the Normative response *banot* 'girls', unlike *naSim* 'women', which only reached three-quarters Normative responses in middle childhood: *naSim* 'women' is not as frequent in children's language as *banot* 'girls'.

The work of Secondary Rote is apparent in the Oblique Pronouns Category. Two types of distinctions were noted in this system—basic vs. derived, and singular vs. plural, along with various changes in the form of the stems themselves. These require the speaker to select suitable strategies to handle a variety of unmotivated forms. Consider *bli* 'without', with the bound form *biladey* activating Secondary Rote, the only item of its kind, which can only be handled by rote. This results in a marked form favored by literate speakers, hence the disparity between the Normative responses given by the high-SES vs. low-SES subjects. Secondary Rote is also necessary in changing the bound forms of *et* 'Accusative marker' and *kmo* 'like', *ot-* and *kamo-* respectively. Even the choice between the three second-person singular feminine forms *-ax, -ex,* and *-áyix* (cf. *ot-ax* 'Acc-you,Fm', *mim-ex* 'from-you,Fm', and *al-áyix* 'on-you,Fm') is partially aided by Secondary Rote: while the plural *-áyix* form is related to other forms in the paradigm, the choice between *-ax* and *-ex* is synchronically unmotivated and must be learnt by rote, so that it is indeed a sociolinguistic variable separating the educated from the Nonstandard dialect. My spontaneous speech data-base contains many examples of the *-ax/ex* problem, e.g. *leyad-ax* instead of *leyad-ex* 'by-you,Fm' [3;0,SAM]; *elex* for *el-áyix* 'to-you,Fm.' [4;6,SAM]; *al-ex* and *ot-ex* for *al-áyix* 'on-you,Fm.' and *ot-ax* 'Acc-you,Fm' [32,SAM]; and *biglal-ax* for *biglal-ex* [2;3,OBS]. They are typical of, though not exclusive to, children and low-SES speakers.

Another example of Secondary Rote is Backformation in animal terms. Two of these names, *para* 'cow' and *tarnególet* 'hen', require simple back-formation to derive the masculine *par* and *tarnegol* respectively. In a third, *kivsa* 'sheep,Fm' the masculine form *kéves* belongs to the corresponding pattern *CéCeC*; while *tarnególet* 'hen' gets very high Normative results from early on, the other two achieve ceiling only in high school (Appendix C). The reason is the over-use of Secondary Rote in a test situation.

Kinship animal terms often form suppletive paradigms, e.g. *ez/táyiS/gdi* 'goat/he-goat/kid'; *par/para/Sor/égel* 'bull/cow/ox/calf'; and *arye/levi'a/kfir* 'lion/lioness/lion-cub' etc, and the names of the young are generally suppletive. Subjects usually had no trouble with the masculine form of *tarnegol* 'rooster', the only colloquial form.[64] But they gave a wide range of mostly male animal-names, both mature and young for *para* 'cow' and *kivsa* 'sheep'. The high-SES 5s responded with *sus* 'horse' and *Sor* 'ox', while subjects eight years and over gave *táyiS* 'he-goat', *égel* 'calf', *áyil* 'ram', *Sor* 'ox', *ya'el* 'gazelle', *tale* 'lamb', and *ez* 'goat'. This tendency re-appeared in the low-SES adults. With the development of lexical specificity there is a greater need to employ Secondary Rote as with animal-terms. Moreover, the experimental situation may have led subjects to give suppletive forms, that is, use a retrieval system to tap a given list of items, rather than employ structural devices such as backformation.

5.2. FORMAL SIMPLICITY

A basic predisposition speakers rely on when required to perform structural operations is for Formal Simplicity (henceforth FS), which yields a strategy involving the preservation of a base form when modified by affixes (Clark 1981, 1982, Clark & Berman 1984). The test findings, as well as the spontaneous data and independent studies, show this to be a fairly basic strategy, employed across the board in childhood. It is also a major preference of adults when faced with opacity in linear structures, employed much more by uneducated adults than by linguistically sophisticated ones, which accounts in part for the large discrepancies between high- and low-SES Normative scores, as well as for the consistent statistically significant similarities between low-SES older and high-SES younger groups.

FS is best exemplified in linear structures, where a stem is modified in a morphological operation, e.g. the English suffix *-ity* that triggers the Trisyllabic Shortening Rule in, say, *divine/divinity* (Chomsky & Halle 1968, Halle 1973). We would thus not expect to find it deployed in areas of Classical Hebrew derivational morphology where a discontinuous Semitic root requires non-linear affixation of vowels to form a word (Berman 1987c, Gesenius 1910, McCarthy 1981, Rosén 1956). Rather, reliance on FS is compatible with two sets of morphophonemic processes: (a) Inflectional processes of affixation such as number (e.g. *matos/metos-im* 'airplane/s'), gender (e.g. *kaxol/kxul-a* 'blue/Fm'), and person (e.g. *yiSmor/tiSmer-u,* 'will-guard/2nd,Pl'); and (b) the more analytic, relatively recent lexical device of linear suffixation (e.g. *báyit/beyti* 'house/domestic', *téva/tiv'i* 'nature/natural') (Attias 1981, Di-Nur 1979, Nir 1981). The type of changes involved in linear affixation in Hebrew include stress-shift, e.g. *xalom/xalomot* 'dream/s' (Podolsky 1987) plus (i) vowel-reduction or deletion, e.g. *zaken/zkena* 'old/Fm' (Ravid & Shlesinger 1987a), (ii) vowel change (*xec/xicim* 'arrow/s', (iii) stop/spirant alternation (*daf/dapim* 'page/ s'), (iv) stop deletion (*sakit/sakiyot* 'bag/s', and (v) vowel metathesis and vowel shift, e.g. *simxa/smaxot* 'joy/s' (Berman 1981c).

Two of the test categories exemplify the use of the FS-motivated base-preserving strategy: *Stem Change* and *Backformation*. FS was deployed in other linearly modified test items in *Weak Final Syllable* and *Stop/Spirant Alternation*, as well as some in *Lexical Exceptions*, and *Oblique Pronouns*. Comparison of these two facets of the same process—increasing complexity by modifying a stem and decreasing it by backforming from a complex form—demonstrates the essential unity of such linear operations (Ravid 1990).

FS strategies take two forms: (i) no stem change and (ii) partial stem change. The first is very childish, and can be regarded as an extension of Repetition with an analytic marker, in much the same way that agglutinating and analytic structures occupy different places on the same continuum. Above we saw the reproduction of the cue item with the added semantic content given by a lexical item, e.g. *harbe iparon* 'many pencil'. In contrast, FS(i) involves retention of the base form, with a grammaticized semantic marker linearly attached at the end of the stem without affecting it, e.g. *iparón-im* for *efron-ot* 'pencils' (Bar-Adon 1959, Borokovsky 1984, Levy 1980), or *rax-a* for grammatical *rak-a* 'soft,Fm'. In doing so, the child gradually moves towards incorporating new semantic information within the word, the crux of grammatical development. The shift from Repetition into FS(i) thus reflects the transition from Rote into grammar. This strategy is clearly at work in the three and five-year-olds in producing *iparon-im* 'pencil-s' for adult *efronot,* and is also responsible for Non-Normative responses in the older low-SES as well as some cases in the high-SES population. My spontaneous data contain several examples of the simplified plural *iparon-im* by children 2;10 and 3;7 respectively [SAM]. But none of the children doing so preserved the stress-pattern in plural *iparon-im:* They all correctly shifted stress to the plural suffix *-im*. Patterns of stress-assignment in stem-modification processes operating on ultimately stressed stems are part of children's earliest grammatical knowledge.

Even at this stage FS(i) does not operate alone, but interacts with other Operating Principles as well as with structural factors. What determines the incidence of deviations following the tendency to leave the stem unchanged depends on its structural properties which either check or promote FS. For example, the other members of the Stem Change category, *éven* 'stone' and *adom* 'red', as well as the Stop/Spirant item *cahov* 'yellow' seem to be unaffected by FS(i), as only a few three-year-olds gave the Nonstandard plural forms *éven-im, adom-im* and *cahov-im* (cf. grammatical *avanim, adumim,* and *cehubim* respectively). This is due to competition with both Saliency and Semantic Coherence (see below). But Nonstandard responses rise with age in the low-SES population, where FS overrules Formal Consistency.

Relative frequency is another factor competing with FS, with high frequency words like *bat* 'girl' and *aba* 'daddy' resisting it from early on in all groups, while less frequent *dli* 'pail' (Nonstandard plural *dliy-im* for *dlay-im*) offers less resistance. The effect of FS on *dli*, lacking Semantic Coherence, lasts into middle childhood, and even into less educated adulthood. Finally, FS is one of the Principles that underlie the quick and easy acquisition of forms such as *taklit/taklit-im* 'record/s' in Weak Final Syllable, so that almost half of the members of the youngest age group already had the Normative plural form *taklit-im* instead of Nonstandard *takliy-ot*. The nature of FS(i) which leaves the stem absolutely intact, as a predominantly childish strategy, is further demonstrated by the spontaneous data-base, e.g. *Snéynu abah-ot* (singular *ába*, compare *imah-ot* 'mothers') for Normative *Snéynu av-ot* 'we're both of us fathers' [2;8,DIA]; *zaken-a* for Normative *zkena* 'old,Fm', (cf. masculine *zaken*) [2;3,DIA]; *ábah-im* (from *ába*) and *iS-ot* 'women' (singular *iS-a*) for *av-ot* 'fathers' and *naS-im* 'women' [2;8,SAM]; *karon-im* (singular *karon*) instead of *kron-ot* 'wagons' [2;6,SAM]; *kapit-im* for *kapiy-ot* 'teaspoon-s' [2;0,OBS]; *Satix-im, kaf-im* and *gavi'-im* (singular *gavía*) for *Stix-im* 'carpets', *kap-ot* 'spoons' and *gvi'-im* 'goblets' respectively [4;3,4;6,OBS]; *iS-im* for *anaS-im* 'men', [2;10,4;0,SAM]; and *gamal-im* instead of Normative *gmal-im* 'camels' [2;10,SAM].

One typical childhood strategy noted for Hebrew is the tendency to leave the verbal stem (3rd person singular, with a zero morph marking 3rd person singular) intact in past-tense number, gender and person inflection (Bar Adon 1959, Berman 1985). This works fine in the common *Pa'al* verb-pattern, e.g. *safár-ti* '(I) counted' (cf. 3rd person singular *safar*). But when stem-modification is needed, as in *y*-final roots, FS yields a deviation e.g. *yará-ti hamon til-im* instead of *yarí-ti* '(I) shot lots-of rockets', (cf. 3rd person singular *yara*); and *damá-ti le-nahag Sel ótobus* for *damí-ti* 'I was like a bus driver', from 3rd person *dama* by FS(i) [3;1,DIA]. Few children produced such forms on the test, as this is a very juvenile strategy, but Bar-Adon's report that this is a general tendency in young children (1959:83) is supported by a wide range of *CaCa-* *y*-final verbs in spontaneous child speech, e.g. *alá-nu la-matos* '(we) went-up to-the-plane', (for *alí-nu*, root ע *-l-y*) [3;2,OBS]; *talá-ti et ze* '(I) hung Acc it', for *talí-ti*, root *t-l-y*; and *ma kana-t li?* 'what (did you) = bought,Fm for-me' for *kanit*, root *q-n-y* [2;9,SAM], and [2;6,SAM]. And similarly *ata kaná-ta et ze?* '(did) you bought Acc it'? for Normative *kaní-ta*, of the same root [2;1,DIA]; *Satá-ti Sóko* '(I) drank chocolate milk', for *Satí-ti*, root *S-t-y* [2;6,SAM]; *yará-ti* '(I) shot', for *yarí-ti*, root *y-r-y* [2;10,OBS]; *saxá-ti ba-máyim* '(I) swam in-the-water', for *saxí-ti*, root *s-H-y* [3;7,OBS]; *kala-t* '(you,Fm) roasted' for *kalit* [2;8,SAM]. I encountered one late example of this kind of my daughter Sivan in a play-session, a verb she rarely used, *yará-ti* for *yará-ti* '(I) shot', root *y-r-y* [6;3,DIA].

Children sometimes persist in applying FS into middle childhood, especially in opaque forms with underlying "double" roots which surface in modification or require vowel change, e.g. *lev-im* for Normative *levav-ot* 'hearts', root *l-b-b*, from singular *lev* [3;5,DIA; 6;7,OBS], or *cilim*[65] instead of *clalim* 'shadows', from singular *cel*, root *ṣ-l-l* [6;3,DIA]. At a later stage, FS(ii) (partial stem change) takes over, especially where there are several changes in the stem whose motivation is not apparent to the speaker, typically a child or a speaker of the Nonstandard sociolect. The following are three examples from the test of such partial stem change in which features of the stem, such as the *bkp/vxf* alternant or the original stem vowel, are retained: (i) the change from singular *iparon* 'pencil' to plural *efronot* involves lowering the initial *i* into *e*, due to the underlying initial pharyngeal *y*; spirantizing *p* into *f*; *a*-deletion; and suffixation of the plural feminine allomorph *-ot*, common in stems ending with *-on*. From age three up into adulthood, failing to perform a number of these operations accounts for the many Non-Normative responses found in the low-SES groups: *iparonot, ipronim, ipronot, efronim, ifronot*. Note, however, that from age 5, subjects always performed vowel deletion. Similarly (ii) the few deviations from the Normative plural *cehubim* (singular *cahov* 'yellow') did not violate vowel-deletion and vowel change ($o \longrightarrow u$), but retained the spirantized *v* of *cahov*, yielding *cehuvim*. A final example (iii) is Normative *avanim* 'stones' occurring as *evanim* (cf. singular *éven*) in the low-SES 5s who failed to perform vowel lowering required by the initial glottal stop.

Another, more sophisticated type of partial stem retention is the tendency to preserve the base form in plural forms of *CóCeC* nouns. At a very early age we find *bosam-im* for *besam-im* 'perfumes', from singular *bósem* [2;6,Rec]. In adult speech FS(ii) tends to take place in the less obvious *CóCi* and *CóCaC* variations of *CóCeC*, so that instead of the required Junction form of *CCaC-im* (e.g. *tófes/tfas-im* 'form/s,') they take the form *CoCaC-im*, e.g. *koSay-im* instead of *kSay-im* 'difficulties' from *kóSi* (Moreshet 1969, Donag-Kinrot 1978) or *tóar/toar-im* for *tear-im* 'adjectives', *nóhal/nohal-im* for *nehal-im* 'procedures'. This Non-Normative alternation occurs in certain established forms as well, e.g. *SóreS/SoraS-im* 'root/s' (Avineri 1976).

To sum up this section: FS operates on structures where (especially non-sophisticated) speakers fail to perceive underlying motivation for stem modification, foci of opacity in Modern Hebrew that can be resolved by attaching a suffix with little or no change in the base form.

FS in Backformation

A "basic" form need not necessarily be non-complex: some nouns most frequently occur in their inflected, usually plural or dual form, e.g. *zeytim* 'olives', *anavim* 'grapes', *klayot* 'kidneys', *garbáyim* 'socks-dual', *kubiyot* 'blocks', *xaruzim* 'beads', *dma'ot* 'tears', *cdafim* 'shells' and *eynáyim* 'eyes Dual' (Berman 1985, Borokovsky 1984, Dromi & Berman 1982, Levy 1980). For the purposes of FS, the inflected structure then serves as a basic form to operate on. This was noted for Junction forms, in which several singular forms converge in a single plural structure *CCaC-im/ot*. When speakers regard such plural forms as basic, and have difficulty in relating the plural to the singular form, they may resort to therapeutic re-analysis to link the free singular form back to the bound *CCaC-* stem. An additional factor is the sheer number of possible singular forms of *CCaCim/ot* which drives the speaker to the most transparent singular *CCaC-* even when the plural is not basic.

The easiest and most natural strategy would be to follow FS in reverse: by removing the plural suffix and leaving the bound stem intact, optionally attaching the feminine suffix to feminine-marked stems, naive speakers follow the simplest possible path from Junction plural to singular forms, e.g. *cdaf-im* —→ *cdaf* 'shells/shell' (cf. Normative *cédef*); *dma'-ot* —→ *dma'a* 'tears/tear' (Normative *dim'a*). This strategy is especially prevalent in the 3s and among the low-SES, and accounts for about 30% of the responses in the adults-b, yet is found in the more established population as well in the spontaneous data: almost all backformed items beyond early childhood in my records are of the Junction structure, where the free and the inflected forms are not readily related, and the plural is pragmatically basic, e.g. a 25-year-old storyteller told children in a story that *ha-par herim tlaf exad* 'the-bull lifted one paw', backforming from dual *tlaf-áyim*, for Normative *télef*; or *elohim bara et xava me-ha-cla Sel ha-adam* 'God created Eve from-the-rib of the-Adam', for Normative *céla* 'rib', backformed from plural *cla'ot* [7;6,OBS]; *brag, xlak* instead of *bóreg* 'screw' and *xélek* 'part', from plural *bragim* and *xalakim* respectively [3;6,OBS]; *zot xaraka?* asked about a bee, feminine gender, backformed from *xarakim* 'insects', for Normative *xérek* [3;6,DIA]; *afilu lo hor exad?* 'not even one parent?' inquired [5;2,SAM] when told not to bring parents to a children's party (backformed from *horim* 'parents' for *hore* 'parent'); *asav* instead of *ésev* 'grass', from plural *asavim* [3;10,SAM]; *kraya* instead *kirya* 'city' from plural *krayot*[66] [11,SAM]; and *levava* from *levavot* 'hearts' for Normative *lev* [4;0,SAM]. Note also colloquial *Slav* 'phase' instead of Normative *Salav,* backformed from plural *Slabim.* Plural forms may become pragmatically prominent in immediate discourse, for example spontaneous *pitre* 'mushroom', back-formed from plural *pitriyot* (cf. grammatical singular *pitriya*) in *nafal, nafal pitre exad. Sivan, yeS po od pitriya, yeS od pitre* 'one mushroomBK has fallen. Sivan, there's one more mushroom here, there is one more mushroom*BK*'—with the child fluctuating back and forth from the back-formed *pitre* to grammatical *pitriya* [2;2,DIA].

In the low-SES population, FS is retained to adulthood in feminine Junction items, and some of these constructions are also common in collo-quial usage among high-SES speakers, especially when the basic form is in the plural, e.g. *klaya*[67] 'kidney', *SmaSa* 'window-pane' from plural *klayot* and *SmaSot*. The clearest example of a changing standard due to FS in Backformation, however, is that of *cdaf* 'shell', backformed from plural *cdafim*. For the low-SES speakers, it was the only form, and in the high-SES groups it was only at early puberty that 70–80% responded with *cédef*.

This is clearly a case of "pretended normativity" since everything indicates that *cdaf* is the Standard for a (sea) shell. In most cases, adult subjects hesitated for some time before giving *cédef*, some of them saying explicitly that "*cdaf* is what you find on the beach, while *cédef* is the stuff jewelry is made from (mother of pearl)."[68]

As in the inflection of the basic form, FS competes with other strategies. We have already seen that the interfering factor in *para* and *kivsa* is Secondary Rote, with subjects eager to retrieve Rote-learned kinship terminology that is not always appropriate. Therefore, *para* 'cow', which requires the simplest backformation operation, has ceiling scores only in the high-SES high-school and adult groups, very much like *kivsa* 'sheep', where the operation required (*kivsa/kéves* 'sheep Fm/Masc') is much more complex. How can we explain, though, the fact that very few, and only the youngest, backformed the ungrammatical *kivs* for *kéves* 'sheep, Masc' from *kivsa*? Why is *kéves* resistant to change? A similar comparison may be made between *dma'ot* 'tears', which reaches Normative ceiling by age 12, and *acamot* 'bones' which does so already by age five in the high-SES. Note that change-resistant *écem* 'bone' and *kéves* 'sheep' both take the highly salient *CéCeC* pattern. But other factors contribute to early mastery of *écem* as well: Firstly, unlike *dma'ot* 'tears' and *cdafim* 'shells', which always occur in the plural, speech input contains as many occurrences of singular *écem* 'bone' as of plural *acamot*, especially in Israeli homes where chicken is major fare in any form. Frequency of input thus reinforces the singular form (Slobin 1985a). Secondly, Backformation would yield a feminine *acama*, highly distinct from established *écem* 'bone'. This is too costly a clash, as Hebrew attaches heavy weight to the external marking of gender (Berman 1985). But backforming from *dma'ot* 'tears' results in *dma'a*, an already existent noun pattern (cf. *braxa* 'blessing'), and gender is not violated.

Moreover, as long as the external gender marking is clear, the internal construction of vowel-patterning seems to carry less weight, especially in Junction structures: vowels in CVCVC structures are often in a state of variability in endstate usage. An example from my supplementary material is *anáxnu mesaxakim be-xravim* 'we (are) playing with swords' (cf. grammatical *xaravot*, [3;2,DIA]), from singular *xérev* 'sword'. Adults are uncertain whether the word for 'insect' is *xarak* or *xérek*; whether *madad* or *méded* means 'index', and whether the word for 'a cut' is *xatax* or *xétex*, (or even *xétax*, re-analyzing the final *k*-derived *x* as *H*-derived); and alongside *cdaf/cédef*, there are examples of CCaC/CéCeC/CáCaC structures such as Normative *saxar* and Non-Normative *sxar* 'wages' (Ravid & Shlesinger 1987a). Note that historically *CéCeC* and *CCaC* were corresponding patterns in Aramaic (Avineri 1976), and were interchangeable in the ancient Yemenite dialect of Hebrew, mostly used today in prayers (Morag 1963). Similarly, there are adult fluctuations in *CiCCa/CCaCa*, e.g. *veda*/ Normative *vaada* 'committee', *seara*/ Normative *saara* 'a hair', *baaya*/ Normative *beaya* 'problem'.

Thus the relative weight of vowels, in general lower in Hebrew due to the basically consonantal structure of its lexicon, is especially diminished in Junction constructions, where there is a certain fuzziness in the distinctions between forms sharing the prefixless CVCVC(V) form, and being linked in plural form as well. This fuzziness is often resolved by employing full or partial FS in backformation.

5.3. FORMAL CONSISTENCY

Strategies favoring FS refer mostly to linear processes: they guide the child in the treatment of a base and a linear morpheme attached to it. However, the very application of rules to structures—both linear and nonlinear—is no less essential in normal morphological development. For example, FS preserves the base *iparon* 'pencil' in plural inflection (cf. adult *efron-ot*), but the decision to attach the less marked masculine plural suffix *-im* rather than the required feminine plural *-ot* derives from a strategy that handles rule application, pursuing Formal Consistency. Speakers are led to seek Formal Consistency (FC) or grammatical regularity in systems, described for child language in Hooper (1979) and Slobin (1985a/c), for language-processing models by Bates & MacWhinney (1982) and Garner (1974), and for diachrony in terms of "the allomorphy reducing trend" by Kiparsky (1982), Vennemann (1972a). Strategies based on FC either complete partial paradigms or collapse rules that produce dissimilar results in superficially identical contexts. These regularizing tendencies may operate on either major or relatively minor inflectional paradigms.

Consistency in Final Weak Syllables

This principle accounts for many of the deviations in *Final Weak Syllables,* where phonetically identical segments behave differently in the paradigm, with those derived from gutturals or pharyngeals attracting low vowels. Speakers, especially the linguistically naive, tend to alleviate opacity by extending the unmarked form to the whole paradigm. There are two main Final Weak Syllable domains where FC is used mainly by linguistically immature or unsophisticated speakers: (i) regularizing penultimately-stressed structures, and (ii) failing to attach final *a*.

FC in the Segolates

Segolate penultimately stressed forms typically contain a double *e* (e.g. *yéled* 'boy', *mirpéset* 'balcony', *bodéket* '(she) checks') which lowers to *a* in the environment of a guttural e.g. *sáar* 'storm', root *s- y -r; mikláxat* 'shower', root *q-l-H;* and *gováhat* '(she) gets taller', root *g-b-h*. Since the basic *e* occurs in the unmarked forms, linguistically naive speakers extend its occurrence across the board, e.g. the Nonstandard response *niftéxet* given by a quarter to a third of the young and uneducated groups for *niftáxat* 'opens,Fm', root *p-t-H* (cf. *niSpéxet* 'spills,Fm', root *S-p-k*). This response is absent in the older, more sophisticated groups. My spontaneous data contain many such forms motivated by FC: *ani roce la-káxat it-i et ha-ekdax le-bet-mirkéxet* 'I want to-take with-me Acc the-gun to-the-drug-store' (cf. Normative *bet-mirkáxat*, root *r-q-H*) [3;2,DIA], said after the child had heard *bet-mirkáxat* said several times; or playing with Lego: *ha-délet Sel-o lo niftéxet. at ro'a, axSav ha-délet Sel-o niftexa, ve-axSav hi nisgéret* 'Its door (does) not *open*. You see, now its door (*has*) *opened*, and now it *is-closing* [2;9,DIA]. Note how the child alternates marked *niftáxat* 'opens', root *p-t-H*, which he regularized to *niftéxet*, with past-tense *niftexa*, and a regular present-tense feminine verb, *nisgéret*, showing what he already knows about the structure of present-tense penultimately stressed feminine verbs, and so why he regularized *niftáxat*. Parallel examples occur among young children and low-SES speakers, e.g. *kSe-ani soger et ha-délet hi niftéxet* 'when I close the door it opens,Fm', [2;11,DIA]; and also [12;6,SAM]; *ma at moréxet? ma at moréxet kol hazman?* 'What (are) you,Fm smearing,FM, what (are) you,Fm smearing,Fm all the time?' [3;4,DIA], (cf. Normative *moráxat*, root *m-r-H*); *im ma at mitgaléxet?* 'with-what (are) you,Fm shaving,Fm'? (cf. Normative *mitgaláxat*, root *g-l-H*), again failing to lower the *e* to *a*; and *ha-mexonat-kvisa Selax lo mucléxet* 'your washing-machine is not good,Fm' (cf. Normative *mucláxat*, root *ṣ-l-H*) [38,OBS]. I also found residual regularizing by mature educated adults: *aval ha-korelácya ha-zot lo muxéxet* 'but this correlation is not proved', (cf. *muxáxat* root *y-k-H*) [electronics engineer, 32, SAM]; and *zxuxit mefuyéxet* 'dark glass' (Normative *mefuyáxat*, root *p-y-H*) (said over the radio by an astronomer on how to use glass in an eclipse) [adult,OBS]. And fifty years ago Dolzhansky (1937) noted that children regularize verbs with *H* according to the *x* (kaf) paradigm, e.g. *soléxet* instead of *soláxat* 'forgives,Fm', root *s-l-H*, *Soléxet* for *Soláxat* 'sends,Fm', root *S-l-H*; and *Soxéxet* regularized from *Soxáxat* 'forgets,Fm', root *S-k-H* (1937:45).

FC in Epenthetic-a Structures

A second common regularization is failing to insert an epenthetic *a* before final low guttural or pharyngeal: compare regular *lomed* 'studies', root *l-m-d*, with *govéa* 'gets taller', root *g-b-h*, *lokéax* 'takes', root *l-q-H*, and *yodéa* 'knows', root *y-d-* ʕ . This salient *a* is missing especially in the speech of very young children, e.g. the test item *kadax/kodéax* 'drilled/drills', root *q-d-H*, regularized to *kodex* by a few very young children and some low-SES adults. Spontaneous examples include *hu lo cixcex* 'he (did) not polish', (cf. Normative *cixcax*, root *ṣ-H-ṣ-H*), [3;6,DIA]; *lama ata kodex?* 'why (are) you drill(ing)?', (cf. Normative *kodéax*, root *q-d-H*) [2;9,DIA]; *at yodáat le-napex balon?* '(Do) you,Fm know (how) to-blow-up (a) balloon'? (cf. adult *le-napéax*, root *n-p-H*) [3;9,DIA]; *ha-léxem ha-ze lo marux* 'this bread (is) not spread', (cf. Normative *marúax*, root *m-r-H*) [7;4,OBS]. Similarly *patux* for *patúax*, '(is) open', root *p-t-H* [2;4,DIA], and *potex* for *potéax* 'opens' from the same root [3;0,DIA]. All these involve the merger of *H*- and *k*-derived *x*, and the tendency to regularize towards the unmarked *k*-derived *x* (For other aspects of this process, see Donag-Kinrot 1978). Children also fail to attach *a* before segments other than *H*, e.g. *ani lo yode* 'I (do)n't know', (Normative *yodéa*, root *y-d-ʕ*) [2;0,DIA]; and *ani cove* 'I('m) painting', for *covéa*, root *ṣ-b-ʕ* [5;9,DIA]. Both the experimental and the spontaneous data as well as Bar-Adon's 1959 findings indicate that FC(a) is confined mainly to very young ages. Note, however, that Non-standard *niftéxet* occurred more on the test than Nonstandard *kodex*, since the internal vowels in *niftáxat/niftéxet* are less salient than the more external attachment of *a* in *kodéax*. The ends of words usually carry important information (Slobin 1973).

Consistency in Double-*a* Stems

FC also constitutes one explanation for the double *a* in *-y* final stems in early child language, e.g. childish *kanáta* 'you bought' for *kaníta*, root *q-n-y*. These roots share an open syllable past-tense 3rd person form of *Paʼal* with *ʔ*-final roots, e.g. *maca* 'found', root *m-ṣ-ʔ*, and *raca* 'wanted', root *r-ṣ-y;* but they differ when inflected for person: *macá-ti* 'I found', *rací-ti* 'I wanted'. The present forms of these two stems are also identical open syllable forms (*moce* 'finds', *roce* 'wants'), and so the young child extends the dominant pattern to yield, say, *racá-ti* instead of *racíti*, (see similar reports in Avineri 1946 and Bar-Adon 1959). Construal of the *a-a* stem as more basic is aided by the frequency of the general *Paʼal* pattern, and by the fact that *a* is the commonest vowel in Modern Hebrew (Bolozky 1991), as well as the least marked morphologically (Ravid 1990). Further evidence is provided by other examples of uncalled for usage of *a* in other verb patterns, e.g. in *Piʼel: kabáti et ha-gaz* '(I) turned-off Acc the-gas (stove)', for *kibíti*, root *k-b-y* [2;4,SAM]; *nikat* '(you,Fm) cleaned', for *nikit*, root *n-q-y* [3;7,OBS]. The final-*ʔ* stem, not common in *Piʼel*, would take the form of *CiCe-* here, e.g. *mile* 'filled', so the use of *a* in the above verbs does not stem from analogy to any *álef*-final form. The childish double *a* may occur even in verb patterns that have no *a*, e.g. *havat* '(you,Fm) brought', for *hevet*, root *b-w-ʔ*, in *Hifʼil*, and *hitxabánu* '(we) hid', for Normative *hitxabénu*, root *H-b-ʔ* [2;8,SAM]. Even a non-weak stem took the *a-a* pattern, e.g. *xabast et zeʔ* '(did you,Fm)wash it?', for *kibast*, root *k-b-s* 'wash' [2;3,SAM]. Though Formal Simplicity is sufficient to explain overexten-sion of the *a-a* pattern in *Paʼal*, it cannot explain its use in other patterns. Thus regularizing with the *a-a* pattern is an example of young children seeking maximal regularity in structures, using an existent pattern as their starting-off point and overusing it across the board to achieve Formal Consistency.

Reconstructing Missing Root Radicals

A third example of FC is the tendency to complete defective roots in cases where one radical or more do not surface. Contrary to Schwarzwald's (1981) claims that speakers may perceive some roots as bi-literal, I found that children and uneducated speakers tended to "complete" defective roots to three radicals. The test item *soxe* 'swims' was introduced to find whether subjects would give *soxétet* for *soxa* 'swims,Fm', compensating for the final weak segment of the root, as reported by Bar-Adon (1959:328) and Berman (1981a) for very young children (cf. *sogéret* 'closes,Fm', root *s-g-r*), and following the two spontaneous data examples of *soxétet* as the feminine suffix for *soxa* 'swims,Fm' [3;4,6;7,OBS]. A few such examples occurred among the 8s(!) and only there. But I did find other examples of root-completion in the very young and in the low-SES groups, e.g. *soxévet*, lexicalized as 'drags,Fm'. Immature speakers evidently try to complete a defective root by adding a segment from the Weak Final Syllable category—e.g. *?, t,* or the vowel *a.* Here are a number of examples of speakers completing defective roots: *osat* 'makes,does,Fm', for *osa,* root *y -s-y* [3;0,SAM]; *haytu* 'were', for *hayu,* root *h-y-y* [4;1,SAM]; *Satetu* 'drank,Pl' for *Satu,* root *S-t-y* [8;6,SAM]; *li-róa* 'to-shoot', for *li-rot,* root *y-r-y* [7;2,OBS]; and *koréet* 'reads,Fm', for *koret,* root *q-r-?* [5;1,OBS]. Root-completion occurs when *?, y* and *y* surface as Ø, which results in bi-consonantal roots. This follows a general tendency in Modern Hebrew to upgrade the unity of the root as a distinct entity by completing the defective root (see the tendency for new words to employ full roots in Ravid 1978, 1990, Schwarzwald 1980a).

Consistency in Choosing *y*-Final Stem Vowels

FC underlies the choice of *e* over *a* in *y* final stems, especially in the *Pi'el* verb-pattern, as a very distinctive marker of Nonstandard usage, e.g. *xike* 'waited', for Normative *xika* root *H-k-y;* and together with Formal Simplicity they explain forms such as *nikéti* '(I) cleaned', for *nikíti,* root *n-q-y.* In a sense, *y*-final and *?*-final stems form a separate minor paradigm in *Pi'el,* and the strategy of choosing one vowel *e* in all forms shows regularization within a subsystem (Table 44). Nonstandard *nise* is the result of FC working to reduce apparently unmotivated allomorphy by collapsing two partial paradigms (*y*- and *?*-final) into one, very similar to the regular conjugation (cf. *sider* 'arranged') and to *?*-final roots (cf. *kine* 'envied'). Moreover, *e* is the final dominant vowel throughout the *y*-final paradigm (cf. *menase* 'is trying', *yenase* 'will try'), so that in fact the past form (e.g. *nisa* 'tried') is the only exception to the otherwise dominant *e*-final stem.

Nisé-ti is the further work of FS attaching an inflectional suffix to the stem with no stem modification. Such analogical changes between these two sets of roots have been noted for Biblical and Mishnaic Hebrew

Table 44. Declension of past-tense regular and irregular verbs in
Pi'el

Root-type	Root	Gloss	3rd person singular	1st person singular
regular	*s-d-r*	arrange	*sider*	*sidárti*
?-final	*q-n-?*	envy	*kine*	*kinet*
y-final	*n-s-y*	try	*nisa*	*nisíti*
y-final Nonstandard	*n-s-y*	try	*nise*	*niséti*

(Schwarzwald 1980c), while Bar-Adon (1959) reports such forms as prevalent in child language alongside with *a*-structures.

Only children and low-SES subjects employed this strategy on the test. The Nonstandard responses *nikéti* '(I) cleaned' and *xike* 'waited' were prevalent in all young high-SES and low-SES groups, virtually absent in the older high-SES. Such forms also strongly characterize childish and/or Nonstandard usage in the spontaneous data-base, e.g. *xikénu* '(we) waited', and *nisénu le-hadlik* '(we) tried to light', for Normative *xikínu*, root *H-k-y*, and *nisínu*, root *n-s-y* respectively [3;3,SAM]; *gilet* '(you,Fm) found-out', for Normative *gilit*, root *g-l-y* [4;8,SAM]; *Sinet* 'you,Fm changed,Tr', for *Sinit*, root *S-n-y* [50,OBS]; *rime* 'cheated', for *rima*, root *r-m-y* [6;2,SAM]; and *xiséti* '(I) covered', for *kisíti*, root *k-s-y* [5;4,SAM].

Paradigm Leveling in Future Tense Verbs

A final example of allomorphy-reduction by FC is the use of the 3rd person *yV-* prefix on 1st person future tense verbs. The Normative future first-person singular prefix differs from the others in most verb patterns in taking a lower vowel, reflecting the historical initial glottal stop *?*, typically deleted in General Israeli Hebrew. Speakers, however, regularize the paradigm and eliminate the marked *álef* by adopting the 3rd person prefix *yV-*, e.g. *ani ye-daber* 'I 3rd-will-talk' and *ani ya-gid* 'I 3rd-will-say' for *ani a-daber, ani a-gid*, with the 1st person prefix. This is an example of a morphologized phonetically-based rule, since it may have started as assimilation from the final *i* of *ani* 'I', but the spontaneous examples indicate that *yV-* forms occur in environments where assimilation is not possible, e.g. ani *axSav yira (ire)* 'I now will-shoot', *ani lo yice (ece)* 'I won't-go-out' [5;9,DIA]; *ani gam iten (eten)* 'I also will-give' [3;7,DIA]; *ani yaale (eele) al kise ve-yasim (asim) et ze* 'I will-climb on (a) chair and-will-put Acc it' [3;3,DIA]; *ani lo yiStok (eStok) lexa* 'I not will-be-quiet to-you' [50,SAM]. In these, some other element separates *ani* 'I' and the verb.

This is a non-salient language-change environment of the kind noted by Naro (1978), and this regularization conforms to Manczak's (1980) laws of analogy, since it spreads from the basic, unmarked 3rd person singular to other future-tense forms. Here allomorphy is leveled off among closely related forms, all members of the same paradigm in the same tense distinguished only by markers of person, number and gender, shown to be "non-autonomous" in a large number of languages (Bolozky 1980, Bybee 1985). This is the prevalent form in children's and low-SES recorded data usage: only speakers who are very self-conscious about their usage, e.g. Hebrew language teachers, or lecturers, enunciate the glottal stop clearly. Most others choose a middle path between regularization and precise marking of ʔ by either retaining the first person singular vowel or using the 3rd person vowel without preceding it by a consonant. The situation is summed up in Table 45.

The test results reflect this situation in flux: The test sentences included the free pronoun *ani* 'I' separated from the future-tense verb by *maxar* 'tomorrow', so as to eliminate any possibility of assimilation (see Appendix A). Only the educated adults score Normative ceiling on the two items reflecting this sub-category, *kotev* 'writes' and *lamdu* 'studied,Pl'. Bar-Adon (1959) claims that the juvenile 1st person future form *yV-* is especially typical of grade-schoolers, which is compatible with my findings. (Bar Adon suggests that *yV-* regularization may stem from the fact that most input to the child is in 3rd person, but I have found no evidence for this.) Before school age, children do not make wide use of future-tense forms, while over 12, less adherence to FC, together with literacy and principled knowledge of language structure reduce the use of this juvenile regularization strategy.

Two further areas affected by Formal Consistency are (i) the choice between *e/a* in vowel-alternating structures in *Hifʔil* e.g. *merim/mapil* 'lifts/drops', where the high degree of opacity leaves speakers with no clues; and (ii) the choice between pronominal suffixes, especially between the suffixes *-ax/-ex* in 2nd person feminine singular. Here, again, there are no semantic cues, and the only Operating Principle to rely on is Formal Consistency, adopting one or the other of these two suffixes. These issues are discussed in the final chapters.

In sum, the nature of the particular subsystem involved determines the type of Operating Principle to be employed by the child and the unsophis-

Table 45. Regularizing person marking on future-tense verbs

Root *y-z-b* 'leave', *Paʔal* verb-pattern 'I won't leave' Root *p-t-H* 'open', *Paʔal* verb-pattern 'I won't open'		
Full Regularization Children & Low-SES	Semi-Regularization Educated Adults in Colloquial Usage	Normative Form Selfconscious Adults
ani lo yaazov	*ani lo aazov*	*ani lo ʔeezov*
ani lo yiftax	*ani lo iftax/eftax*	*ani lo ʔeftax*
3rd person prefix	No prefixed consonant	1st person prefix
3rd person vowel	3rd or 1st person vowel	1st person vowel

ticated adult. In the case at hand here, the problem is basically structural, hence the solutions aim at minimizing seemingly random allomorphy.

5.4. SEMANTIC TRANSPARENCY

The principle that leads speakers to seek a one-to-one correspondence between meaning and form is well-known in the psycholinguistic literature (Bates & MacWhinney 1982, Clark 1981, 1982, Hooper 1979, Karmiloff-Smith 1979, Slobin 1973, 1977, 1985a), in the study of pidgins and creoles (e.g. Naro 1978) and in diachronic studies (Kiparsky 1982, Lightfoot 1979, 1981, Vennemann 1972b). When a basic form in a paradigm becomes fixed as the only carrier of a meaning-complex, the child resists assigning that same meaning-complex to other forms, and attempts to reduce the relationship between meaning and form so that a given structure should carry a certain meaning uniquely. Such a structure is transparent, and children follow strategies that enhance transparency. This study provides several examples of opacity-reducing strategies which may lead to deviations from the norms of the Hebrew Language Establishment. For example, the explanation some adult subjects thought of as to why they said *cdaf* for *cédef* 'seashell' ("*cdaf* is what you find on the beach, while *cédef* is the stuff jewelry is made from") relies crucially on Semantic Transparency (ST): one meaning (count or mass noun) for one form. Similar cases indeed occur in Hebrew: Hebrew scholars insist on analyzing two opposite meanings in the Mishnaic dyad *alul asuy* 'may', a negative and a positive one respectively, despite contradictory usage by Hebrew revivers (Avinery 1964:450). ST also underlies the well-known tendency of children to use the *-im* masculine plural endings for all non-feminine nouns, e.g. *vilonim* 'curtains,Fm', for Adult *vilonot* (cf. unmarked *vilon*)[69] [2;6,SAM], or *levavim* 'hearts' for Normative *levavot* (cf. unmarked *lev*) [6;2,SAM]. The feminine plural *-ot* is then applied only to nouns morphophonologically marked in the singular for feminine gender, e.g. *beycot* 'eggs' for *beycim*, from feminine singular *beyca* [3;3,OBS]; or *nemalot* 'ants' for *nemalim*, from feminine singular *nemala* [8;4,OBS]). This is why children attached the masculine ending *-im* instead of the required feminine suffix *-ot* to *iparon* 'pencil' on the test. The gradual disappearance of childish *ábaim* 'daddies' from singular *ába* is also due to Semantic Transparency: As speakers grow more sensitive to levels of usage with maturation, they distinguish both the plural forms of *av/avot* 'father/s' and *ába/ábaim* 'daddy/s' and abandon Formal Simplicity for the sake of clearer marking of separate semantic values.

Test structures that exemplify the push to Semantic Transparency include the phonematicization of the stop/spirant *bkp* alternants; redundant present-tense marking with *m-* and past-tense marking with *hi-;* regularization of *CaCeC* and *CaCoC* forms in *Pa'al*, Lexical Exceptions; and difficulties with Case-Marked Pronouns. The Predisposition for ST is associ-

ated with the principle of Semantic Coherence, which facilitates the acquisition of members of semantically and morphologically well-defined
classes.

Spirantization and Semantic Transparency

We have seen above the inherent opacity in *Stop/Spirant Alternation*. A
basic strategy employed by speakers faced with it is to adopt a single *bkp*
alternant that appears in a basic form, e.g. *tafar/li-tfor* 'sewed/to-sew', for
Normative *li-tpor*, root *t-p-r*. The motivation for this strategy results from
the function of the Semitic root in Modern Hebrew. The Semitic root has
been shown to have two distinct functions in Modern Hebrew (Ravid
1978, 1990), relating to Aronoff's (1976) distinction between old and
new words: In old words, it serves as a redundancy rule, linking words
sharing the same basic meaning and consonantal structure, none more
basic than the others, e.g. the root *b-d-d* 'alone' in Table 46.

In new words the function of the root is less abstract. New words are
constructed from existing words, with the consonantal root carrying over
the precise meaning and structure of the base word, relating these two
words alone. For example, the word *hanfaSa* 'animation' violates normativistic demands in manifesting a surface *n*, which should delete in root-
initial position in a cluster, and a spirant *f* instead of a stop *p* following a
non-vowel. These two are necessary since otherwise *hanfaSa* would no
longer be related to *néfeS* 'spirit, soul', from which it directly derives (cf.
theoretical **hapaSa*, like *hapala* 'abortion', root *n-p-l*). In new words, then,
the root is an active go-between linking two separate lexical entries. For all
speakers, the root in derivational morphology is an entity which uniquely
represents the contents of the base word. Any failure to reflect sequence of
consonants from the base word, such as using a different stop/spirant
alternant, violates Semantic Transparency. Accordingly, speakers of all
backgrounds tend to phonematicize root *bkp* across lexical entries, especially in new-word formation or when having problems in retrieval, as in
the test situation, leading to distinctions between roots such as *hiStabec*
'found one's proper place' from *miSbécet* 'square', root *S-b-s*, vs. colloquial
hiStavec 'had a stroke', from *Savac* 'stroke', root *S-v-c* (Fischler 1975).

Table 46. Words sharing the root *b-d-d* 'alone'

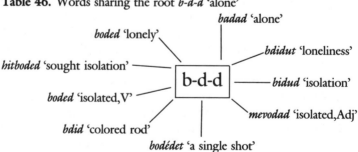

Semantic Transparency and Tense-Form Splitting

Overmarking the Present-Tense Form

Tense offers a different example of the role of ST in language acquisition—redundant marking of present and past tense forms. Past tense verbs almost always differ from present-tense verbs structurally. In most cases, the present-tense verb takes a *mV*- prefix, e.g. *Pi'el me-vater* 'gives up', root *y-t-r; Hif'il ma-dlik* 'lights', root *d-l-q;* and *Hitpa'el mit-palel* 'prays', root *p-l-l*. past-tense verbs either have a different internal vocalic pattern (e.g. *Pa'al lamad/lomed* 'studied/studies'; *Pi'el limed/melamed* 'taught/teaches'), or start with *hi-* (*Hif'il hixtiv/maxtiv* 'dictated/dictates'). There are two places in the verb system where past and present-tense forms coalesce: In *Nif'al* e.g. *nirdam* 'fell/falls asleep' and in glide-medial roots in *Pa'al*, e.g. *kam* 'got up/gets up'. Many examples are found in the spontaneous data of marking present-tense with *mV*- to maximize ST, e.g. *mizahéret*, for *nizhéret* 'is being careful' and *miSa'énet* 'leans,Fm' for *niS'énet* [2;10,SAM]; *miSa'er* 'stays' for *niS'ar* [4;2,SAM]; *mariv* 'fights' for *rav* [4;6,SAM]; *axSav ani masim et hakubiya* 'now I('m) putting the block', for *sam* [2;9,DIA]; *hu mipaca* 'he (is) getting-hurt' for *nifca* [3;9 DIA]; and note how clearly the child differentiates between past and present forms in the following: *ani mikanes le-ze, nixnásti le-ze* 'I('m) entering into-it, I (have) entered into-it', for adult present *nixnas* [2;6,DIA]. These data were collected from young children usually under 3;6, never above 4;6, and even the youngest subjects of the test hardly ever produced these forms.

The way children treat this area is one of the most fascinating examples of young children's inexorable search for ST. They cannot tolerate a single form representing two meaning units (past and present tense), so they "correct" this situation by adding a prefixed *mV*- to these structures (see also Bar Adon 1959, Berman 1983, Kaplan 1983, Rosén 1966). The prefix *mV*- is a salient marker of present tense in three out of five non-passive verb-patterns (e.g. *mesaper, maskim, mitvakéax* 'tells, agrees, argues' in *Pi'el, Hif'il* and *Hitpa'el* respectively. In addition, it occurs in both Passive participial verb-forms, e.g. *meluxlax* 'dirty' and *mulbaS* 'dressed'; and it occurs in seven productive noun patterns, e.g. *mitbax* 'kitchen' and *maSpex* 'funnel' (Clark & Berman 1984, Ravid 1978, 1990).

The forms that children assign to their marked present-tense verbs are not accidental either. In the three non-passive *binyanim,* the future-tense and the present-tense forms are identical, except for the prefix, thus: *mesaxek/yesaxek* 'plays/will play, *Pi'el'; makSiv/yakSiv* 'listens/will listen, *Hif'il'*; and *mitlabeS/yitlabeS* 'dresses/will dress, *Hitpa'el'*. the childish present form of *Nif'al* (for instance, *miSa'en* 'leans', for adult *niS'an*) mirrors *Nif'al* future-tense form, *Ci-CaCeC,* in precisely the same way, e.g *yigamer* 'will-end'. The child thus achieves Formal Consistency across *binyan* forms in addition to ST, and creates a structurally coherent paradigm in *Nif'al* as shown in Table 47.

Each of the tense-forms is clearly and overtly marked, while the discrepancy between the past/present and future forms is "corrected," thus following FC within the *binyan* form as well. What children do with *Pa'al* is even more interesting: not only do they attach a prefixed *mV-* to present-tense medial-glide verbs; they also give this new creation the form of present-tense verbs in the *Hif'il* verb-pattern, as in the following example, root *r-y-b* 'fight': Table 48.

The choice of of the *Hif'il* present-tense form is not accidental either: it so happens that the future forms of *y*-medial verbs in *Pa'al* is homophonous with *Hif'il* glide-medial verbs. Compare, for example, *Sar/yaSir* 'sang,sings/will-sing', (root *S-y-r*, *Pa'al*) with *herim/merim[70]/yarim* 'lifted/lifts/will-lift' (root *r-w-m*, *Hif'il*). Children create the *maCiC* form in *Pa'al* glide-medial verbs under two conditions: (i) if the verb contains a medial *-y-*, (otherwise its future form is *ya-CuC* rather than *ya-CiC*, e.g. *yakum* 'will-rise', root *q-w-m*), and (ii) if this form does not occur (to the child's knowledge) in *Hif'il*. If it does, then the *maCiC* form in *Pa'al* is preempted by homonymy (Clark & Clark 1979). Given the small number of *y*-medial roots, and the existence of corresponding *Hif'il* forms, it is not surprising that the redundant *ma-* present-tense forms in *Pa'al* are so few, limited to *maSir* for *Sar* 'sings', *masim* for *sam[71]* 'puts' and *mariv* for *rav* 'fights'. It is thus clear that even this juvenile strategy of differentiating between past and present forms requires a considerable amount of knowledge about the Hebrew verb system on the part of the young child.

Overmarking the Past-Tense Form

The mirror-image method of differentiating between identical past and present forms is overmarking the past tense verb with a prefixed *hi-*. This is a rarer juvenile strategy, since only two out of five non-passive verb patterns take *hi-* (*Hif'il*, e.g. *hipil* 'dropped,Trs', and *Hitpa'el*, as in *hitraxec* 'washed'), while *Pi'el* and *Pa'al* mark past tense through vowel alternation: *diber/medaber* 'talked/talks, *Pi'el*', and *katav/kotev* 'wrote/writes, *Pa'al*'. Ex-

Table 47. Children's construal of the *Nif'al* paradigm

Past tense: *ni-CCaC* e.g. *nixnas* 'entered'
Present tense: *mi-CaCeC* e.g. *mikanes* 'enters' (adult *nixnas*)
Future tense: *yi-CaCeC* e.g. *yikanes* 'will-enter'
Infinitive: *le-hiCaCeC* e.g. *le-hikanes* 'to-enter'

Table 48. Children's construal of glide-medial roots in *Pa'al*

Past tense: *CaC* e.g. *rav* 'fought'
Present tense: *ma-CiC[72]* e.g. *mariv* 'fights' (Adult *rav*)
Future tense: *ya-CiC* e.g. *yariv* 'will-fight'

amples of over-marking past tense are completely absent in this experimental study and the following are spontaneous data examples: *kódem baxíti ve-axárkax hiragáti* 'first (I) cried, and-then (I) calmed down', for *nirgáti* [2;11,DIA]; and *hu hisim et ha-ragláyim* 'he put Acc the-legs' for *sam* [2;3,OBS]. Both may also be examples of paradigm completion by FC: Childish *hiraga* follows the future and infinitive colloquial *Nif'al* forms *tiraga/le-hiraga* 'will/to-calm down', while childish *Pa'al hisim* completes the *Hif'il*-like *yasim* 'will-put' and childish *masim* 'is-putting' (see above). Note, moreover, that a common form in the speech of low-SES school-children reported by teachers is *herik/marik* for Standard *yarak/yorek* 'spat/ spits', root *y-r-q*, explained by their need to mark both the past and present forms clearly and coherently, overriding the *Pa'al* paradigm which only uses vowel alternation for this purpose.

Yaxol *'Can'*

A similar strategy is employed by speakers across age and SES boundaries to maximize ST by keeping past and present forms apart in the modal verb *yaxol* 'is able' whose Normative masculine singular form is identical in past and present tense (Rosén 1956, 1966). In forms other than the unmarked masculine singular *yaxol*, the suffixed markers of person, gender and number (e.g. *-ti* for 1st person singular, or *-a* for 3rd person feminine singular) serve as past-tense markers, e.g. *yaxól-nu* 'we could'. But in this study I made it difficult for subjects to rely upon these markers, since the cue question was *ha-yom ha-yéled yaxol la-vo, ve-gam etmol hu* . . . 'today the-boy can come, and-also yesterday he . . .', directing the subject towards the masculine singular form. Interestingly, the number of Normative responses at young ages is larger than among older subjects, as the young children often used the task-induced strategy of repetition, responding with the cue item itself. But subjects eight years old and over used two main strategies, both resulting in maximized ST: Either they produced *yaxal* as the past-tense form of *yaxol*, or else they used the copula *haya* 'was' in *haya yaxol/yaxol haya*. The first strategy follows the general *Pa'al* paradigm (compare regular *lomed/lamad* 'studies/studied'). This is the favored form among highschoolers both on the test (80%) and in the spontaneous speech samples.[73] The change in the vowel pattern of the verb both adheres to ST and also regularizes this exceptional verb by FC. The second strategy, favored by literate adults, exploits the fact that *yaxol* is perceived as an adjective, shifting the burden of tense-marking to the copula *haya* 'was'.

Semantic Transparency in Pa'al: CoCel *and* CaCel *Present-Tense Forms*

A classical case of following ST is that of *yaSna* 'slept,Fm', rendered *yoSénet* for Normative *yeSena* 'sleeps,Fm' by many subjects. The major present-tense verb pattern in *Pa'al* is *CoCeC,* e.g. *loveS* 'wears', *gonev* 'steals'. A minor pattern now denotes mainly adjectival state verbs, whose past and future forms are usually not in use, e.g. *ayef* 'tired', *Samen* 'fat', *ra'ev* 'hungry'. Since *yaSen* 'sleeps' is not perceived as a state verb, it is assigned the regular *CoCeC* rather than the adjectival *CaCeC* form. Thus a one-to-one correspondence is achieved between *CoCeC*/activity verbs and *CaCeC*/state verbs. In fact *yoSénet* is the prevalent form in the young and uneducated population, the standard form up to age eight, quite common later on as well. The only group that reached Normative ceiling were the adults. Examples of this usage in the Spontaneous Data are usually from children, e.g. *hi yoSénet* 'she('s) sleeping' [2;4,DIA], and *ha-tinóket yoSénet, oxélet vegodélet* 'the-baby girl sleeps, eats and grows', for Normative *yeSena* and *gdela* [8;4,OBS]. In one recorded conversation among children aged three to four in a kindergarten, *yoSen/yoSénet/yoSnim* occurred all 13 times the root *y-S-n* was used in *Pa'al* out of 254 utterances. This suggests that a new standard is forming in the younger generation.

Overmarking Semantic Content

The Predisposition to maximize transparency may lead to overmarking of semantic features (see OP:Maximal Substance, Slobin 1985a), as in the above-mentioned example of replacing *Pa'al yarak* 'spat' with *Hif'il hirik* in *ha-mora, hu hirik al-ay* 'the-teacher, he spat on-me' [7;2,OBS]. Various studies report the redundant overt marking of semantic features, e.g. Karmiloff-Smith (1979), Kuczaj (1978). Erbaugh (1986) reports overmarking of classifiers with both number and noun by young children in Mandarin. In Hebrew, young children have been reported to overmark plurality on nouns already marked for the plural (Levy 1980). My spontaneous data show that children overmark either nouns which typically occur in the plural e.g. *zeytímim* for *zeytim* 'olives', singular *záyit* [3;3,SAM]; or mass nouns, e.g. *gézerim* 'carrots' (cf. *gzarim* for a few carrots, singular mass *gézer* for a larger amount) and *késefim* for non-count *késef* 'money' [3;7, SAM] (but cf. *ksafim* 'moneys').

Semantic Coherence

ST operates not only on lexical items and morphemes, but also on whole classes, and knowledge of word-class membership is essential to a child faced with different forms of allomorphy (Slobin 1985c). A pattern which is recognized as both semantically and structurally coherent, and so carrying unique semantic value in a non-ambiguous structure, is easily learnt and retained, and overcomes other Mapping Preferences. One example is the *CaCoC* adjective pattern, mainly denoting color-terms, e.g. *yarok* 'green', *CCuC-* in inflection, e.g. *yeruka* 'green,Fm' (Rubinstein 1981). The test had two such items—*cahov* 'yellow' and *adom* 'red', both with high Normative scores from early on. In *cahov* 'yellow', over two thirds of the youngest group adhered to correct *cehubim* 'yellow/s', with only 5% leaving the base spirant *v* in *cehuvim*. Very few of the eight-year-olds failed to change the spirant to a stop, in contrast to a quarter in *rax/raka* 'soft/Fm'. The acquisition of *adom* 'red' is even more precocious, since there were fewer features to change: Close to 80% of the three-year-olds correctly gave *adumim* as the plural form, with Normative scores reaching ceiling by age five. Why didn't FS operate in these two cases to yield *cahovim* and *adomim* respectively, as it did in *rax/raxa* 'soft/Fm' instead of *raka*, or *iparon/iparonim* 'pencil/s' for *efronot*? The stem change from *cahov* to *cehubim* involves both vowel-deletion and vowel change as well as spirant/stop alternation, so the answer cannot lie in the number of operations performed on the stem. It lies in the semantic coherence of this pattern, which relates a well-defined structural operation, $CaCoC \longrightarrow CCuC\text{-}$,[74] to a distinct semantic category of color-terms. Compare other noun and adjective *CaCoC* patterns, e.g. *karov/krovim* 'close/Pl', *lakóax/lakoxot* 'customer/s' to find that the typical *o/u* change takes place only in the color pattern CaCoC.[75] This special association of form and meaning overcomes FS. This is not true, however, of items in the same pattern that are not names of colors, as shown by mistakes such as *ani roce li-lboS gufiya aroxa* 'I want to put-on (a) long,Fm undershirt,Fm', for Normative *aruka* (cf. masculine *arox*), [3;10,DIA]. Note, moreover, that rarer, formal adjectives in the same pattern which do not denote color terms now follow the general *CaCoC/CCoC-im* rather than the original *CaCoC/CCuC-im* form in adult language, e.g. *xason/xasonim* 'sturdy/Pl' (Normative *xasunim*) and *avot/avota* 'dense (foliage)/Fm' (Normative *avuta*);[76] while colloquial *ratuv/retuva* 'wet/Fm' (Normative *ratov/retuba*) has been reanalyzed as passive-completive *ratuv*, following the three-edged active *Pa'al*/verbal passive *Nif'al*/adjectival passive *Pa'ul* system as in *laxac/nilxac/laxuc* 'pressed/was pressed/under stress', thus achieving both ST and FC. This evidence points to the *CaCoC/CCuC- im* alternation being restricted now to color terms. Other studies both on child language and on diachrony also point to the fact that coherently marked patterns resist structure-preserving strategies and consequently change (Berman 1981b, Ravid & Shlesinger 1987a), and see Erbaugh's (1986) review of studies showing early marking of items in coherent classes such as flowers, animals, books etc.

5.5. SALIENCY

Saliency is the property of a structure that is perceptually distinct from its environment, constituting a principle that has been shown to govern operations in both child language and diachronic studies. In diachrony, non-salient structures are more subject to change: " . . . syntactic change tends to sneak through a language, manifesting itself most frequently under those circumstances in which it is least salient or noticeable" (Naro & Lemle 1976:237). In child language, salient structures are more easily learned and retained (Peters 1985): "A child will begin to mark a semantic notion earlier if its morphological realization is more salient perceptually" (Slobin 1973:202). Some of the puzzling facts about my findings are resolved by this principle. This is particularly true of the *CéCeC* pattern (e.g. *bérez* 'tap', *mélex* 'king').

Saliency in the Segolates

CéCeC (and its related form, *CóCeC*) differs significantly from other noun patterns because of its stress and vowel pattern. It is the only masculine pattern with penultimate stress, and its vowel pattern—a double *e*—is also distinctive. Historically, *CéCeC* was the commonest noun-pattern in Biblical Hebrew, accounting for nearly one-quarter of the masculine radical nouns in the Bible, and one of the three richest noun patterns in Mishnaic Hebrew. Today, items in this pattern constitute some 10% of all radical nouns[77] in Hebrew (Avineri 1976). The old words in *CéCeC* lack coherent semantic value, often denoting basic objects, e.g. *éven* 'stone', *léxem* 'bread', *géSem* 'rain', *béten* 'stomach', *béged* 'garment' and *kémax* 'flour'. In Modern Hebrew, however, many denote abstract nouns and even action nominals, e.g. *récef* 'sequence', *récax* 'murder', and *dáxaf* 'urge' (Ravid 1978). In their bound singular form, *CéCeC* nouns revert to their historical *CVCC-* form, still evidenced in Arabic, e.g. *sifr-i* 'my book', (cf. free *séfer*) or *malk-o* 'his-king', (cf. *mélex* 'king') (Gesenius 1910). But they generally retain their *CéCeC* form in the construct state, e.g. *béged yam* 'swimsuit'. In the plural, *CéCeC* nouns take the universal Junction form *CCaC-im/ot*, e.g. *géver/gvarim* 'man/men'. The picture is of a salient, highly frequent singular form, covering a range of semantic fields (Ravid 1990). As such it is easily perceptible and general in applicability (Bybee 1985).

It comes as no surprise that *CéCeC* has a special status in Hebrew morphology, with an independent identity that asserts itself early on. For example, compare the early acquisition *éven/avanim* 'stone/s', with the late acquisition *iparon/efronot* 'pencil/s'; or the easy access youngsters had to *écem* 'bone' from plural *acamot*, compared to the inaccessibility of *dim'a* 'tear' from plural *dma'ot* (cf. juvenile backformed *dma'a*). Note that by FS it should have been harder for children to derive *écem* 'bone' from its plural form *acamot* because the initial *y* attracts the low vowel *a*. Moreover, feminine *dma'ot* 'tears' is easily linked with feminine singular *dim'a*, whereas *écem*, though feminine, belongs to a generally masculine noun pattern. Finally, note the early and successful acquisition of masculine *kéves* 'sheep' (cf. feminine *kivsa*). The backformed *kivs* was restricted to very few small children. Accessing *kéves* should have been more difficult than *par* 'bull' from *para* 'cow' and *tarnegol* 'rooster' from *tarnególet* 'hen', which involve simple backformation.[78] The surprising success of the youngsters indicates a gradual realization of the link between the *CéCeC* and *CiCCa*, which is also indicated in the shared plural form *CCaC-im/ot* (Avineri

1976). Thus a number of separate items that undergo different grammatical processes indicate that *CéCeC* is an especially salient noun pattern, resisting strategies deriving from Operating Principles which may lead to change. Independent evidence of the special status of *CéCeC* is given in Ravid (1990) concerning the vowel pattern assigned to acronyms: The two unmarked patterns are either *CaCaC* or *CéCeC*. The *CéCeC* pattern and *a* thus seem to share the status of basic default vocalizing devices.

Saliency in Present-Tense Marking

One reason why young children choose *mV-* to mark present tense is its saliency: It attaches to stems at initial position, a perceptually salient point, and it fulfills a number of grammatical functions. In much the same way French-speaking children overuse the salient particle *de* (Karmiloff-Smith 1979).

Salient *t*

We have already seen that *t* is often used to complete irregular roots, e.g. the Nonstandard *soxétet* for *soxa* 'swims', root *s-H-y*. Other examples from the Spontaneous Data include *nisxat ba-máyim* '(we) will-swim in-the-water', for *nisxe*, root *s-H-y* [2;10,DIA]; *kantu ota ba-xanut* 'They (impersonal) bought it in the store' for Normative *kanu* (cf. *kanta* '(she) bought') [3;6,DIA]; *maStu oto me-ha-máyim* 'They drew him out of the water', for Normative *maSu* (cf. *maSta* '(she) drew out') [3;9,DIA], and in Bar-Adon (1959), Dolzhansky (1937:45); *hi Sivta li* 'she swore to-me', with wrong *Pi'el* for *Nif'al niSbe'a*, root *S-b- y* , [10,OBS]; *haytu* 'were', for *hayu*, root *h-y-y* (cf. *hayta* '(she) was' [4;1,SAM]; *Satetu* '(they) drank' for *Satu*, root *S-t-y* (cf. *Sateta* '(she) drank') [8;6,SAM]; *le-hitxabot* 'to-hide', for Normative *le-hitxabe*, root *H-b-?* (cf. *le-hitkasot* 'to-cover oneself', root *k-s-y*) [10,OBS]; and *le-malot* 'to-fill' for *le-male*, root *m-l-?* (cf. *le-nakot* 'to-clean', root *n-q-y*) [40,OBS]. Thus *t* is used by speakers both to complete irregular roots in childhood and to mark postulated grammatical functions in adulthood.

Salient *t* stands for two morphological entities, historical *T* and *t*, represented by the letters *Tet* and *taf* respectively. The basic difference between the two is one of morphological function: while *Tet* occurs only as a root radical, *taf* may function as a root radical in addition to having multiple grammatical functions; it has a number of morphophonological functions as in (i) replacing final *a* when an affix is added to the word, e.g. *miSxa/miSxat-eynáyim* 'ointment/eye-ointment', *Salva/Salvato* 'calm/his-calm'; and (ii) occurring in various morphophonological phenomena related to *y*-final roots, e.g. in the infinitival form (*likn-ot* 'to-buy', root *q-n-y*), in 3rd person feminine singular past-tense verbs (*cip-ta* '(she) expected', root *s-p-y*; cf. *limda* '(she) taught'), as well as in the *y*-related suffixes *-it* (see below) and *-ut*, e.g. *eyx-ut* 'quality', *xan-ut* 'store' (root *H-n-y*). It is an inflectional and derivational marker serving as (i) a pronominal tense affix, e.g. *Samar-t* '(You,Fm) guarded' and *te-tayli* '(you,Fm) will-stroll'; occurring in (ii) the feminine plural morpheme *-ot* as in *smixa/smix-ot* 'blanket/s'; indicating (iii) feminine gender on adjectives ending in *-i*, e.g. *tiv'i/tiv'it* 'natural/Fm'; and in (iv) the salient *Hit-pa'el* prefix, being the segment that metathesizes with stridents; (v) serving as a derivational affix in a number of noun patterns, e.g. *tiCCóCet*, (*tikSóret* 'communication'), *taCCuCa*, (*taxbura* 'transportation'), *taCCiC* (*taxtiv* 'dictation'); specifically, (vi) it occurs in the salient feminine suffix *-et* at the end of penultimately stressed noun patterns, e.g. *CiCócet*, (*sipóret* 'fiction'), *CaCéCet* (*kalévet* 'rabies'), *CCóCet* (*któret* 'incense'). In all of these cases, *t* occurs in a perceptually salient location (at the beginning or the end of a word); it is the only obstruent in the morpheme, and so it carries most of the semantic content, particularly in a consonant-oriented language like Hebrew; and it carries distinct grammatical functions. In short, it is a very salient segment.

As a result, surface *t* manifests two types of behavior: A stable root radical which always occurs on the surface, mostly deriving from *T* (e.g. roots *T-p-l* 'treat' and *m-l-T* 'escape'); and an unstable *t*, always *taf*), an affix obstruent that may or may not occur on the surface, fulfilling root as well as various grammatical functions. Compare, for example, the roots *s-H-T* 'squeeze' and *s-H-y* 'swim' in Table 49.

The behavior of *t* seems erratic: It occurs across the board in the conjugation of *s-H-T*, whereas in *s-H-y* it appears in the past tense feminine and the infinitival forms. The behavior of *t* in this example certainly defies ST and so should lead to considerable deviation. But errors of the *soxétet* type (for *soxa* 'swims,Fm') are rare, and confined to the very young, whereas errors confusing *t* in *y*-final and other, especially ?-final stems, are quite common, especially among the low-SES speakers. For example, the Nonstandard deviation *kinta* for Normative *kin'a* 'envied,Fm', root *q-n-?*, was found in all test groups save one. "Completing" the root radicals by the addition of *t* is a Transient usage, while attaching *t* on a ?-final stem is Nonstandard, gradually spreading in the higher-SES population.

The difference is due to awareness of notions like Root and Affix involving the different kinds of salient *t*: Children realize the different radical/affixal functions of *t* quite early on, due to its extreme saliency, and they avoid deviations which otherwise would have been the natural outcome of mapping preferences. Forms such as *soxétet* disappear very quickly as the

Table 49. *s-H-T* 'squeeze' and *s-H-y* 'swim' in *Pa'al*

| | Past Tense | | Present Tense | | |
	Masculine	Feminine	Masculine	Feminine	Infinitive
s-H-T	*sáxat*	*saxata*	*soxet*	*soxétet*	*li-sxot*
s-H-y	*saxa*	*saxata*	*soxe*	*soxa*	*li-sx-ot*

speaker understands that if *t* is the third root radical, its behavior should be consistent, and it should always occur on the surface. Once this separation of the two functions of *t* is under way, juvenile mistakes like *soxétet* disappear. But in forms like *kinta* 'envied' instead of *kin'a* the speaker realizes the grammatical function of *-t*, yet has trouble separating the two types of roots due to their extreme resemblance. The saliency of *t* as an affixal obstruent leads to its adoption even in ?-final stems, hence *kinta*.

Salient-*it*

Another salient segment is the feminine suffix *-it*. This occurs (i) as an inflectional feminine suffix, e.g. *sapar/saparit* 'barber/Fm', and in a variety of derivational roles: (ii) as a diminutive suffix, e.g. *kos-it* 'a little glass'; (iii) as a suffix on *y*-final stems in the *taCCit* pattern, e.g. *tafnit* 'turning', root *p-n-y;* (iv) as a word formation suffix on *y*-final stems, e.g *maal-it* 'elevator' from *maale* 'ascent', root *y-l-y;* and (v) as a general word-formation suffix, e.g. *matl-it* 'rag'. Relating the singular and plural *-it* forms is problematic, as the singular suffix *-it* is replaced by plural *-iyot,* e.g. *tavnit/tavniyot* 'pattern/s', *mapit/mapiyot* 'napkin/s'. FS guides young children to retain the base form with *-it* (as Levy 1980 shows they do with final *-ut*), e.g. *kapit/ kapitim* 'teaspoon/s', for *kapiyot,* and *xanut/xanutim* 'store/s', for xanuyot [2;0,SAM]. However, children abandon FS once they realize the unstable nature of the final *-t*. Now FC takes over, to consistently relate *y*-final *-it* to *-iyot* in the plural, e.g. *taglit/tagliyot* 'discovery/s', root *g-l-y*.

However, a *taCCiC* structure may actually contain a stable *T*[79] radical, e.g. the test item *taklit* 'record', root *q-l-T* (cf. *talmid* 'pupil', root *l-m-d*), and so the final segment *-it* would obviously be retained in the plural: *taklit-im* like *talmid-im*. The child must discover this systematic behavior of *t*-radicals and *t*-affixals or end up with *takliyot* for *taklitim* 'records'. Interestingly, *takliyot* proved to be the product of a transient strategy, occurring in less than 20% of the responses of the youngest group, and only in 5% of those of the kindergarteners. The spontaneous data yield two examples, both fairly uncommon words, between ages three and four: *maciyot* 'lighters' for *macitim,* root *y-ṣ-t* [3;3,SAM], and *Sarviyot* 'batons' for *Sarvitim,* with final *Tet* [3;7,SAM]. It seems that the saliency of *-it* leads children to focus on it early on and pay attention to its unique behavior patterns, hence the small amount of deviations. Frequency and familiarity help too: *taklit* 'record' occurs frequently in child language,[80] which helps classify the *-it* as non-changing, aided by ST maintaining the internal integrity of the root *q-l-T* 'absorb' (used in well-known words such as *hiklit* 'recorded', *haklata* 'recording', *maklet* 'receiver', and *kalétet* 'cassette') by keeping its components on the surface. Knowledge of root and pattern, salient features, familiarity and frequency of an item all come together to resist the leveling effects of FC.

Salient -it *and Backformation*

Another common operation in *-it* structures is Backformation following Formal Simplicity. The plural suffix *-iyot* derives both from *-it* and from *-iya*, e.g. *sifriya/sifriyot* 'library/s'. Children typically backform by the shortest path to formally simple *-iya* by removing the feminine plural ending *-ot*, e.g. *kariya* for *karit* 'pillow' from plural *kariyot* [3;3,SAM]; *álef ze ha-otiya ha-riŠona* 'alef is the first letter', for *ot* (cf. plural *otiyot*) [4;7,DIA]. As we saw above, such backformation is more likely to take place when the *-iyot* plural form is the less marked one, as in the case of *otiyot* 'letters'. The developmental path for *-it* nouns is summed up in Table 50.

   In conclusion, three main salient units have been identified for Modern Hebrew: The noun pattern *CéCeC* and the segments *m-* and *t*. Their saliency restricts the application of other Operating Principles, usually resulting in earlier and more successful acquisition.

Seeking Analytic Structures

A highly salient way to mark information is to encode it in a separate word, distinct from its environment as an analytic free form (Clark 1981, 1982, Clark & Berman 1984, Hooper 1979, Slobin 1985a). This strategy is especially significant in Hebrew, a language rich in bound, often fused, morphemes. My findings indicate that speakers employ such a strategy either at a very young age or when faced with a particularly opaque structure. Test-induced tactical measures sometimes took the form of such analytic structures, with the child assigning each semantic value a separate word, e.g. *exad cdafim* 'one shells', instead of *cdaf/cédef* '(a) shell'; or the tendency of the 3s and 5s to use the free forms of the preposition and pronoun, e.g. *mimxa* 'from-you' was rendered as *mi-ata* (Berman 1981c). Similar findings are reported by Rom & Dgani (1985) for children aged 2;6–3;0. They used the correct preposition and pronoun required by the test, but in analytic free form, and difficulties in the acquisition of case-marked pronouns seemed to be morphophonemic rather than semantic.

Table 50. Strategies and errors in the development of *-it*

Step 1: *Formal Simplicity* 2–3 years *-it* ⟶ *itim*	*kapit* ⟶ *kapitim 'teaspoons' (adult *kapiyot*) *taklit* ⟶ *taklitim* 'records'
Step 2: *Formal Consistency* 3–5 years *-it* ⟶ *iyot*	*kapit* ⟶ *kapiyot* *taklit* ⟶ *takliyot (adult *taklitim*)
Step 3: *Formal Simplicity* 3–5 years *-iyot* ⟶ *iya* backformation	*gufiyot* ⟶ *gufiya* 'undershirt' *mapiyot* ⟶ *mapiya 'napkin' (adult *mapit*)
Step 4: *Saliency of -it* 3 years and over	Separating *-it* structures into classes, following knowledge of root, pattern, affix; familiarity and frequency

Older subjects used the same strategy when faced with the more difficult preposition *bli* 'without', whose bound form is *biladey-*. This may be because *bli* (like *kmo* 'like') may take a clausal complement, e.g. *bli Se-at taazri li* 'without (that) you,Fm will-help me', so that its occurrence as a free form more than other prepositions (due to its adverbial history, Even-Shoshan 1979), may reinforce separating *bli* and the pronoun. Rabinowitch (1985) found such analytic preposition and pronoun sequences only in young bilingual children, and she attributes this to an earlier stage in acquisition which monolinguals have already undergone.

Analytic marking of grammatical notions is found not only in child grammars, but also in phylogenetically developing pidgins and creoles and has been suggested as a transitional stage in the formation of human Language (Bickerton 1990, Givón 1979a, Sankoff & Brown 1976). Thus in both Papiamentu and Palenquero (Spanish and/or Portuguese-based creoles spoken in Curaçao and Palenque de San Basilio, Colombia, respectively), plurality is expressed by the article or the numeral, and not by affixation (Lenz 1926, Montes 1962); and there are many cases of lack of plural markers, and obligatory deletion of plural with numerals, in Caviteno and Zamboagueno (Spanish creoles of the Philippines), and in Portuguese creoles such as Macaista (Whinnon 1956). Finally, in nonstandard uneducated speech in Puerto Rico, there is a tendency to use *mucha gracias* instead of *muchas gracias* 'many thanks', and *son mi sufrimiento* instead of *son mis sufrimientos* 'these/those are my sufferings' (Alvarez Nazario 1961).[81] This strategy is common in young children, e.g. *od exad agilim* 'another one earrings' [2;0 DIA]; (Mother) asking child *biSvil mi ha-mita* 'for whom (is) the-bed'?: (Child) *ani* 'I' instead of *biSvili* 'for-me', impossible in Hebrew (Berman 1985) [1;11,DIA]; *kmo hu* 'like him' in free form, for *kamóhu*, *néged hu* 'against him', for bound *negdo*, and *bli at* 'without you,Fm', for *biladáyix* [3;11,SAM]; Similarly, *bli anáxnu* for *biladéynu* 'without-us' [4;8,SAM]; *ze dome le-ani* 'it resembles (to)-me' for *ze dome li* [4;10,SAM]; a child, about a new doll: *kama Se-hi yafa! kmo ani!* 'how pretty she is! Like I' for *kamóni* 'like-me' [5;1,DIA]; *ani yaxol la-sim et ze meaxorey-ani* 'I can (to-)put it behind-I', for adult *meaxoray* 'behind-me' [3;4,DIA]; and finally, a child demanding attention, with self-repair: *tagídi lo Se-yiten exad gam biSvil ani, gam exad biSvili* 'tell him to give one also for I, also one for-me [4;1,DIA]. Employing the analytic form strategy keeps the preposition and the pronoun easily recognizable, with their semantic content separate and distinct.

Sometimes, the child overmarks the case-marked pronoun, employing one bound and one free preposition e.g. *el oto* 'to-Acc-he', instead of *elav* 'to-him' [4;0,SAM]; *hirámti le-lo* '(I)-picked to-to-him' for *oto* 'Acc-him' [2;5,DIA]; and *axotex Selo* 'sister-your of-him' instead of *axoto* 'his sister?' [3;3, OBS]. Overmarking in addition to giving free form of the preposition ensures that the message comes through, as in French children overmarking possessive structures (Karmiloff-Smith 1979).

5.6. TYPOLOGICAL CONSISTENCY: ATTENDING TO CANONICAL SENTENCE STRUCTURE

The last predisposition to be discussed here is children's sensitivity to the basic word order that their language manifests. Children have been shown to have no difficulty in processing different word-orders in their native tongues, such as English SVO and Turkish SOV, as long as these represent the minimal-presupposition, most neutral sentence word order in main clauses (Givón 1976, Lightfoot 1991). Children are attuned to the most unmarked word-order in their language, and adopt it as a canonical sentence schema (Slobin & Bever 1982). Hebrew speakers are thus attuned to the unmarked word orders of Israeli Hebrew, with certain morphosyntactic consequences.

Let us for the moment recall the results of the test: they showed subject-verb agreement to be one of the least stable categories—3rd from bottom overall and in the low-SES population alone, and second from bottom in the high-SES population. Despite the experimental situation, conducive to self-monitoring, most groups had low Normative scores on most agreement items. However, this was found only in V(O)S structures, e.g. *ko'ev lo ha-béten* 'hurts,Masc to-him the-stomach,Fm' (for *ko'évet,*Fm), but not **ha-béten ko'ev lo*. Since the Agreement items were presentative predicates (*yeS* '(there) is', *le-haS'ir* 'to-leave', *li-x'ov* 'to-hurt', *le-hiSaver* 'to-break,Int'), and deictic *ze* 'this',[82] they were natural candidates for foregrounding the predicate to sentence-initial position (Giora 1982) and consequent violation of concord. I would now like to provide an on-line processing account for this violation which is embedded in a typological framework.

The linguistic literature usually posits a single unmarked order in the main clause for every language (e.g. Croft 1990, Greenberg 1966b). However, Modern Hebrew has two unmarked orders: (i) "Dynamic" and "equative" SVC (C = Complement), and (ii) "Stative/presentative" P-first (P = Predicate).

SVC Order

One major word order occurs in two types of sentences: (i) Dynamic sentences with a verbal predicate, e.g. *dan ganav et ha-tik* 'Dan stole AM the bag', which display Accusative characteristics (Comrie 1981, Greenberg 1966a); and (ii) identity/attribute "equative" sentences with a copula relating the subject and the predicate, e.g. *dan haya/hu/yihye ba-mesiba* 'Dan was/is/will-be at-the-party'. The canonical, unmarked order of elements in such sentences is SVO (or SVC—Subject-Verb-Complement, to cover a wider range of possibilities), with the subject noun governing agreement within the NP and in the VP (Berman 1980a, Givón 1977, Ravid 1977). According to Givón (1976) this is the final destination of all word-order diachronic drift. The canonical, basic type here is transitive, with a human subject-agent and a definite direct object obligatorily marked with Accusative *et* (Berman 1978a). Basic SVC structure is flexibly altered by preposing various elements, since as an inflectional language Hebrew can afford movement of NPs and other material in the sentence, the basic relationships expressed explicitly by agreement and object-marking. The position of preposed elements depends on relative topicality when introducing new material, as well as on stylistic register (Ben-Horin 1976, Giora 1982).

P-First Order

An equally prevalent unmarked order is P-first, with a typically nonverbal predicate denoting mainly existence (*yeS eS ba-xéder* 'there (is) fire in-the-room'), possession (*yeS lánu para* 'is to-us (= we have) a cow'), modality and experience (*mutar lexa la-léxet* '(It's) allowed for-you to-go' = 'You're allowed to go'; *na'im le-daber itxa* '(It's) pleasant to talk to you'; *kar po* '(it's) cold here') (Berman 1979, 1980a, Borer & Grodzinsky 1986, Rosén 1966, E. Ziv 1976, Y. Ziv 1982). For these structures, the P-initial order is not a variation of some other basic ordering, but rather the only order that is neither ungrammatical nor topicalized. For instance, the following are two topicalized versions of *mutar le-xa la-léxet* '(It's) allowed to-you to-go': (i) *le-xa mutar la-léxet* '*You* may leave, but somebody else may not'; and (ii) *la-léxet mutar le-xa* 'You may *leave,* but not do anything else'. In general, P-initial structures contrast sharply with verbal sentences both semantically, as they denote state rather than dynamic action or equative attribute, and syntactically, since (i) the predicate is the first element in the sentence and (ii) they tend not to manifest agreement with the subject. The latter case results naturally from the fact that the canonical P-first predicate *yeS* (indicating both possession and existence as well as modality) and modality/experience adjectives are "neuter" segments (Rosén 1966), and moreover P-initials lack "true" agreement-endowing subjects (Berman 1980a, E. Ziv 1976). Note that the present-tense copula that may optionally occur in verbless sentences, carrying agreement, is barred in an unmarked P-initial sentence. Compare, for example, *dan hu tayas* 'Dan is (a) pilot' with **mutar hu le-xa la-léxet* '(It) is allowed to-you to-go' or any other version with the copula.

Consequences

The fact that the input contains these two different unmarked word orders leads Hebrew speaking children to become attuned to both of them, with a number of consequences for language acquisition and language processing.

Following the salient action/identity Accusative SVC order, for a child acquiring Hebrew a "subject" is an argument that basically appears to the left of the verb, with a predicating nucleus that agrees with it in (at least) number and gender.[83] It may have full surface realization, e.g. *hi katva lexa* 'she wrote to-you' or occur in a pronoun-incorporating (PRO-drop) construction which obligatorily manifests agreement, e.g. *katávti lexa* '(I) wrote,1st to-you'. Any NP which neutrally occurs to the right of the verb is interpreted as complement, not subject, and the speaker finds no counter-indication in unmarked state P-initial constructions with neuter predicates.

Located between transitive SVC and state P-initial structures is a group of intransitive ("unaccusative") verbs that denote physical entrance onto the scene or change of state in "presentative" constructions (Givón 1976) whose prototypical member is the *yeS* possessive/existential. They serve as the "link unto the scene or . . . 'relevance to context'" via time or location adverbials (Givón 1976:155), e.g. *nixnas li koc la-yad* 'entered to-me (a) thorn (in)to-(my)-hand', or *ba ha-dóar* 'arrived the-mail'. In direct on-line discourse the P-initial presentative order prevails, e.g. *-ma kara?* 'What (has) happened?' *-nafal alay ha-séfer Selxa* 'dropped on-me your book', while in reported "distanced" speech the natural order would be SVC, e.g. *ha-séfer Selxa nafal alay* 'your book dropped on-me'. The SVC order always entails subject-verb agreement, but in the P-initial structure, lack of agreement between subject and verb is tolerated, except in carefully monitored speech or writing (Berman 1980a, Gil 1982), e.g. *nigmar ha-máyim* 'ended,Sg the-water,Pl'.

Consider the following spontaneous speech examples: *ko'ev li ha-yad* 'hurts,Masc. to-me the-hand,Fm = my hand hurts', for feminine *ko'évet* [3;7,DIA]; *mikódem nitfas li ha-safa* 'earlier caught,Masc to-me the-lip,Fm = my lip caught (on something) earlier', for feminine *nitpesa* [2;11,DIA]; *kvar haya lánu kubiyot ka'éle* 'already was to-us (= we already had) blocks like these', for *hayu* 'were' [3;8,DIA]; *etmol kSe haya kar axár-kax haya SémeS xazaka* 'yesterday, when (it) was cold, later (there) was,Masc sun,Fm strong,Fm. [3;7,DIA]; *nafal li ha-sfarim* 'fell,Sg to-me the-books = my books dropped', for plural *naflu* [2;8,DIA]; *kSe higía ha-dimdumim az natnu li mástik* 'when came,Sg the-twilight,Pl, then (they) gave me chewing-gum', for plural *higíu* [3;10,DIA]; *ole al ha-acic harbe nemalim* 'is-climbing on the-vase many ants,Fm', for plural feminine *olot*, and *barax lo kol ha-kadurim* 'escaped,Sg to-him all the-bullets', for plural *barxu* [5;6,SAM]; *Se-lo yihye lánu carot* 'that not will-be,Sg to-us (= we shouldn't have) troubles', for plural *yihyu* [DIA,5;2]; *nofel ha-sikot* 'falls,Sg the-pins', for plural feminine *noflot* [3;6,DIA]. And examples from adults: *axSav nigmar ha-hafsaka* 'now (has) ended,Masc the-break,Fm', for feminine *nigmera* [17;6,SAM]; *ba-cava avar aléynu xavayot meragSot* 'in-the-army passed,Sg on-us (= we had) experiences exciting', for plural *avru* [21,SAM]; *kvar Savúa Se-ko'ev li ha-Sináyim* '(it's been) already (a) week that hurts,Masc to-me the-teeth,Fm = I've had a toothache for a week', for plural feminine *koavot* [35,OBS]; *nigmar li ha-ugot ba-mekarer* 'is-finished to-me the-cakes in-the-refrigerator', for plural *nigmeru* [30,OBS]; *al tiSali—haya lánu teuna* '(do)n't ask, was to-us (we had an) accident,Fm', for feminine *hayta* [30,SAM].

Such lack of P-initial concord is also found in Biblical Hebrew, which had unmarked VS order (Bendavid 1967, Gesenius 1910, Givón 1977, Meyuchas 1928). For example יהי מארות ברקיע השמים 'will-be,Sg lights in the heavens = Let there be lights in the heavens' (Genesis 1,14). All of these are instances of P-initial structures with presentative verbs indicating existence, possession or change in physical state, almost always accompanied by adverbs of time and place (Givón 1976).

The test findings, together with the spontaneous data, demonstrate that Hebrew speakers are definitely sensitive to rules of agreement (Berman 1985, Levy 1980, Rosén 1966, 1977, Schwarzwald 1979); and deviation from concord in P-initial constructions is not in fact a "violation," since speakers perceive the NP to the right of the verb as an object rather than a subject, and consequently do not assign the verb its grammatical features.

This claim is supported by another process manifested in the free speech data: insertion of the Accusative Marker *et* before the right-hand NP in P-initial constructions, e.g. *katuv et ze ba-séfer* 'is-written Acc this in-the-book = it's written in the book' [6;5,DIA]; *haya et ze ba-iton* 'was Acc this in-the-paper = it was in the paper' [18,SAM]; *niS'ar et kol ha-mikrim ha'ax-erim* 'remains Acc all the-other,Pl cases' [33,OBS]. Such sentences often lack Subject-Verb Concord too (see the last example from the spontaneous data-base). Nor is this a new phenomenon either: Even-Shoshan (1977) lists at least 60 such cases out of the 9,228 occurrences of *et* in the Bible, that is, close to 1%, e.g. וטוב את אשר עדן לא היה 'and-good . . . Acc that to-them not was = And the one who did not reach them is better' (Ecclesiastes 4,3). Given the vast productivity of *et* in transitive constructions, this number is not insignificant. Note that, in the prototypical existential and possessive *yeS* subclass of P-initial structures (Borer & Grodzinsky 1986, Ziv 1982), *et* insertion is obligatory if the NP is definite, e.g. *yeS lo et kol ha-tasritim Se-bikaSt* 'be to-him (= he has) Acc all the-scripts that you-asked (for)'. This requirement is clear with pronouns, which occur in their free form only in the Nominative case. Compare *yeS li oto* 'be to-me (= I have) Acc-it' with ungrammatical **yeS li hu* 'be to-me (= I have) it'.

The three phenomena—P-initial structures, lack of subject-predicate agreement and *et* insertion—are closely interrelated. This has been noted by several researchers, from different perspectives. Some emphasize the pragmatics, tying P-initial and lack of agreement to presentation of new information, and stressing the special logical-communicative character of P-initial possessives (Givón 1976). Others, either within the GB framework (Borer & Grodzinsky 1986) or within a typological framework (Berman 1980a) maintain that these constructions are essentially subjectless. Another approach to *et* insertion in non-transitive sentences is phonological size (Gil 1982). The classical psychological explanation of non-concord in P-initials is of on-line processing (Meyuchas 1928): starting with the verb, the speaker has to go forward to check number and gender specifications on the NP, and then go back to the verb to mark it accordingly, which causes problems in processing.

My interpretation of these phenomena combines a psycholinguistic processing explanation with a typological approach: in *dynamic* and *identity* constructions, Hebrew shows the Accusative traits of subject-verb agreement (unlike ergative languages, where the verb may agree with the object) and direct object marking (ergative languages mark the agent NP). Children, sensitive to the specific typological features that characterize their language, learn very early to do the first (Levy 1980). Moreover, *et* is a salient marker in Hebrew, and the first "word" a child says in Hebrew is often *edze*, a combination of Accusative *et* and the deictic pronoun *ze*, in pointing to objects (Berman 1978b, Dromi 1987). Both operations depend on recognizing the syntactic function of the NP. Given this word order as well as the P-initial subjectless, verbless constructions in Hebrew (Berman 1980a), intransitive presentative constructions take either word order following pragmatic considerations: if the verb is placed in initial position, the sentence is construed as subject-less, and so the NP to the right is interpreted as a direct object. This entails (i) lack of Subject-Verb agreement, and (ii) marking the NP to the right with *et* if definite. If, for pragmatic reasons, the structure is SVC, there is no problem in identifying the subject, and marking it accordingly with subject-verb concord and no *et* insertion. Compare, for example: (i) *etmol be-Séva hitraxácti ba'ambátya. ha-máyim nigmeru li ve-niS'arti im sabon* 'Yesterday at-seven (I) was washing in-the-bathroom. The-water,Pl finished,Pl to-me and-(I)-was left (covered) with soap' and (ii) *ma kara? nigmar/nigmeru li ha-máyim!* 'What (has) happened? Finished,Sg/finished,Pl to-me the-water (= I've run out of water!)'. In (i), the context of the narrative past, information is given in a sequential series of events with no sudden focus on any new information, and the order is SVC. In (ii), the context is direct speech, with sudden focus on the fact that there's no more water, so that word order changes to P-initial. *ha-máyim* 'the-water' is no longer perceived as the subject, and so concord may be violated, and *et* inserted. Violation of subject-verb agreement is noticeable only when the NP to the right of the verb is in plural and/or feminine, but it could be that cases such as *haya séret yafe ba-televízya* 'was movie nice (= a good movie) on-television' also involve potential concord violation. Since a subject like *séret* is masculine singular, the verb takes the unmarked zero 3rd person singular, and no violation is observed. But the principle is the same.

5.7. SUMMARY

The last few chapters have discussed implications of the findings of the test and supporting evidence from everyday spoken usage. The results on a variety of morphological facts of Modern Hebrew show a complex interaction between factors of Structural Opacity, Operating Principles in language acquisition and in language processing, as well as typological properties of the target language. These in turn were shown to be directly influenced by the impact of chronological maturation and level of education respectively. The concluding chapters discuss synchronic variation in Modern Hebrew as reflected in the distribution of deviations in the population, and the roles of different age/SES sections of the speech community in promoting language change.

6

Linguistic Variation and Cost

These last two chapters aim to integrate the central factors motivating synchronic variation and eventually diachronic change: surface opacity interacting with propensities towards Consistency, Transparency and Saliency. These are checked by Maturation, by the conservative force of Literacy, and by the evaluation measure of Cost, to explain the disappearance, partial retention, and fossilization of the deviations described above. For Modern Hebrew, this means that old standards are giving way to new in a language that was artificially revived but which is nonetheless shaped by the same factors as underlie the evolution of all human languages.

Let me define first a number of factors which promote or hinder adherence to norms.

(i) *Deep vs. Shallow Grammar*: The ability to perceive deep-level relationships that underlie superficial disparities, and deep-level distinctions that underlie superficial similarities, characterizes a Deep Grammar. For example, classifying the final *-it* on *sakit* 'little bag' and *taklit* 'a record' as suffixal and stem-internal respectively; or relating *écem/acamot* 'bone/s' despite stem-change. A Shallow Grammar seeks guidance in the direction of regularity and transparency in Operating Principles more frequently than a Deep Grammar. Two factors contribute to creating a Deep Grammar: Maturation and Literacy.

(ii) *Maturation:* The natural process of cognitive growth, specifically referring here to the development of language knowledge and linguistic abilities in interaction with language input. Maturation triggers adherence to and abandonment of Operating Principles according to a predetermined order.

(iii) *Literacy:* The result of education in its broadest sense—both formal and informal. It is the ability to find one's way in both the written and the spoken language. The literate Hebrew speaker has access to all levels and periods of language usage (Berman 1987b), including the all-important orthography. The Hebrew alphabet contains letters representing lost phonological groups which supply motivation for surface alternation. A greater awareness of Hebrew orthography motivates Language Establishment norms and therefore promotes language conservatism and avoidance of change.

Below I propose the additional notion of Cost to explain the hierarchy of instability established earlier and to motivate the distinction between different kinds of deviations from classical linguistic norms: Strictly Juvenile, sociologically motivated or Nonstandard and Language Change, characterizing the most unstable categories. More general linguistic and psycholinguistic implications are then reviewed.

6.1. LINGUISTIC INSTABILITY: SOME ANSWERS

The hierarchy of instability, established above and reviewed in Table 51 below, reflects on-going processes of change in Hebrew, expressed as deviations from the Norm, where in some cases the Standard form is no longer the one assumed by normativists.

Most of the categories illustrate more than a single phenomenon, or the same phenomenon along various parameters. For example, Verb Tense covers redundant present and past tense markers as well as regularized 1st person future-tense. Different types of "deviations" and unstable phenomena thus cut across this category, which manifests both a Transient (redundant tense marking) and a Nonstandard phenomenon (1st person future marking). Nor are the types of deviations totally distinct, but rather they form a continuum with each type fading into the other (Berman 1987b). This is particularly true of the relationship between Nonstandard and Language Change forms, where the differences may be expressed as a matter of degree in the two sub-populations.

Why Does Language Change?

In such a fluid situation, we might understandably ask ourselves what is the nature of a linguistic deviation, or, *What is an error?* To find an adequate definition, we must first pose a number of questions about language change. At the fundamental level, we might ask why language changes in the first place. What causes it to undergo alteration? Given that Language

Table 51. Instability revisited

Category Content	Rank Ordering from least to most stable
Vowel Alternation	1
Lexical Exceptions	2
Subject-Verb Concord	3
Stop/Spirant Alternation	4
Case-Marked Pronouns	5
Backformation	6
Weak Final Syllable	7
Verb-Tense	8
Verb-Governed Prepositions	9
Pre-Suffixal Stem-Change	10

is "one of the countless adaptive mechanisms that have developed in the species in the course of evolution" (Bickerton 1990), the answer to this should be given in evolutionary terms: The natural state of Language as an evolutionary entity is to undergo change, in a manner analogous to the way living organisms undergo change: In the same way that existing gene pools always contain a number of variants, so does Language; and changes in the pool occur both spontaneously (mutations) and as a result of evolutionary pressure, which is a reflection of the forces that shape language.

Why Do Specific Language Domains Undergo Change?

This study is concerned with the results of a type of evolutionary pressure we termed Structural Opacity, which determines why certain linguistic structures are more prone to change than others. Language is always in a state of flux affected by two rival factors: Rule and Rote. For instance, adherence to Backformation by Formal Simplicity yields the backformed deviation *yabala* 'corn' from *yabalot* 'corns' [56,SAM]. The literate woman that produced this form was certainly aware of the rote-learned correct form *yabélet*. However, at that particular moment she failed to retrieve it, and instead, using the plural *yabalot* as a base form, produced a regularized rule-governed form. Such regularization stems from the tendency to be clear and semantically coherent, and so to favor clearly marked structures which obliterate opacity (Givón 1985). However, this tendency operates in concert with the Principle of Least Effort (Martinet 1955, Zipf 1949), in the attempt to condense as much information as possible into a unit of speech, as long as comprehensibility is retained and the speech unit remains processible in ongoing conversation. This helps achieve quick and easy communicability but also results in opacity (Halle 1962, Slobin 1977). Thus a certain degree of opacity is inherent in every linguistic system (Bates & MacWhinney 1982), since every natural language is in a state of flux, with several variations existing side by side. And morphological fusion of elements, reflecting their degree of semantic relatedness, is manifested in regular and irregular allomorphy, portmanteau morphs, and suppletion (Bybee 1985, Slobin 1977). In fact, Karmiloff-Smith (1986a) has shown that it takes children ten years to slowly shift from a unifunctional construal of grammatical markers, producing long, redundant but transparent utterances, to a plurifunctional adult system which enables them to express the same thoughts in economical form.

Phonological Erosion

In many cases, opacity is created at the phonological level, when systems "drift" (Aronoff 1976, Labov 1972c, Venemann 1975), leading to the gradual phonological erosion known as "sound change" (Aitchison 1974, Andersen 1974, Hocket 1965, Kiparsky 1982, Labov 1981, Martinet 1955, Wang 1969). Phonological erosion leads to a loss of the motivation for morphophonological alternation. When a structure is no longer processible in terms of its constituent parts, or when different structures collapse into a single surface form, communicability breaks down unless the Transparency Principle is applied to perform therapeutic reanalysis (Lightfoot 1979, 1991) and thus restructure the relevant morphological unit (Bybee 1985). This basic process may be accelerated by factors such as language contact, or by the impact of other subsystems where changes are underway, as well as by factors such as maturation, social stratification, and literacy (Kemp 1984, Labov 1982).

I have shown Modern Hebrew to be characterized by all of the above due to the special circumstances of its revival as a spoken language: In Hebrew phonological erosion has taken a radical, non-gradual form, since the language was revived as a spoken medium using a new phonological system only loosely related to that of Classical Hebrew (Klar 1951), with entire phonological classes being obliterated (Izre'el 1986, Rubinstein 1981, Tené 1969, Weiman 1950). Therefore Hebrew morphophonology is pervaded by opacity.

Other Questions Relating to Change

Given this, the next set of questions relates to the specific direction and spread of language change: Why are some sections of the population, especially children and low-SES adults, more apt to produce deviations than others? Why are certain changes "successful," that is, become established in the speech community, whereas others are blocked? Why are some changes restricted to certain segments of the speech community, especially less educated speakers and children, while others spread quickly throughout the whole population?

Young Children and Language Change

Deviations from the norm, such as in Modern Hebrew, reflect speakers' effort to "correct" subsystems that do not convey grammatical information according to the internal organizing principles that shape morphosyntactic space. Children are the least tolerant of irregularity because they are least able to perceive underlying relationships, have a "local" construction of grammatical systems, and are unaware of orthographic conventions (Bentur 1978, Ehri 1985, Karmiloff-Smith 1986a). They most frequently rearrange linguistic units in patterns more compatible with an ideal "blueprint" of language (which may indeed occur in other languages) in keeping with psycholinguistic principles of Consistency, Simplicity and Transparency. But these attempts to remedy inherent opacity are doomed to early disappearance, because they "cost" too much in terms such as: loss of saliency, a high degree of markedness, going against conventionality and rote-learned information, and the creation of opacity in other, major areas. In other words, young children's reanalyses fail to stick because they are too radical and "harmful." They seek a black-and-white linguistic reality that does not correspond to the adult system. Such "expensive" juvenile deviations go counter to important operating principles or typological propensities, and they exercise therapeutic influence on the subsystem involved while causing damage in other, related systems. I suggest that this is the way the evaluation measure of Cost determines whether a reanalysis should or should not survive as language change: by positing "profit" against "loss" in global systems in terms of transparency, saliency, consistency and communicability.

Literacy and Language Change

"Errors" that survive to adolescence and adulthood must have some beneficial effect upon the system and relatively low "cost." These corrective efforts made by older speakers result in reanalyzed structures that deviate from the educated norm without impinging on other systems, to yield a situation of synchronic variation. The more deviations per category or per item, the less stable it is. The more deviations per speaker, across a group of speakers, particularly at older ages and in more advanced SES groups, the more likely it is that such a deviation reflects more than synchronic variation, and constitutes ongoing change.

Children's errors are Transient, and uniquely juvenile, functioning in synchronic variation along the axis of age alone. For example, childish *takliyot* for *taklitim* 'records' from singular *taklit* (cf. *sakit/sakiyot* 'bag/bags') is almost totally absent by age 5. Nonstandard phenomena, by contrast, characterize both children and adults, although in the latter case, only the uneducated. However, "uneducated usage" is a very vague term, applying to more or less all (but certainly not only) low-SES speakers. Such deviations also apply to some extent to speakers defined as high-SES, especially adolescents, and hence vary synchronically along both the axes of time (age) and of social stratification (Labov 1969, 1972b). A typical example is *nikéti* for Standard *nikíti* '(I) cleaned', root *n-q-y* (compare *kinéti* '(I) envied', root *q-n-?*), used by three-quarters of the adolescent and adult low-SES population, compared with less than one-tenth of the high-SES.

Language-Change Phenomena

Language-change phenomena, pervasive in the sense that they characterize the entire population across the board, serve as a link between synchronic variability and diachronic change. They reach levels where they can no longer be regarded as deviations, but rather as representing a new Standard. The only way such pervasive forms can be seen as deviations is by accepting the norms set by the Hebrew Language Establishment; but this is no longer valid, since only language-specialists (i.e. members of that establishment) may claim to know what they are.

One criterion determining whether a domain is indeed undergoing language change is the fact that high-SES subjects are not able to falsify normativity in it, compared to their ability to do so in domains with Literacy phenomena. For instance, in the case of Nonstandard *yoSénet* for *yeSena* '(she) sleeps' (compare *yoSévet* '(she) sits'), the adult high-SES subjects produced the Normative form 100% of the time (even though they may not always do so in everyday usage) precisely because they were aware of the existence of a norm. Faced with the experimental situation, educated adults presented a carefully monitored, self-conscious linguistic image to the tester. But this did not happen in *Vowel Alternation,* for example: All Normative scores were low, because speakers *were not aware of making a "mistake."* In this category, the Normative form is no longer accessible either unconsciously or through formal monitoring. People simply have no norm to refer to in such cases, not even under the rigorous conditions of a test in Hebrew grammar, where students in many cases learn each *mVCiC* form by rote.

Table 52 represents the relationship between the three types of deviations, the variables of age and SES, and synchronic variation vs. diachronic change. Deviations along the continuum in Table 52 can be characterized from two perspectives, across and within populations: (1) *Across*

Table 52. Variation in Modern Hebrew

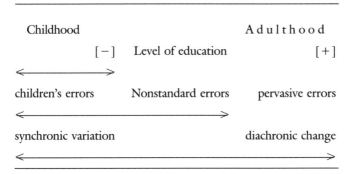

populations, errors can be further subdivided into three classes: (i) Those that are confined to children, and never occur in the speech of adults, e.g. *Satáti* for adult *Satíti* '(I) drank', root *S-t-y* (cf. *macáti*ʿ(I) found', root *m-c-?*); (ii) those typical of low-SES usage and occurring only negligibly in the speech of the high-SES population, e.g. *yilboS* for Normative *yilbaS* 'will-wear' (cf. *yixtov* 'will-write'); and (iii) those that occur in the population as a whole—e.g. lack of *Verb-Subject Concord*. (2) *Within* populations, those errors that occur across the board in child language, and those whose occurrence gradually diminishes with the rise in age and SES. The best example is the phonematicization of *bkp/vxf* alternants within inflectional paradigms: Children use this strategy almost exclusively for every paradigm that manifests *Stop/Spirant Alternation,* even extending it to the "parasites" that do not alternate, e.g. *ba-xufsa* for *ba-kufsa* (orthographic non-spirantizing *q* (Berman, personal communication)).

6.2. TRANSIENT DEVIATIONS

Transient phenomena do not affect the structure of adult language, since they are so short-lived (Hooper 1979). In fact, the spontaneous speech evidence suggests that during early acquisition these forms resist input counterevidence, relying almost exclusively on and adhering strictly to internal constructs resulting from built-in Operating Principles, due in part to lack of a more comprehensive understanding of formal systems underlying principled linguistic behavior (Karmiloff-Smith 1986a) and to unfamiliarity with conventional forms (Berman 1986a).

Maturation, which brings awareness of the final shape of endstate grammar plus a gradual detachment from innate Propensities, allows children to learn from external evidence and teaches which deviations are too costly to retain. Childish errors of this kind include the following: Analytic structures; redundant marking of present-tense; the double-a strategy; regularizing *-it* suffixes; completing defective roots; and confusing pronominal suffixes on prepositions.

Analytic to Synthetic

A very early strategy has children lexicalize information, e.g. *exad cdafim* 'one shells', *ába para* 'daddy cow', with the grammatical categories of number and gender kept analytic, so having distinct semantic information on separate lexical items. This also explains the rare occurrences of free preposition and pronoun combinations, e.g. *le-ani* 'to/for me' for *li* which, except for cases of prepositions that change shape radically (e.g. *biladáyix* 'without-you,Fm' from *bli* 'without'), both our test and spontaneous data show to disappear very early on. This is due to a clash with the fundamental typological character of Hebrew in the two grammatical systems of gender/number marking and Case-marked Pronouns, another manifestation of the propensity towards Typological Consistency noted above.

Although Modern Hebrew is more analytic than Biblical Hebrew, this is usually manifested as a preference for agglutinative to fusional devices, e.g. the external agent/instrument noun suffix *-an* rather than the affixal noun pattern *CaC(C)aC*[84] (Clark & Berman 1984), both, however, synthetic rather than periphrastic devices. In fact, Hebrew speakers have been shown to avoid compounding as a major analytic device for Hebrew word-formation (Berman 1987a). Inflectional morphology usually allows the speaker far less choice, since in most cases the bound form is obligatory (Matthews 1974). A marked exception is possessive marking on nouns, where the literary bound form *xulcat-i* 'shirt-mine' is replaced by colloquial periphrastic *ha-xulca Sel-i* 'the-shirt of-me'. But *Sel-i* itself has the same obligatorily bound character as other case-marked pronouns. So analysis of bound structures goes only as far as the language allows, and children realize this quite early on. Inflecting words for gender and number is an early grammatical operation in Hebrew (Levy 1980), obligatory across nouns, verbs, adjectives, demonstratives and numerals. Hence grammaticization of number/gender is a fundamental typological feature of Hebrew violated only by children in the pre-grammatical stage of acquisition (Borokovsky 1984).

In the case of Oblique Pronouns both prepositions and pronouns in Nominative case do occur in free analytic form, as in *ha-buba al ha-Sulxan; hi yafa* 'the-doll (is) on the table; she (is) pretty'. Cognitively there is no reason why children should not go on expressing case relationships on pronouns as in English (e.g. on me, to you, without him). It is rather the nature of the typological input to children's developing grammar that determines the early shape of this particular area of their grammar (Shatz 1982). In fact, what they may be doing in initially separating prepositions and pronouns is ontogenetically recapitulating an earlier phylogenetic stage of the language. Inflectional morphemes often derive from separate words which gradually reduce phonologically to clitics and then to bound morphemes (Bybee 1985, Givón 1979a, 1979b, Sankoff & Brown 1976). The reason they originally fused may be the high degree of relatedness of prepositions and pronouns, as shown by their close proximity in the sentence. English-speaking children put separate emphasis on auxiliaries that are usually contracted, e.g. *I will* instead of *I'll*, or *she has* instead of *she's* (Brown 1973). This corresponds to young Hebrew speakers separating preposition from pronoun. The difference is that Hebrew totally disallows separate preposition-pronoun sequences (except for demonstrative *ze*, e.g. *al ze* 'on this') whereas pronoun and auxiliary can be enunciated (and are typically written) separately in English. Children are well-prepared for either fusional and/or periphrastic expression of semantic content in a sentence (Slobin & Bever 1982). Hebrew adherence to bound forms of oblique pronouns provides further evidence for the impact of the input data on the child acquiring a native tongue.

Redundant Tense-Marking

A typical juvenile form yielded by adherence to Semantic Transparency is redundant marking of present-tense *Nif'al* and (glide-medial) *Pa'al* verb-patterns with the salient *mV-* prefix to differentiate homonymous past and present tense forms. Instead of the adult paradigm with a single form for past and present forms, the child has a nicely differentiated one with three different forms (e.g. *nilxam/milaxem/yilaxem* 'made war/makes war/will-make war', for adult present-tense *nilxam*) (Berman 1983).

My findings reveal childish forms with redundant *mV-* to disappear by age 3;6. This is generally in line with Bar-Adon (1959:340-355), although he claimed that *miCaCeC* forms occur in free variation until school age. Bar-Adon suggests that young children introduce the *miCaCeC* structure to distinguish past- and dynamic present-tense forms, so regularizing the present-tense system, but he fails to explain why children abandon this strategy so early, beyond mentioning the influence of their linguistic environment. Nor is it made clear why this influence failed to operate from the start, or why children soon pay attention to this, but not to other linguistic categories. I propose that children abandon this strategy so early, even though it presents a sound solution to a problem of opacity, because it is too "costly." In terms of gain and loss, redundant *mV-* is profitable because Transparency is enhanced within the inflectional paradigm, with two forms kept apart for two tense-meanings. But it entails an even greater loss: The resulting *miCaCeC* form is exactly similar to the childish rendition of the present-tense form of another verb-pattern, *Pi'el,* e.g. *misaxek* for adult *mesaxek* 'plays' (Berman 1983). These two *binyan* verb-patterns are totally unrelated, belonging to two different sub-systems (Berman 1975b, 1980b, Berman & Sagi 1981, Ravid 1990). Thus greater transparency in the inflectional paradigm gives rise to opacity across lexical systems. In terms of Cost, it is not worth retaining a strategy which keeps tenses distinct while merging two *binyan* forms, in line with diachronic research showing that more opacity is to be found within inflectional paradigms (Thomason 1976).

Other arguments include the following: First, the childish change produces a form which differs radically from the adult system. A change succeeds when it is minimal, or else the disparity between adult and childish system is too great to preserve communicability (Halle 1962, Kiparsky 1982). Here, not only is the internal vowel structure altered (*miCaCeC* for *niCCaC*), but so is the external prefix (*mi-* for *ni-*). And as demonstrated above, Hebrew tolerates changes in internal vowels but not in the far more salient external affixes. Second, maturation reduces the power of Transparency, allowing children eventually to accept fused, portmanteau morphs (Bybee 1985). It is the rule rather than the exception for Hebrew inflectional morphs to convey more than one notion. Third, the *Nif'al* present-tense form may persist precisely because it has the unique, clearly marked prefix *nV-,* making it distinct from other verbal forms in Hebrew (Naro &

Lemle 1976). Besides, as noted by Manczak (1980), present tense is among the forms that are more frequent in discourse and which remain unchanged diachronically. Finally, identity between past and present is reduced to a few forms with increasing use of forms inflected for other persons (e.g. *nirdema/nirdémet, Sáru/Sarim*). Thus, in the struggle between Rule and Rote, the conservative, more opaque rote-learned form wins out, despite the superficial temporary advantage in marking tenses separately.

Another redundant *mV-* present marker, that of glide-medial roots in *Pa'al* (e.g. *mariv* for adult *rav* 'fights', root *r-y-b*), takes a little longer to disappear, as retaining it causes less disturbance in the system. Recall that the future form of *y*-medial roots in *Pa'al* (e.g. *yariv* 'will-fight', cf. *rav* 'fights') is identical with the future-tense form of *Hif'il* (e.g. *yarim* 'will-raise', cf. *herim* 'raised'). Here, the syllable structure is not violated since both prefix and vowel structure are compatible with the *Hif'il* verb-pattern paradigm. Therefore children provide a second identical present-tense *Pa'al* form to *y*-medial roots, with redundant *mV-*. Besides, there is a productive relationship between *Pa'al*, a basic verb-pattern, and *Hif'il*, a (usually) derived pattern denoting either Causativity or Inchoativity (Berman 1975b), so it is less "costly" to retain the *mV-* in *Pa'al* than in *Nif'al*. Eventually, by school age, this strategy too is abandoned so that overall redundantly marking present-tense with the salient prefix *mV-* is a Transient phenomenon which merges lexically distinct systems.

Contemporary Hebrew manifests another process where homonymous past and present forms became distinct. The Normative conjugation of many stative *CaCeC* verbs had identical 3rd person singular past and present forms, e.g. *yaSen* 'slept/sleeps' (Barkali 1962, Goshen-Gottstein et al. 1977), marking the endpoint of a historical process by which regular sound change collapsed the inflected forms of past-tense *CaCeC* verbs with their *Pa'al* counterparts, leaving the *e* in the second syllable only in the 3rd person masculine singular stem. Today, across Israeli Hebrew use, the past tense of stative verbs like *yaSen* 'sleeps' and, *zaken* 'becomes old' is identical to that of *Pa'al* (i.e. *yaSan* 'slept' and *zakan* 'became old', cf. *barax* 'escaped'), indicating that the stative patterns of *CaCeC* are in general being collapsed with *Pa'al* past-tense forms (Blau 1981c). The fact that speakers now distinguish past and present *CaCeC* forms which were once the same appears similar to what children do with the *miCaCeC* forms. But there are the following differences: (i) The only change in *CaCeC* verbs was in the vowel, $e \longrightarrow a$, not in syllable structure; (ii) collapsing the *a-a* and *a-e* vowel patterns in past tense allows speakers to follow both Semantic Transparency and Formal Consistency by regularizing a minor rule to the predominant vowel pattern within the same *binyan*; and (iii) no damage was caused to any structure outside the *Pa'al* paradigm, since the *a-a* verbal vowel pattern is unique to *Pa'al*. This is an example of a "cheap," therefore successful, morphophonological change, which is purely beneficial. The childish *miCaCeC* innovation, in contrast, is quite "expensive," and hence short-lived.

The Double-*a* Strategy

Another typically juvenile structure is the double-*a* vowel pattern in past tense with *y*-final *Pa'al* verbs, e.g. *yaráti* for adult *yaríti* '(I) shot', root *y-r-y*. Children abandon the *a-a* pattern around the time they master verb inflection, by 3;6 (Berman 1985). Above I invoked Formal Simplicity which conserves the 3rd person singular stem, e.g. *yará-ti* '(I) shot' for *yarí-ti*. I find this to be a more convincing argument than the (in essence Formal Consistency) claim of collapsing two defective patterns together in analogy to the *a-a* pattern of *álef*-final roots in *Pa'al*, e.g. *macáti* '(I) found' (Bar Adon 1959). Indeed, both *y*-final and *álef*-final roots produce weak final syllables, and have alternated with one another for hundreds of years (Schwarzwald 1980c). However, the number of ?-final roots is one-fifth of that of *y*-final roots; and the number of ?-final roots taking the *a-a* pattern in *Pa'al* is 11, six of which do not occur in child language, e.g. *b-r-?* 'create', *H-T-?* 'sin' and *k-l-?* 'imprison', compared with 71 *y*-final roots (Goshen-Gottstein et al. 1977). In fact, only five *a-a* *álef*-final roots occur in children's usage: the formulaic *maxa* (*kapáyim*) 'clapped (hands)', *yaca* 'went out', *maca* 'found', *kara* 'read', *sana* 'hated'[85] and *kafa* 'froze,Int'. Not counting *áyin*-final verbs (with a varying phonetic distribution in the population), the overwhelming majority of Weak Final Syllable verbs in *Pa'al* is thus *y*-final, so analogy to the *Pa'al* ?-final pattern alone cannot explain why children take the *a-a* structure as basic. Moreover, overgeneralizing ?-final structure in *Pi'el*, for example, would yield *e* not *a* as in *kinéti* 'I was jealous', while in fact we get *nikáti* for adult *nikíti* '(I) cleaned', root *n-q-y*. Therefore it is Formal Simplicity working across the board from the third person singular, which always takes a final -*a* in past-tense *y*-final stems, e.g. *kana* 'bought'; and *nika* 'cleaned', *hifna* 'referred'.

In fact the juvenile final *a* here is a particular example of a general interim strategy between two early stages in the child's acquisition of the verb system: (i) producing verbs without their final person markers, e.g. *ani giraS guk* 'I chased-away(-1st) (a) cockroach' (cf. adult inflected *geráSti juk*) [2;0,DIA], or *ani ala po* 'I went up(-1st) here' for properly inflected *alíti* [2;3,OBS], and (ii) adjusting the internal morphophonology of the stem after addition of the person agreement marker, e.g. *siper/sipárti* 'told/ (I) told', root *s-p-r* in *Pi'el* and *bana/baníti* 'built/(I) built', root *b-n-y*, in the *Pa'al* verb pattern.

Between these two, the "*Satáti*" period indicates realization of the need for external inflection, without the ability to make the necessary morphophonological adjustments. Children opt for the 3rd person singular form as their model, since it is the least marked and so the most likely to itself resist change and to cause change in other derived structures (Manczak 1980). This is in fact another example of grammaticizing a notion without altering the base form, as in *iparon/iparonim* for adult *efronot*. The early disappearance of *Satáti* '(I) drank' (for *Satíti*) indicates that with the establishment of morphophonological knowledge, children no longer need to rely upon the default structure of the 3rd person singular once they have a more generalized construal of the verb system, with the final-*y* subsystem recognized as a salient entity in its own right, with its own specific rules.

-*it* Structures

Stabilization of -*it* structures occurs very early, with children abandoning Formal Consistency (resulting in the -*iyot* suffix for every noun ending with -*it*) in favor of general notions related to other systems in Hebrew. Consistently deriving -*iyot* from -*it* has the advantage of classifying all -*it* nouns together, but entails losing the critical gender distinction, as well as the distinction between stable root radical and unstable affix. Subsequently, literacy helps speakers to identify unstable *t* with orthographic *taf* and stable *t* with orthographic *Tet,* where morphophonology reflects difference in grammatical function. Then, too, losing a radical impairs the semantic coherence of the root. Besides, learning to distinguish between stem-internal and stem-external -*it* is independently motivated by the fact that stem-external vowels are very salient. Finally, learning to distinguish between -*it* nouns means learning to identify morphological classes, to tell the difference between a linearly attached meaning-carrying suffix and the interwoven construction of a pattern. The linguistic phenomena related to the emergence of -*it* as a coherent entity are thus powerful factors impelling the child to abandon Formal Consistency at an early age.

However, the reverse operation—Backformation from -*iyot* to -*iya*—is not Transient. When a base form naturally occurs in numbers, its diachronically backformed singular structure reflects its derived rather than basic status in the mental lexicon. In such cases, where the plural form is more basic pragmatically, FS may be responsible for language change: For example, the words *ugiya* 'cookie', *maciya* 'cracker' and *karciya* 'lichen' originally had the diminutive suffix -*it* (Even Shoshan 1979), the relationship being especially clear in *uga/ugit* 'cake/cookie' and *maca/macit* 'matso bread/cracker'. The plural -*iyot* suffix conceals the original diminutive -*it* so that Semantic Transparency does not compete with Formal Simplicity, paving the way for language change.

Defective Roots

Children are sensitive to the Semitic root as a formal and semantic core of the word (Berman & Sagi 1981, Ravid 1990, Walden 1982). Though consisting of discontinuous elements, it is perceived as a single whole. This unity is violated in the case of defective roots, especially those ending with a final weak syllable, e.g. *kone* 'buys', root *q-n-y* (cf. *moxer* 'sells', root *m-k-r*). Completing final weak syllable roots (e.g. *soxétet* 'swims,Fm' for adult *soxa*, root *s-H-y*) is another juvenile strategy typical of early grammatical acquisition. This means that with an increasing knowledge of grammatical function children learn to accept that some roots do not have the fully transparent triconsonantal structure. Completing the root gains children a structurally consistent form, but this is too "expensive" in terms of other generalizations, such as (i) obliterating the distinction between root-*t* and function-*t*, since a *CoCéCet* structure allows for three root radicals plus a final *t* to mark feminine gender; (ii) violating number/gender distinctions (for example, *maStu* '(they) drew out' for *maSu*, root *m-S-y* [3;9,DIA] violates the stipulation that only feminine 3rd person stems carry an extra *t*); and (iii) completing a discontinuous structure is not compatible with the salient external marker of gender. Modern Hebrew marks feminine gender on present-tense verbs either with a final -*t* or with a final vowel *a*, e.g. *lovéSet* 'wears,Fm', root *l-b-S* and *xola* 'ill,Fm', root *H-l-y* (Schwarzwald 1982a, Sharvit 1987).

Y-final stems usually take the external vowel suffix, e.g. *more/mora* 'teacher/Fm', root *y-r-y*. In sum, this strategy disappears early on because the various features characterizing the coherent class of *y*-final roots interfere with the childish strategies that aim to regularize its morphophonology. This is not simply a question of learning idiosyncrasies by rote versus applying a general rule, but rather learning that the *y*-final class of roots is marked in comparison with the general full-root system, and also with other classes of weak final syllables.

Pronominal Suffixes

The last Transient deviation noted here is pronominal suffixes on prepositions restricted to the usage of small children. Once children learn to fuse prepositions and pronouns, they master the simpler or more common combinations; but the high degree of opacity of the system prevents them from producing only Normative forms. For instance, childish *alo, aléhu* or *alóhu* 'on-it' for adult *alav* were found only among the three-year-olds and the low-SES five-year-olds. The structure of these juvenile forms is analyzed below to determine why they are abandoned at an early age.

The (historically) plural preposition *al* 'on' takes the suffix -*av* (cf. 'his eyes'—*eynav*, from plural *eynáyim*—'eyes'). Children pursue Formal Consistency by generalizing the unmarked 3rd person singular pronominal suffix -*o* which occurs on familiar and frequent case-marked pronouns such as *Sel-o* 'of-him', *it-o* 'with-him' and *ot-o* 'Acc-him' (Dromi 1979, Rom & Dgani 1985). A second childhood strategy is using the bound stem *aley*- which occurs with other pronominal suffixes, e.g. *alé-ha* 'on-her', *aléxa* 'on-you', and *alénu* 'on-us', yielding *aléhu* 'on-him' (*aléhu* is a combination of both strategies). In employing both strategies children thus refer to either the external or the internal paradigm available to them, as presented in Table 53.

These two points of reference—the paradigm-internal bound stem *aley*- and the paradigm-external suffix -*o*—determine the shape of the childish case-marked pronoun.

Table 53. General points of reference in childhood strategies: The preposition/pronoun network

Internal Paradigm (Referring to the prepositional stem) *aley-*	*on*	*he*	External Paradigm (Referring to the pronominal suffix) *-o*
alé-xa	'on-you'	*Sel-o*	'of-him'
alé-ha	'on-her'	*lo*	'to-him'
alé-nu	'on-us'	*it-o*	'with-him'
alé-xem	'on-you,Pl'	*ot-o*	'Acc-him'
ale-hem	'on-them'	*tor-o*	'his-turn'
Result: *alé-hu*		Result: *al-o*	

al + hu

The spontaneous samples yield similar examples, e.g. *ani rácti axaro* 'I ran after-him' for adult *axarav* [5;4,DIA], and *bil'ado* 'without-him' for *biladav* [4;2,OBS] (cf. *lo* 'to-him'); *kafácti meala* '(I) jumped over-her', for *mealéha* (cf. *ita* 'with-her') [5;1,SAM]; *ima, tifxadi miméha* 'mummy, fear from(=of)-her' for *miména* (cf. *aléha* 'on-her') [3;7,DIA]; *mitaxta céva adom* '(there's) under-her (a) red color', for *mitaxtéha* [5;0,DIA]; *ani roce laSévet aléax, alax* 'I want to-sit on-you,Fm, on-you,Fm' for adult *aláyix* (cf. *itax* 'with-you,Fm') [2;5,DIA]; *sími et ze ali, alóhi*[86] 'put Acc this on-me, on-me' for adult *alay,* with the external marker *i* in the first occurrence (cf. *bi* 'in-me'), and the modified stem in the second [5;2,DIA]; and *ima, matay telxi mimáynu, miméynu?* 'mummy, when (you) will-go from-us, from-us?' for the difficult adult form *meitánu,*[87] by the general bound stem (cf. *miméni* 'from-me') [3;10,DIA].

These two Formal Consistency strategies actually work (Zager 1982), so that most of the time the child following them produces forms that do not differ from adult ones. Only when the system "surprises" children with unexpected idiosyncracies do they produce deviant forms. But by middle childhood children have learnt to handle most of these idiosyncracies and minor rules. The most frequent case-marked pronouns are memorized by Secondary Rote and reinforced by constant use, e.g. *mimex* 'from-you,Fm'. Rote does not operate alone, since by now children are aware of the most marked class of plural prepositions. While historically original prepositions differ from derived prepositions only in the 2nd person feminine singular, and only in one vowel, plural prepositions differ from others both in internal structure and the type of pronominal suffixes they take in a number of persons (Table 54).

Typical children's errors occur both across singular and plural forms. But adults' deviations from the Language Establishment norms occur almost exclusively in original and derived prepositions in singular persons (e.g. *ot-*

Table 54. How plural prepositions differ from other prepositions

	Preposition Type		
Person	Original *le-* 'to'	Derived *biSvil* 'for'	Plural *lifney* 'before'
1st Sg	*l-i*	*biSvil-i*	*lefan-ay*
2nd Sg	*le-xa*	*biSvil-xa*	*lefan-éxa*
2nd Sg Fm	*l-ax*	*biSvil-ex*	*lefan-áyix*
3rd Sg	*l-o*	*biSvil-o*	*lefan-av*
3rd Sg Fm	*l-a*	*biSvil-a*	*lefan-éha*
1st Pl	*l-ánu*	*biSvil-énu*	*lefan-éynu*
2nd Pl	*l-axem*	*biSvil-xem*	*lifney-xem*
3rd Pl	*l-ahem*	*biSvil-am*	*lifney-hem*

ex for Normative *ot-ax* 'Acc-you,Fm'). Children stop overregularizing plural prepositions because they soon come to construe this group as unique in having radically different stem and suffix structures, and also because they eventually learn to reconstruct the underlying *-ey* occurring in most persons. It is too "expensive" to regularize a paradigm which is so radically different from the others, and which does not require re-analysis since the underlying form is close to the surface. It is, however, worth regularizing in the other paradigms, which is what adults do (see below).

In sum, six types of Transient phenomena which disappear before school age were noted. None takes part in language change, since they are short-lived re-analyses, mainly found among children under five. Such structures, though following the dictates of natural Mapping Preferences, are all abandoned early on because they clash with major language-specific classes and rules, such as root, pattern and other bound structures; grammatical agreement in number, gender and person; distinctions between affix and root segments, salient and frequently occurring grammatical morphemes, and favored vowel alternations. They are also abandoned since they are characterized by too-radical changes in structure which impair communication between generations. Finally, childish structures solve local problems at the cost of creating opacity elsewhere, where it would be intolerable. They are local remedies which resolve a paradigm-internal problem, yet may give rise to serious problems on a larger scale. Hence, Cost does not permit them more than a temporary existence.

6.3. NONSTANDARD FORMS: LITERACY-RELATED PHENOMENA

Nonstandard Phenomena are deviations which are Transient for the literate section of the speech community that has access to all levels and registers of language usage. For these middle/high-SES speakers, the forms discussed below disappear around puberty and sometimes before, while they remain fossilized in the low-SES sociolect. We will see how the latter speakers contribute to language change by sustaining medium-cost deviations beyond childhood. The distinction between Transient and Nonstandard is not clear-cut, however: some of the Nonstandard forms gradually "creep" into high-SES usage, constituting a type of "errors" which, unlike Transient phenomena, plays an active role in language change, since it is not excluded from the usage of any age or SES group.

Such deviations are tolerated by high-SES speakers (in various degrees) more than childish errors, but they do not form a part of all sociolects in the same way as Language Change phenomena do (Householder 1983). Nonstandard phenomena characterize the speech of the less-educated, who may be young children, at the initial stages of formal schooling, or less literate older speakers. In fact, this is a classical example of Bailey's synchronic variation reflecting diachronic processes: "Linguistic changes begin variably in relatively restricted environments, being later extended—at first variably—to more general environments" (1973:32). The notions of "literate" and "non-literate" are quite fuzzy, so the distribution of Nonstandard phenomena should be placed on a continuum, depicting highly literate speakers at one end, and illiterates at the other, with intermediate possibilities in between (Table 55).

Like Transient deviations, Nonstandard deviations derive from the need to solve local problems of opacity, irregularity and allomorphy in paradigms. Like Transient Phenomena, such deviations follow innate Mapping Preferences, evidenced by the fact that *they arise independently in the speech of children from both a literate background who may never get them in their input, and those who come from uneducated background and so may hear them often.* One main concern is why they disappear (though not completely) from literate, but not from uneducated adult usage. This is not entirely a question of two different dialects, each with its own parameters selected out of the universal stock (Lightfoot 1991, Riemsdijk & Williams 1986): The fact is that low-SES adults consistently make the same morphological choices as school-age children, showing this is one sociolect employing the

Table 55. Distribution of Nonstandard Phenomena

Amount of Nonstandard deviations	
−	Highly literate language specialists
⏐	Well-educated adults
⏐	Adolescents
↓	Semi-educated adults + grade-school children
+	Non-literate adults + preschool children

same innate principles in on-line language processing that children do in language acquisition, and coming up with the same results, as against another sociolect that manifests far less reliance on these principles. I propose that high-SES speakers are moved by Literacy and Conventionality (Bates & MacWhinney 1982), conservative forces which inhibit the application of Mapping Preferences. The limited distribution and often total absence of Nonstandard deviations in this usage is due to the interaction of Opacity, Cost and Literacy.

Literacy, combined with broader linguistic experience and growing metalinguistic control, renders areas of instability in Modern Hebrew less opaque to literate speakers, so that they may perceive a pattern where the less literate, working only with shallow grammars, may not. Literate speakers may also be aided by Secondary Rote, a conservative strategy that preserves suppletive and/or idiosyncratic members of paradigms such as *xamor/aton* 'donkey/she-donkey', and by their tendency to select marked forms, as against a less sophisticated trend to reduce allomorphy.

Nonstandard Phenomena typically occur across the board in children, and decrease in frequency in direct proportion to the rise in both age and literacy. They are thus more common in the speech of younger than older high-SES, but not low-SES speakers: The 12s-b scored highest Normative in the low-SES population, and the gap in Normative responses between peer groups with different SES background was much larger in the adult groups. The test results consistently indicate the following ranking in Normative results for low-SES subjects: 12-year-olds < Adults < 5s.

The low-SES 5s were clearly constrained by both maturational and socio-economic factors, but I had expected the low-SES adults to perform better than the 12-year-olds by virtue of maturity and greater linguistic experience. (Recall that high-SES 12s consistently occupy the same statistical domain with the other adult groups, with very high results! This means that 12-year-olds are equivalent to adults from the point of view of morphological maturation (Karmiloff-Smith 1986a)). However, the low-SES 12s are in fact more literate than adults with the same background, since they have already attended school regularly for seven years, which cannot be said for all low-SES adults, and have been exposed to newer and better teaching methods than the older subjects. They have also grown up with a more consolidated second- to third-generation Hebrew, while older subjects were usually first/second-generation speakers. These two factors may have made pattern recognition easier for our adolescent than for the adult low-SES subjects, enabling them to find principled regularity where surface structure was opaque.

Nonstandard forms discussed below include: *Weak Final Syllable* stems; *Stop/Spirant Alternation; Stem Changes;* future-tense person markers; *CaCeC* verbs; *Lexical Exceptions;* and 2nd person *Case-Marked Pronouns*.

Weak Final Syllable Stems

Recall that *Weak Final Syllable* (WFS) stems display two kinds of opacity: (i) A weak root radical may or may not occur on the surface, and (ii) phonetic mergers cause what appears to be the same weak segments to have different behaviors in the same environment. Given that, it was reasonable to expect speakers to re-analyze the resulting opaque forms and create a general area of instability and change. This is only partially true: WFS is in fact only 3rd from the most stable test category (51). What it does is sharply demarcate the literate from the Nonstandard sociolect. Why then is this category, which violates Transparency and Consistency, not subject to fullscale re-analysis and shift in Standard? Moreover, why are some items within this class more subject to re-analysis than others, and what characterizes typically Nonstandard usage? The answers to these questions demonstrate the interaction of local opacity with other variables that promote or retard change.

Firstly, the situation here is not strictly speaking one of full phonetic merger. True, gutturals and pharyngeals either do not surface at all or merge in General Israeli Hebrew, but speakers of this dialect have at least three potential ways of accessing them: (i) Speakers of "Oriental Hebrew" (not isomorphic with the Nonstandard sociolect) pronounce some, in extreme cases all, of the gutturals and pharyngeal obstruents (Ben-Tolila 1984). Speakers of both Oriental and General Hebrew intermingle in all facets of Israeli life and institutions, so that all of them are able to recognize gutturals and pharyngeals when they hear them. (ii) Gutturals/pharyngeals are concretely realized in Arabic, spoken by a large minority of Israelis—both Jews and non-Jews—and by over a million residents of the Occupied Territories, as well as in surrounding countries, and Arabic is readily accessible on radio and television. (iii) Gutturals/pharyngeals are represented in the Hebrew orthography and serve as crucial motivation for morphophonological alternations (Bentur 1978, Schwarzwald 1981), e.g. lowering of vowels in *náar* 'youth' (Oriental Hebrew *ná y ar*), compared with *yéled* 'boy' of the same pattern; or *koráat* '(she) tears', root *q-r-y*, vs. *kotévet* '(she) writes', root *k-t-b*, both in present-tense *Pa'al*. In reading aloud, speakers may enunciate them carefully even if they do not do so in their everyday usage. This gives rise to a special morphophonological situation of partial merger in production, distinct segments in comprehension, rendering the underlying structure of WFS stems syllables more accessible than that of other merged segments.

Another factor that facilitates learning WFS is knowledge of morphological rules and classes. One reason young children abandon trying to "complete" roots with final weak segments (e.g. *soxe/soxa* 'swims/Fm', juvenile *soxévet* or *soxétet*) is the knowledge they acquire of "full" paradigms such as *CoCeC/CoCéCet* e.g. *lomed/lomédet* 'studies/Fm', vs. "defective" ones such as *CoCe/CoCa(CoCet)* which are in complementary distribution—e.g. *kone/kona* 'buys/Fm' and *moce/mocet* 'finds/Fm' (Schwarzwald 1982a, Sharvit 1987).

Moreover, speakers tend to eventually learn "favored" stem-internal vowel alternants, tolerating what amounts to a variable rule subject to morphophonemic criteria (Bailey 1973, Labov 1969, 1982, Sankoff & Labov 1979). Such favored alternants are *i/e* (e.g. Normative *nisíti*, vs. Nonstandard *niséti* '(I) tried', root *n-s-y; hevéti* vs. *hevíti* '(I) brought', root *b-w-?*) and *e/a* (e.g. *nisa* vs. *nise* '(he) tried', root *n-s-y; mile* vs. *mila* '(he) filled', root *m-l-?*,[88] and see also *e/a* alternation in *Hif'il*), unlike impossible *i/a* as in *Satíti* '(I) drank', childish *Satáti*. In terms of Cost, making an error within the favored alternation is not very "expensive," and the way is open for Nonstandard usage and/or for language change. Making an error within a non-favored alternation, however, is soon corrected, since it is too "costly" (See MacWhinney 1985:1115 on weak allomorphy).

Low open-syllable segments are responsible for a wide variety of morphophonological phenomena, mostly involving vowel lowering, e.g. *e*———>*a* in *CéCeC*, as in *pérax* 'flower', root *p-r-H*, and *táam* 'taste', root *t- y -m* (cf. *bérez* 'tap'); or *i*———>*e* in future-tense *Nif'al*, e.g. *yehares* 'will-be-destroyed', root *h-r-s*, or *yealem* 'will-fall silent', root *?-l-m* (cf. *yisager* 'will-be closed', root *s-g-r*). We will now take a look at a number of specific WFS processes to see the interaction of Structural Opacity with Maturation, Literacy and Cost.

Overgeneralized and Hypercorrect H

One WFS phenomenon typical of the less literate sociolect is regularizing segolate structures with surface *x*. Formal Consistency entails choosing double *e* over double *a* in penultimately stressed patterns with gutturals/pharyngeals, e.g. *niftéxet* 'opens,Fm,Int', for *niftáxat,* root *p-t-H* (cf. *nisgéret* 'closes,Fm', root *s-g-r*). In order to perform vowel-lowering the speaker must recognize *H* despite its surface identity with *k*-derived *x,* again, an underlying relationship manifested in different morphophonological behavior, e.g. epenthetic-*a* insertion (see below). Perceiving such underlying networks demands a measure of autonomy for the language system as a formal problem space.

Knowledge of the orthography, making a clear distinction between *Het* and *xaf,* helps keep the two subsystems apart as well. Moreover, literate speakers are attracted to the marked form with lowered vowels. It not only marks the (phonetic) environment more clearly, but also serves as a hypercorrecting force known to play a role in language change (Labov 1972a:136–142, Ravid & Shlesinger 1987a). This is shown by results on the present-tense verb *dorex* 'steps', root *d-r-k*. The hypercorrect form *doráxat* (for *doréxet*) occurred in all the groups, as well as in the spontaneous data (cf. the very common *oráxat-din* '(woman) lawyer' for *oréxet-din,* root *y -r-k* [58,SAM]; *láma at moSáxat et ze* 'why (are) you pulling,Fm Acc it?' for Normative *moSéxet,* root *m-S-k* [35,OBS]; *niftéxet* 'opens,Fm' for *nif táxat*, root *p-t-H* [12;6,SAM], and *hi koráxat et ha-sfarim* 'she binds,Fm Acc the-books' for Normative *koréxet*, root *k-r-k* [58,SAM]). Neither type of deviation is pervasive, showing that both populations are able to differentiate *Het* from *xaf* with varying amounts of success. But quantitative claims aside, the very existence of such examples is indicative of how high-SESs deal with opacity; they will often favor the marked segment.

a- Epenthesis

a-epenthesis occurs before final orthographic *Het, he,* and *áyin* (historical *H, h* and *y* respectively) in the environment of a non-low vowel,[89] e.g. *mitkaléax* 'showers', root *q-l-H* (cf. *mitkalef* 'peels', root *k-l-p); gavoá* 'tall', root *g-b-h* (cf. *gadol* 'big', root *g-d-l*); and *maSmía* 'sounds', root *S-m-y* (cf. *maSmin* 'grows fat', *S-m-n*). Since both orthographic *he* and *áyin* emerge as either phonetic zero or glottal stops in the General Israeli pronunciation, the child has to learn to distinguish their behavior in the same environments from that of (truly) ?-final and *y*-final stems, e.g. *korea* 'tears', root *q-r-y* vs. *kore* 'reads', root *q-r-?*, and *kore* 'happens', root *q-r-y*. In the same way, *H*-final stems must be distinguished from *k*-derived *x*-final stems, e.g. *moSéax* 'applies oil', root *m-S-H*, versus *moSex* 'pulls', root *m-S-k*. This is one more example of an underlying network of abstract segments that are responsible for what otherwise seems random behavior of surface elements, as depicted in Table 56. Until the child's system of underlying phonemes responsible for surface alternations stabilizes, there are bound to be errors, especially in the unmarked direction of non-epenthesis. This is in line with other childish/low-SES reliance rendering *niftáxat* 'opens,Int' as *niftéxet*, despite the low radical *H*. Children soon abandon Formal Consistency, collapsing such forms, as evidenced by the following two examples: *li-róa* 'to-shoot', for adult *li-rot*, root *y-r-y* [7;2,OBS], and *li-mSóax* 'to-pull' for *limSox*, root *m-S-k* [51,SAM], because otherwise they miss the crucial distinction between guttural/pharyngeal and other segments that underlie so many vowel-lowering processes in Hebrew (Blau 1981c, Bolozky, to appear).

Vowel lowering occurs in both verbs (in all tenses) and nouns, as well as in adjectives and some prepositions, and is thus a general process that applies in all word-classes. Failing to insert final epenthetic *a* means ignoring other major processes related to *groniyot*, thus failing to perceive a major morphophonemic class. Moreover, in this case Saliency upholds the marked final vowel (epenthetic *a*) at the end of the word in the face of Formal Consistency, and wins out early on.

Regularizing y-Final Stems

The next two examples are of the related *y*- and *álef*-final stems. Consider, first, low-SES regularization of *y*-final stems, e.g. *menaka* 'cleans,Fm', root *n-q-y*, and *mexake* 'waits', root *H-k-y*, to past tense *nikéti* '(I) cleaned' for

Table 56. Phonetic mergers and epenthetic *a*

1.	[0/?]	derives from / *y* / and /*h*/ [+ *a* epenthesis]
		derives from /?/ and /*y*/ [− *a* epenthesis]
2.	[*x*]	derives from /*H*/ [+ *a* epenthesis]
		derives from /*k*/ [− *a* epenthetis]

nikíti and *xike* 'waited' for *xika*. Bar Adon (1959:78) reports such forms in child language, but gives no account of their prevalence among older less-educated speakers. As we saw above, there are fewer (12) ?-final roots than (25–30) *y*-final verbs in *Pi'el*. ?-final verbs normatively end with *e* in *Pi'el* (e.g. *kine/mekane/yekane* 'envied/envies/will-envy', root *q-n-?*), while *y*-final verbs take *a* in past tense and *e* in other forms (e.g. *kiva/mekave/yekave* 'hoped/hopes/will-hope', root *q-w-y*). But here both Standard and Nonstandard usages depart from the required norm: While low-SES speakers alone adopt *e* for *y*-final verbs in *Pi'el* (e.g. *nise* 'tried' for Normative/Standard *nisa*, root *n-s-y*), speakers in general, and high-SES in particular, shift to final-*a* in both ?- and *y*-final verbs (e.g. *mila* for Normative *mile*, root *m-l-?*). This study shows Nonstandard *e* for Normative *a* in *y*-final stems to be a sociolinguistic variable (Ben-Tolila 1983), common in the usage of children up to age eight, and in that of low-SES speakers. (Word-medial Nonstandard *e* (*nikéti* '(I) cleaned' for Normative *nikíti*) also occurs to a lesser extent in the usage of high-SES adolescents). Thus we can see a change taking place in three age/SES groups out of four: children, low-SES speakers, and, less widely, adolescents. Only the high-SES adults totally refrain from this strategy.

"Silent" ? and *y* form a sub-set within WFS differing from the more accessible *y*, *h* and *H* which attract lower vowels much more generally. The ?- and *y*-final collapse here is thus a local phenomenon, and does not cause radical disruptions in other systems. This explains why analogies between ?-final and *y*-final stems have existed since Biblical times (Schwarzwald 1980c). In choosing *e* over *a*, speakers follow Formal Consistency despite the quantitative difference between ?-final and *y*-final stems, as *e* is the regular case both within the *y*-final paradigm (present and past tense) and in the *Pi'el* pattern in general (cf. *kibel/mekabel/yekabel* 'got/gets/will-get', root *q-b-l*), while *a* occurs only with final *y*; and in all other *binyan* patterns, except for *Pa'al*, *y*-final stems Normatively take *e* when inflected, (e.g. *Hif'il hifna/hifnéti* 'directed/(I)directed'). In short, final *a* is the exception to the rule here, so children and low-SES speakers follow what seems to be the rule in rendering *xika* 'waited', root *H-k-y*, as *xike*. Moreover, *e* is phonetically, though not morphophonologically, less marked than *a*, being a more central vowel. The difference between high- and low-SES is also in amount of alternation: While the former alternate *a* and *i* in unmarked stem and inflected form (e.g. *nisa/nisíti* 'tried/(I) tried'), the latter, relying on Formal Consistency, extend the same vowel to the inflected verb (e.g. *xike/xikéti* 'waited/(I) waited', for Normative *xika/xikíti*, and compare *xikénu* '(we) waited', Normative *xikínu; niset* '(you,Fm) tried', Normative *nisit*, root *n-s-y*, [48,SAM]; *xibéti* '(I) turned-off', for *kibíti*, root *k-b-y*, [33, SAM] in the spontaneous database), reducing alternation. A simplified grammar for uneducated speakers thus means both extending the unmarked *e* and reducing alternation. Finally, word-medial *e* (*nikéti*) is much more common in low-SES usage than word-final *e* (*xike*), and also occurs in the high-SES adolescents, highlighting again the reduced significance of stem-internal vowels (noted by Bar-Adon 1959 with regard to child language), as opposed to the increased significance of stem-external vowels, which are more salient and less subject to alternation.

Two factors prevent established speakers from following the same strategies: First, Literacy, especially knowledge of the orthography, eventually re-asserts the underlying difference between ?-final and *y*-final roots. Familiarity with the orthography will help the speaker decide on the alternant vowel, related to a specific letter (*álef* or *he*). Secondly, the literate speaker seeks markedness, special features to characterize the chosen segment. The phonologically marked *a* is chosen over the unmarked *e*, explaining the choice of both Normative *bila* 'enjoyed', root *b-l-y*, and colloquial *mila* 'filled' (Normative *mile*, root *m-l-?*), prevalent among literates. In sum, this subcategory which involves the alternation of two pairs of vowels—*a/e* in the uninflected stem, and *i/e* in the inflected stem—is an example of medium-Cost deviation: Choosing one vowel over the other applies only to these two final syllables, which are related further, e.g. in the infinitive (childish *le-lave* 'to-accompany', for *le-lavot*, root *l-w-y* [4;5,SAM]; colloquial *le-malot* 'to-fill', for *le-male*, root *m-l-?* [35,OBS]; and *likr-o* 'to-happen', for Normative *likr-ot*, root *q-r-y* [40,OBS]). Thus the speaker performs an internal exchange between two subsystems that are anyway related. In fact, in choosing *e* over *a*, low-SES speakers take advantage of an ancient option: Even Shoshan (1977) lists five Biblical occurrences of the root *n-q-y* alone as *nikéti* '(I) cleaned', rather than today's Normative *nikíti*. Yet the fact that high-SES speakers are able to select the Normative forms shows that literacy provides a way of distinguishing between *y*-final and ?-final roots, blocked to less literate speakers.

Redundant t

Further evidence of the convergence of ?-final and *y*-final stems is redundant *t* in past-tense ?-final 3rd feminine singular stems, e.g. *santa* 'hated' for Normative *san'a*, root *s-n-?* (cf. *y*-final *kanta* 'bought,Fm'). The item illustrating this problem is *kine* 'envied' (root *q-n-?*), rendered as *kinta* '(she) envied' for *kin'a* by ⅕ of all speakers in most groups, including the high-SES groups. Again this process has roots in Mishnaic Hebrew (Kutscher 1959, Schwarzwald 1980c). It, too, reflects the complex interplay of ?-final and *y*-final roots, in the misappropriation of salient *t* used with *y*-final roots. Superfluous *t* is restricted even in low-SES usage precisely because it is so marked, occurring in past tense only in the one environment of 3rd person feminine singular, in direct contrast to the usual zero manifestation of surface ?. In the Established sociolect, attention to the orthography prevents these two similar subgroups from coalescing.

hevéti '(I) Brought'

As a further instance of the interchangeable nature of stem-internal vowels: *mevi* 'brings' (root *b-w-?*), with only the first radical *b* surfacing, has two internal vowels in the past tense 1st person singular *hevéti*. Some 10% of the subjects changed this construction to either Nonstandard *hevíti* or *hivéti*. Both types of deviations indicate that *i/e* are interchangeable in stem-internal position, as long as the three consonants carry the semantic composition of this verb—past form, the *Hif'il* verb-pattern indicating Causativity, and the core meaning 'bring' carried by the *b*-derived radical *v* (with the two other underlying radicals *w* and ? lacking surface manifestation).

   To conclude: *Weak Final Syllable* forms emerged as a sociolinguistic characteristic of the Nonstandard sociolect: The responses of children and low-SES subjects manifest adherence to Formal Consistency, re-analyzing phonetically merged segments which display multiform behavior in the same environment. These deviations are local, in the sense that they collapse two rules or structures that were similar to begin with, without causing major re-analysis in related structures, as childish errors do. These "medium Cost" deviations are blocked in the literate population both by reliance on orthographic distinctiveness, and by access to a rich and complex stock of structurally related items.

The New Status of Stop/Spirant Alternation

Above I showed that *Stop/Spirant Alternation* no longer represents a transparent phonological rule, and that speakers' solution for the opacity created is to adopt a single *bkp* alternant that appears in a basic form, e.g. *tilfen* 'telephoned' (Normative *tilpen*) from *télefon* 'telephone' following Semantic Transparency by carrying over the semantic and structural features of the base word, including its precise consonant structure. The literature shows that such phonematicization of *bkp* occurs in all speakers in the derivational component of the lexicon (Fischler 1975). This study, however, tested Stop/Spirant Alternations across inflectional paradigms rather than lexical entries, and in a specific population defined by age and SES. My study shows that phonematicization of *bkp* radicals is restricted in both sociolinguistic terms and in domain of application, so that this strategy sharply delineates child speech and the Nonstandard sociolect from the established sociolect, on the one hand, and inflection from derivation, on the other.

   Consider the fact that high-SES speakers dropped the Transparency-preserving strategy around age 12, while the low-SES population went on producing the Expected response with a single *bkp* alternant to adulthood. For example, the past form of *mefazéret* 'scatters,Fm' was given as *fizra* instead of *pizra* by 60–80% of all low-SES groups, but not by the two oldest high-SES groups.

This reveals a difference between the way the morphological component is perceived by high-SES and low-SES groups respectively. Speakers of the established sociolect regard the grammatical paradigm as a single grammatical space across which *bkp/vxf* stops and spirants function as allophones. This grammatical space includes inflectional categories with closely related members (in the sense of Bybee 1985), such as number (*cahov/cehubim* 'yellow/s'), gender (*rax/raka* 'soft/Fm') and tense (*safar/sofer* 'counted/counts'). Variation is therefore permitted, and is carried out according to a number of morphophonemic rules functioning in varying environments. Thus as segments under inflection, *bkp* have allophonic spirant variations, e.g. *rax/rak-a* 'soft/Fm', *tof/tup-im* 'drum/s'. This perception of the abstract phoneme is promoted by education and access to written language, since the Hebrew writing system does not ordinarily distinguish *bkp* stops and spirants except in texts for beginners. However, as units in lexeme-forming roots, each of the six *bkp/vxf* is construed as a non-alternating independent phoneme, e.g. *s-v-v* is taken as shared by noun and verb in *sivuv* 'curve,rotation' from *le-sovev* 'to-rotate', instead of *sibuv* (surface manifestation of *s-b-b*), required here by the phonetic environment (cf. *kibud* 'refreshment' (root *k-b-d*); and *k-f-?* is taken as shared by both noun and verb in *kifa'on* 'freeze' from *kafa/kafu* 'froze/frozen' (surface manifestation of root *q-p-?*) [38,OBS] for Normative *kipa'on* (cf. *iparon* 'pencil'). By contrast, naive speakers—children, and uneducated adults—lump together lexical entries and grammatical words so that the basic word in a paradigm serves as a lexical prime. Following its structure, all related words are assigned its basic structural skeleton, adopting one alternant of the *bkp* set (see Schwarzwald 1980c on a similar tendency in Mishnaic Hebrew). The notion of a "basic word" is significant here, as in other areas of psycholinguistic research, since it determines what precise alternant is to be used. In nouns and adjectives, the basic form is the free masculine singular, whose structure is retained by Formal Simplicity in inflection in Child Language and the uneducated sociolect, e.g *rax/raxa* 'soft/Fm' instead of Normative *raka*, or *cahov/cehuvim* 'yellow/Pl' with the word-final *v* retained in the plural form instead of the Normative *cehubim*. Note, however, that the Normative plurals *musakim* 'garages' and *masakim* 'curtains' (cf. singular *musax* and *masax*) have been lost from Standard usage for the same reason!

As for verbs, the situation is more complex, since Hebrew verbs lack a basic form similar to, say, English *sleep* or *stay;* Speakers must therefore designate one member of the conjugation as basic. This may be a less complex form acquired early on, such as the infinitival form, which is not marked for number, gender and person. Indeed, Nonstandard *soper* 'counts', occurs instead of the Normative *sofer* in all of the children's and low-SES subjects' responses, with the *p* from *li-spor* 'to-count' transferred to the present form. Similarly, the Spontaneous Data show a reliance on a base form in *ma at xotévet?* (Normative *kotévet*) 'what (are) you,Fm writing,Fm ?', from Infinitive *lixtov* [3;1,DIA]; *verárti* (Normative *berárti*) '(I) found out', from *le-varer* 'to find out'; and *vikaSt* (Normative *bikaSt*), '(You,Fm) asked' from *le-vakeS* 'to-ask' respectively [36,OBS]. The selected basic form may also be a more frequent one, or else pragmatically more basic, including being present in previous discourse. This may be the case in *mefazéret* 'scatters,Fm', with past form *fizra* (Normative *pizra*) arising from either present-tense form or on the infinitival *le-fazer* 'to-scatter'. Children as well adult speakers of the Nonstandard sociolect, however, generally perceive *bkp/vxf* segments as distinct phonemes in both morphological domains, e.g. *xatávti* '(I) wrote', instead of Normative *katávti*, root *k-t-b* [7;8,SAM] (compare: *li-xtov* 'to-write'); (and alternatively, *tiktevi* 'you,Fm will-write', from *katav* 'wrote'—; or *viSalt* '(You,Fm) cooked', instead of *biSalt*, root *b-S-l* [4;2,DIA] (cf. *le-vaSel* 'to-cook', or *mevaSélet* 'she cooks'); and *loked* 'traps' for *loxed* [19,low-SES,OBS] (cf. *li-lkod* 'to-trap', root *l-k-d*). Since this endeavor concerned inflectional alternations the Nonstandard treatment of *bkp* segments resulted in many deviations, while the more abstract treatment of high-SES speakers of this alternation was closer to the Normative.

My findings thus suggest two solutions to the *bkp* problem: *Naive speakers* (children and uneducated adults) seek a base form in both derivation and inflection, entailing the use of the same *bkp* alternant in all derived forms, whereas *educated speakers* mostly seek such a base form in lexical derivation alone, and allow Stop/Spirant Alternation within grammatical paradigms. As a result, *bkp/vxf* each tend to have independent phonematic status in the low-SES sociolect, while in the high-SES sociolect, this tendency holds for lexical derivation but much less for inflection (Table 57).

The variable that determines how far speakers employ Semantic Transparency and Formal Simplicity in *bkp* alternation is the notion of a base word. In general, a word can be produced/analyzed in one of two ways—by the retrieval system, locating a rote-learned form, or by generative production working either forward, to combine stem and affix into a word, or backwards, to analyze a word into stem and affix (Bybee 1985). The former method is how familiar and frequent words are typically retrieved in on-line conversation; the second occurs either when a new word is coined or encountered, or when a formal grammatical or lexical operation needs to be applied to a given base-word. This distinction explains the differential treatments of spirantization by different types of speakers. For the high-SES, a "base word" is a separate lexical item whose meaning and radical structure must be carried over intact to the new word. This includes the type of *bkp* alternant to be adopted. But for uneducated speakers, a "base word" is the input structure to any rule-bound morphological operation, lexical and inflectional alike. In both cases, the alternant in the base word determines its choice throughout the paradigm. A "base-word" may

Table 57. Tracing the status of *bkp* segments in Hebrew

1. HISTORICAL RULE	2. RULE OPACITY	→ 3. RULE TODAY	
		3a. New-word formation	3b. Word Inflection
Phonetically conditioned	Partial loss of members of class ·	Standard: Phonematic status	Allophonic status
12 allophonic variants —→	Loss of phonological environment	Nonstandard and children: ←— Phonematic status —→	
	Introduction of "parasites"		
	Use of root as uniform lexical unit		

155

vary in ongoing conversation, as when a speaker has used both *Sbura* 'broken' (Normative *Svura*) from *niSbar* 'broke,Int', and *niSveru* '(they) broke,Int' (Normative *niSberu*) from *Savar* 'broke,Tr', in the same conversation [15,SAM]. It is this easy reliance on the most convenient form at hand, lexical or inflectional, to serve as a base form, that distinguishes carefully monitored speech from informal, less controlled on-line conversation.

Speakers are also aware of numerous minor morphophonological rules that govern *bkp* segments in specific verb-patterns. For example, in active *Pi'el* and its passive counterpart *Pu'al*, root-initial radicals occur as stops in past tense, and as fricatives in present tense and future tense, e.g.: *biker/ mevaker/yevaker* 'visited/visits/will-visit'; and *bukar/mevukar/yevukar* 'was/is/ will-be visited'. Wider experience with a large number of lexical items and the orthography (in which *bkp* stop and spirant alternants are represented by the same letter) promote reliance on these minor alternations, yielding marked stop/spirant alternations. Three general patterns emerge: (i) The only *bkp* alternant in word-final position environment is a fricative, e.g. *Safax* 'spilled', root *S-p-k*, *hixtiv* 'dictated', root *k-t-b*. (ii) In word-initial position, the old Biblical constraint that required a stop still applies, and sharply divides children and low-SES speakers on one hand, from literate adults on the other: The former violate this constraint, while the latter do not, except for some lexicalized forms, mostly with *x*, e.g. *xibásti* '(I) laundered' and *xibíti* '(I) turned off', for Normative *kibásti* and *kibíti* respectively (see Ben Horin & Bolozky 1972). (iii) Most violations occur in stem-internal position, where in on-line speech even high-SES adults may resort to a base form, or simply use of a variable rule (Barkai 1972). This is because the phonetic environment most markedly violated by the product of the two historical rules is word-internal.

Moreover, word-beginnings and word-ends are more salient than word-medial positions, enabling speakers to perceive frequently occurring patterns more clearly when they relate to beginnings and ends of words. Finally, the type of alternant chosen by literate as well as non-literate speakers across *binyan* patterns is lexically determined, since the relations of Valence and Transitivity they express are derivational relationships; that is, each verb in a *binyan* form signifies a separate lexical item linked to others through those relationships (Berman 1975a,b, Bybee 1985, Ornan 1971). This is demonstrated when a single alternant is used across related verb-patterns, e.g. childish *makfic* 'causes to jump' for *makpic*, root *q-p-ṣ* [3;7,Dir] in *Hif'il* from intransitive *kofec* 'jumps', in *Pa'al* (Berman 1975b, 1980b).

In sum, unity of root is a major goal in linguistically immature speakers, both young and uneducated. Such goals are subsequently superseded by knowledge of the complexity of morphological systems, of derivational patterns, and of minor morphophonological rules. The notion of a "base form" varies in speakers of different age/SES backgrounds: In low-SES speakers and in children, it must be very close to the form produced, in order to preserve a clear semantic relationship. In literate speakers, the base form is construed more abstractly, allowing for morphophonological variations within the grammatical paradigm. The more abstract roots and base forms are for the native speaker, the more adherence there is to norm. The shallower the grammar, the more the tendency to perceive the root as a go-between between two closely related forms, and the more adherence to Operating Principles. Finally, stressful conditions that require re-formation of a structure, such as a test situation, increase the chance of the speaker falling back upon these natural principles.

As I mentioned above, my results are different from those of Schwarzwald (1981), who did not find such great discrepancies between the low- and the high-SES populations, especially not in root-initial *bkp*[90] (1981:43). Too, in her study performance improved in *both* populations with age, while in this study the low-SES adults had results similar to the high-SES 5-year-olds. I believe this gap derives in part from the different methodology.[91] Please note, moreover, that the test results for Stop/ Spirant Alternation are entirely in concord with the rest of the results of this study. And furthermore, my spontaneous data supports my claim for a lower awareness of the underlying rules in the adult low-SES population. Schwarzwald claims that better performance in this category is the result of maturation and more schooling. This is certainly borne out by my results, but "more schooling" is too general a term to explain the differences between inflection and derivation discussed above. Further studies of this fascinating area are no doubt required to determine the interaction between root radical position, lexical/grammatical alternation, and population type.

Stem Changes

In addition to taking a rich array of inflectional suffixes, Hebrew stems often undergo internal changes in pre-suffixal positions. The most frequent types of change are vowel reduction, e.g. *zaken/zken-im* 'old/Pl' (Ravid & Shlesinger 1987a); vowel change, e.g. *mas/misim*; *t*-deletion, e.g. *sakit/ sakiyot* 'bag/s'; Stop/Spirant Alternation, e.g. *daf/dapim* 'page/s'; and radical stem change, e.g. *kélev/klavim* 'dog/s'. Formal Simplicity guides young children to conserve the whole free stem in inflection, but this wears off with maturation. Nevertheless, the bound stems on our test fail to undergo all of the required changes among children and low-SES. Their pattern of stem-changing is as follows:

(i) Without fail *a-reduction* is performed by all groups from age five (e.g. *cahov/cehubim* 'yellow/Pl' and *iparon/efronot* 'pencil/s'). None of them, except for the very young, deviated by retaining *a*. In other words, the old *a*-reduction rule (Gesenius 1910) is still viable in Modern Hebrew, as is compatible with the findings of Berman (1981c) and Ravid & Shlesinger (1987a).

(ii) *Pre-suffixal stem change* occurs where speakers realize it is part of a salient or semantically coherent pattern (Berman 1981c). This was the case in *éven/avanim* 'stone/s' and *kivsa/kéves* 'sheep/he-sheep', belonging to the salient noun pattern *CéCeC*, and in *cahov* 'yellow' and *adom* 'red', in the color terms pattern *CaCoC/ CCuC-*, e.g. *adumim* 'red,Pl'. When speakers fail to make the connection between the lexical item and a certain pattern, they fail to perform the necessary changes, e.g. naive subjects are not aware of the reason for *dli/dlayim* 'bucket/s', historically in the *CéCeC* pattern. Note, however, that Normative *ratov/retuba* 'wet/Fm' is now universally rendered *ratuv/retuva* for the same reason.

(iii) As before, we note here the *lessened weight assigned to stem-internal vowels*, a leitmotif in this study. Thus the major patterns that take the Junction form *CCaCim/ot* are in many cases inter-changeable, e.g. *cdaf/cédef* 'shell' or *dim'a/dma'a* 'tear' (Normative form first). The pilot study indicated that the *CiCCa* pattern was very unstable, regularized in most cases to *CiCCot* in the plural. The test results serve as further evidence of the instability of *CiCCa*.

(iv) *Frequency and familiarity* of a particular item help in its becoming established as idiosyncratic through reinforcement by Secondary Rote (Hooper 1976, Phillips 1984). Thus, for example, both *bat* 'girl' and *iSa* 'woman' have special, non-rule-bound plurals, which prevail in the adult population due to their high frequency and familiarity. Another factor is which of the paradigm members ("grammatical words"—Matthews 1974) occurs more frequently as a base form. This may indicate the frequency and distribution of errors, e.g. the fact that *dma'ot* 'tears' occurs more naturally as a base-form than *acamot* 'bones', thus increasing the chance for backformation from *dma'ot*, especially in the less literate groups.

Stem-change is thus construed by all speakers as an inseparable part of Hebrew morphophonology. But low-SES speakers and children, following Formal Simplicity and Formal Consistency, strive to preserve the input form of root and stem, and are hence more liable to change the form of vowels than that of consonants, which explains why stop/spirant alternation is conspicuously missing even when *a*-reduction or vowel change are performed correctly, e.g. *cehuvim* 'yellow,Pl' for Normative *cehubim*, from singular *cahov*, but not *cahovim*; or *ipronot/ipronim/epronot*, all erroneous forms of Normative *efronot* 'pencils', (singular *iparon*), but not childish *iparonim* which preserves the free stem. Literate speakers perform both vowel-changing and consonant-changing operations because they have "deeper" grammars.

Future-Tense Person Marking

This is a typical example of literacy blocking regularization. We noted that the 1st person singular prefix marking future-tense is specially marked, and that it is regularized by Formal Consistency to the basic and unmarked 3rd person singular future-tense marker *yV-*, e.g. *ani maxar yedaber ito* 'I tomorrow will-talk,3rd with-him' for Normative *adaber* 'will-talk,1st'. All groups, to the exclusion of high-SES adults, rely on this strategy to some extent. Clearly, older, more literate speakers are better able to curb regularization, referred to the orthographic *álef* of the 1st person singular prefix, and guided to select the marked 1st person singular prefix. Literacy obviously exerted more influence over the speaker in the structured experimental situation, evidenced by the numerous regularized samples produced by literate speakers in the Spontaneous Speech data.

Regularizing *CaCeC* Verbs

Present-tense *CaCeC* verbs and adjectives (Morag 1957) constitute an interesting example of ongoing change which derives from the tendency to seek Semantic Transparency, spreading from young and less literate to older and more literate groups. Thus, *yaSen* 'sleeps' takes the regular present-tense *CoCeC* pattern, since it is not perceived as an adjective, and Nonstandard *yoSen* predominates among the young and less literate, and occurs in all groups except high-SES adults. The Spontaneous Speech data confirm Bar-Adon's (1959: 311–314) finding that children shift active *CaCeC* verbs to the *CoCeC* pattern also for the adult population. They include numerous examples of (mostly) children and uneducated adults producing *yoSen/yoSénet* instead of Normative *yaSen/yeSena* 'sleeps/Fm', and even more examples of *godel/godélet* for Normative *gadel/gdela* 'grows up/Fm'. In fact, there is a split between historical *CaCeC* forms perceived as active verbs, taking regular *CoCeC* even in the literate adult population (e.g. *lomed* 'studies' for Mishnaic *lamed*), and those construed as state verbs, retaining the marked *CaCeC* pattern. This is a direct continuation of a historical trend: Biblical Hebrew had many *CaCeC* verbs denoting quality, state or inchoativity (Bergstrasser 1982 lists some 50), e.g. *yaveS* 'dry up', *davek* 'adhere', and *sane* 'hate'. But even in Biblical times there was already a tendency to distinguish state from dynamic verbs by giving the former adjectival patterns, and the latter tended to take the regular *Pa'al* pattern (Bergstrasser 1982). Today there are fewer *CaCeC* verbs, and most of those listed in Bergstrasser now take the regular *Pa'al* form. For example, the root *l-m-d* 'study' is listed in Even Shoshan (1979) as *lamed* 'studies', but as regular *lomed* in Barkali (1962). These *CaCeC/CoCeC* forms can be ranked on a continuum according to Householder's (1983) notion of "kyriolexia": "A form regarded by most speakers as the basic variant, the literal meaning, the normal or correct pronunciation, the in-group form" (1983:2). Deviations from this form may exist, but they are regarded as dialectally or otherwise marked forms, usually as errors, thus: "At least two classes of . . . errors seem to exist: (1) those which provoke reaction of some sort . . ., and (2) those which are silently tolerated by one's listeners. The passage of an error from the first of these classes to the second (in any individual's behavior) may often be the precursor of a linguistic change—if it is not, in fact, the change itself. (1983:2)

Householder's notion of language change thus crucially depends upon individual speakers' perception of forms as "kyriolexia" or not. Nonstandard *yoSénet* 'sleeps,Fm' is perceived by adult literate speakers, including the author of this study, as much "worse" than, say, *godélet* 'grows up,Fm', while *lomédet* 'studies,Fm' is perfectly acceptable. That is, there is a scale of language change involved. I suggest that the criterion of "Stativeness" determines which historical *CaCeC* verb now taking a *CoCeC* present-tense form will belong to Householder's type (1) or (2) respectively, as shown in Table 58.

Table 58 shows that the less stative the *CaCeC* verb, the more likely it is to cross over to the major *CoCeC* pattern. In terms of Cost, it makes more sense to keep stative verbs apart, marking them by the special *CaCeC* pattern. Children may perceive *saméax* 'is happy', as less stative than, say, *ra'ev* 'is hungry', and so produce the Transient form *somáxat* 'is happy,Fm' [4;2, SAM], which disappears in view of endstate classification of *saméax* 'is happy' as an adjective. The verb *yoSénet* 'sleeps,Fm' is more stative than *godélet* 'grows up,Fm', and so is less acceptable to the literate adult (Householder's Type 1), whereas inherently durative *godélet* is tolerated, though not always produced, by established adults. At the other end of the continuum, entirely active *lomédet* is the established Standard for the entire population. While the notion of kyriolexia refers to speakers of the Standard sociolect, for these speakers it is enough for a form to cross the middle line of stativeness to be classified as *CoCeC*. Literate speakers are more sensitive to the semantic nuances of this continuum, possibly because they are more familiar with obsolete *CaCeC* forms in texts from various historical periods, as well as because of their preference for markedness.

Table 58. *CaCeC* Verbs: From error to kyriolexia

[State]—————————————————————→ − [State]				
kveda, mele'a heavy, full	*somáxat* glad	*yoSénet** sleeps	*godélet* grows up	*lomédet* studies
Full adjectives No regularization	Transient childish reg.	Type 1 "jarring" deviation	Type 2 "tolerated" deviation	established standard "kyriolexia"

*Given in the feminine form, where the difference between the Normative and Nonstandard is more pronounced (*yeSena/YoSénet* 'she sleeps' vs. *yaSen/yoSen* 'sleeps').

Lexical Exceptions

The lexical exceptions noted below form a subset of the *Lexical Exceptions* category. Here, we deal with only one phenomenon: The type of future-tense pattern assigned to roots in the *Pa'al* verb-pattern, *yi-CCoC* or *yi-CCaC*. The regular form is *yi-CCoC,* e.g. *yi-sgor* 'will-close' and *yi-msor* 'will-pass,Tr'. Roots with a 2nd or 3rd guttural/pharyngeal take the *yi-CCaC* form with the lowered vowel, e.g. *yi-crax* 'will-scream', root ṣ-r-H; *yi-tba* 'will-drown', root T-b- ʕ , *yi-chal* 'will-rejoice', root ṣ-h-l. But a number of non-guttural stems also take this form, e.g. *yi-gdal* 'will-grow', root g-d-l, and *yi-Skav* 'will-lie', root S-k-b. Historically, the split between *yi-CCoC* and *yi-CCaC* verbs was semantically motivated: Active verbs took the *yi-CCoC* form, while stative *CaCeC* verbs took the *yi-CCaC* pattern. Thus statives verbs differed markedly from active verbs in all three finite verb-forms (Bergstrasser 1982). With the disintegration of the class of statives, it lost its unique semantico-morphological character, and the non-guttural *yi-CCaC* future-tense pattern now seems unmotivated, a lexical exception to be learnt by rote. The test-item *loveS* 'wears' is *yi-lbaS* in future-tense. Since it does not contain a guttural, it was construed by the subjects as a lexical exception, and was thus regularized in some cases by children plus older low-SES speakers to *yi-lboS/yi-lvoS*. The fact that this verb is highly familiar, occurring with great frequency, helps to preserve its rote-learned form in the more literate population. It is not however always easy for a native speaker to decide for less frequent verbs which future-tense form they should take, e.g. (Normative) *yicdak* or *yicdok* 'will-be right'. In such cases, literate speakers may be attracted to the *yi-CCaC* marked form, and non-literates to the *yi-CCoC* regular form.

2nd Person Case-Marked Pronouns

Of the three types of prepositions in Modern Hebrew (original, derived and plural), the historically plural prepositions are the most marked, and hence the most salient and accessible, especially through the free form of the preposition, e.g. *axarey* 'after'. As a result, confusion of plural prepositions with the two other types is usually Transient. Distinguishing between original and derived prepositions is much harder, however, especially in the form of the 2nd person feminine singular, e.g. *Sel-ax* 'of-you,Fm' vs. *biSvil-ex* 'for-you,Fm' (derived preposition *biSvil* 'for'). The historical form is not available, so the speaker must arbitrarily choose between *a* and *e*. Choice of a single vowel would simplify the oblique pronouns construction by collapsing two paradigms that differ in three places: 2nd person feminine singular (*-ax/ex*), 1st person plural (*-ánu/énu*) and 3rd person plural (*-am/hem*). As expected, the less literate population chooses the less marked *e*, which occurs in most everyday case-marked pronouns. Out of the 147 Modern Hebrew prepositions listed in Shlesinger (1985), 35 take the 2nd person feminine singular suffix *-ex,* and only five take *-ax* ! True, these five are the most familiar and frequently-occurring prepositions: The Accusative Marker *et, be-* 'in', *le-* 'to', *im* 'with' and *Sel* 'of'. The great majority takes *-ex,* but those few that take *-ax* are acquired early on (Kaplan 1983, Rom & Dgani 1985) and are thus able to resist regularization.

This equilibrium is reflected in the responses to *et* + 2nd person feminine singular, showing regularization only in the low-SES adults. Indeed, the Spontaneous Data show that regularization towards the *-ex* suffix is much more widespread among low-SES adults and high-SES adolescents than revealed in the controlled test situation, e.g. *alex* 'on-you,Fm', for Normative *aláyix; otex* 'Acc-you,Fm', for *otax; itex* 'with-you,Fm', for *itax;* and *elex* 'to-you,Fm' for *eláyix* [32,SAM].

Note, however, that of the five *-ax*-taking prepositions, only two are regularized: *otax* 'Acc-you,Fm' and *itax* 'with-you,Fm'. The other three— *Sel* 'of', *be-* 'in', and *le-* 'to'—never take the form of **Selex, *bex* or **lex* in any age or SES group. I suspect that it is the highly salient *t* at the end of the bound stems *ot-* and *it-* which is perceived as the bound *t* that surfaces in feminine nouns in inflection (and nouns with 2nd person feminine singular possessive inflection always take the pronominal suffix *-ex,* e.g. *mora/moratex* 'teacher/your,Fm-teacher', or *axot/axotex* 'sister/your,Fm sister'). Now consider that those 35 prepositions take the *-ex-* suffix precisely because they are derived, and mostly from nouns, e.g. *le* + *yad-ex* 'beside-you,Fm', from *yad* 'hand', *biSvil-ex* 'for-you,Fm', from *Svil* 'path'. Thus regularization is not indiscriminate, even among children and uneducated adults. As before, the uneducated follow the regular, frequent, unmarked form—but only to a certain extent. Those case-marked pronouns that are construed as having an independent existence by right are "left alone", so to speak. The literate, seeking the marked and the irregular, follow the highly salient *-ax* suffix. Sometimes this may lead to overmarking of *-ex* prepositions with *-ax,* e.g. *eclax* for *eclex* 'at-you,Fm', which is also found in the speech of literate Hebrew speakers.

To conclude this subsection, the Nonstandard deviations revealed in the study are caused by speakers seeking Transparency, Simplicity and Consistency, as before, but not at such a high Cost as childish errors. These deviations are not as radical as those occurring in child language alone, they do not violate typological constraints, and they do not cause opacity in other grammatical subsystems. But they do demonstrate the clash between universal Mapping Preferences, which typically have the effect of simplifying idiosyncrasy and irregularity, and language-specific characteristics that check these simplifying tendencies through the effects of Literacy and the literate propensity towards marked structures. In a sense, the type of grammar that children and low-SES speakers strive towards is "improved" or "simpler" in the sense of Bever & Langendoen (1971).

As such, although these forms are checked by culture-bound principles of Literacy and are regarded by most educated adults as "errors", they constitute a genuine endstate option. They exist alongside the Standard and Normative options, constituting synchronic variation, creeping into the literate sociolect through the unbuttoned language of adolescents. But this is definitely not the only tendency in language change, nor are the uneducated the only initiators and perpetrators of change, as will be shown below.

6.4. AREAS OF LANGUAGE CHANGE

Language Change phenomena are forms which are neither Transient nor regarded by literate native speakers as erroneous. This occurs when the Standard itself has changed. Seeking a combinatorial device of correction (MacWhinney 1978) is inevitable when literate speakers can no longer perceive the motivation for an opaque structure, and there is no option favored by semantic factors. Language Change phenomena are "beneficial" from the viewpoint of the system as a whole: They repair local opacity by therapeutic re-analysis (Lightfoot 1979), bringing the underlying structure sufficiently close to the surface for speakers to perceive it, without causing opacity elsewhere.

Donag-Kinrot (1978) selected the 85% point as "Standard"; in this study, adult literate speakers had to reach ceiling scores (90% and over) for us to determine that Normative requirements and Standard were one and the same. There are two categories (and two items) on this test for which the Standard now deviates from the Norm, where even literate adults were not able to achieve Normative ceiling, constituting the "least stable" of all categories: *Vowel Alternation* and *Verb-Subject Concord;* and two single items: *yaxol* 'can' and *tistakel* 'look'.

Vowel Alternation in *Hif'il*

A very clear finding of this study is the changing standards in *n*-initial and glide-medial roots in *Hif'il* present-tense verbs, where both roots involve the same basic pattern, *mVCiC*, differing in one vowel: *n*-initial roots Normatively take the form of *maCiC,* and glide-medial roots take *meCiC*. Knowing which vowel to use with which root involves the kind of self-conscious, monitored manipulation of root plus pattern in ongoing conversation equivalent to consciously calculating algebraic vectors to find out where a ball is going to land. Besides, even if this were possible, there is no clue as to the weak link in the root: initial *n*- or medial glide. To know which element has failed to surface, one has to know *nikud,* or pointed orthographic vocalization (Masoretic punctuation) which reflects the way the end-of-the-first-millennium scholars construed the phonological system of Biblical Hebrew (Allon 1984, Aronoff 1985). To this day, *nikud* constitutes the motivation for Normative morphophonological behavior of words. Without this knowledge, available only to those specializing in Hebrew grammar, there is no way of knowing that *Hif'il yakir* 'will-recognize', contains a different kind of root (*n-k-r*) from *yakim* 'will-establish', root *q-w-m*, since Modern Hebrew *a* represents two different historical vowels: *qamas* and *pattaH*.[92] Neither *n* nor glide surfaces at any point in the *Hif'il* paradigm: They may or may not surface in some other verb-patterns (e.g. *hipil* 'dropped,Tr' in *Hif'il; nafal* 'fell', *Pa'al*, root *n-p-l*), and often the two structurally related verbs may have drifted apart so they are no longer related semantically. In any event, it is impossible to check the origin of a root in non-monitored on-line free speech. In simple words, in order to know the root, one must know the *Hif'il* vowel, and in order to access the vowel, one must know the root—a no-win situation. This is an example of total opacity, without even one of the forms being more basic or carrying any semantic load. Moreover, this category contains a large number of high frequency verbs. I counted 35 *n*-initial verbs and 70 glide-medial verbs that occur in *Hif'il* in spoken usage, out of more than 100 listed in Goshen-Gottstein et al. (1977), e.g. *n*-initial *hipil* 'dropped,Tr', *higiS* 'served' and *hikir* 'recognized'; and glide-medial *heki* 'vomited', *heziz* 'moved' and *he'ir* 'woke up, Tr'. The fact that these very common and familiar verbs belong to the lexical core of Hebrew means speakers encounter them early on (Bates & MacWhinney 1982) and so are forced to make a choice.

The three options open to speakers here are the following: (i) Choose *a;* (ii) Choose *e;* (iii) Variable rule. To find out which option is favored, I re-analyzed the responses on *e/a* Alternation (see Item Analysis—Appendix C) in terms of the type of vowel chosen by subjects of each test group for each of the four items: *higía* 'reached', root *n-g-y* , and *hipil* 'dropped,Tr', root *n-p-l; herímu* 'raised,Pl', root *r-w-m,* and *heríax* 'smelled', root *r-y-H.* Table 59 below presents the results of this analysis. A clear tendency is revealed: The young subjects consistently select *a* over *e* in their *mVCiC*

Table 59. *e/a* tendencies in *Hif'il*

Percentage of *maCiC* and *meCiC* forms given by the ten test groups on *e/a* Alternation [N = 188]

Group	% of responses* maCiC	meCiC
High SES 3-year-olds	47	10
High SES 5-year-olds	72	18
Low SES 5-year-olds	57	12
High SES 8-year-olds	48	47
High SES 12-year-olds	41	57
Low SES 12-year-olds	51	38
High SES 16-year-olds	53	46
High SES Adults	21	77
Low SES Adults	34	38

*Percentages rounded to the next decimal point

verbs. Thus most of their *n*-initial forms come out Normative, while their glide-medial forms do not. With maturation, the number of *a*-forms declines and that of *e*-forms increases, until they balance out in middle childhood (8 year olds). Verbs in *maCiC* continue to decline until they constitute only a fifth of the responses of the adults, while *meCiC* forms account for close to 80% of the adults' responses. Thus most of the adults' *n*-initial forms come out deviant, while their glide-medial forms come out Normative. The low-SES groups are as usual slower, but follow the same trends. The high-SES 16s, on the other hand, have had their *mVCiC* forms reinforced by formal rote, especially on *n*-initial verbs, as required by the curriculum (Léket 1972), learning each of the most frequent ones by rote for the school-leaving examination in Hebrew Grammar. This accounts for their higher Normative results on the *n*-initial verbs. It would thus be futile to analyze these verbs solely from the viewpoint of normativity, seeing that what is going on here has nothing to do with Norm. I propose the following solution (Table 59): In the younger ages, children go by the general present-tense *Hif'il* vowel *a,* as in *maxtiv* 'dictates', reinforced by the future-tense *yaCiC* shared by all forms (e.g. *yaxtiv* 'will-dictate', *yapil* 'will-drop,Tr', root *n-p-l,* and *yaríax* 'will-smell', root *r-y-H*). Therefore the number of *maCiC* verbs is much higher in the younger groups, with both Normative *magía* 'reaches', root *n-g-y* and deviant *marim* 'picks up', root *r-w-m,* following the general pattern. As speakers mature, this morphophonological class stands out distinctly because of the one missing root radical, and the way to characterize it clearly is with the morphologically marked (but phonetically neutral) *e.* This is illustrated by students' responses to my questions about the degree of acceptability of *meCiC* and *maCiC* forms: they always respond that *mepil* (Normative *mapil*) sounds OK, while *mavi* (Normative *mevi*) is bad.

This is an example of a minor linguistic change in a less salient segment of the grammar—word-internal vowels. As *n*-initial and glide-medial roots in *Hif'il* are so difficult to relate to other occurrences of these roots, there is no danger of this minor vowel-collapse causing complexity or irregularity elsewhere.

Subject-Verb Concord

This category depicts the sharpest picture of disparity between controlled, self-conscious speech under monitored circumstances, as in a test, and informal, colloquial on-line usage (Bailey 1973, Givón 1979b, Ochs 1979). Recall that there are two unmarked word orders in Modern Hebrew: SVC and Predicate-initial. Subject-Verb agreement is performed without fail in SVO structures, but P-initial structures allow an unmarked 3rd person singular predicate nucleus in sentence-initial position (Berman 1980a, Givón 1976) and in some cases permit (or even necessitate) *et* insertion before the definite subject, re-analyzed as a direct object. The only group that stood out by giving more Normative responses to the test items was the school-going population, more subject to normative pressure than adults because of constant criticism from teachers. Since the accepted view of P-initial structures in schools is that they are VSO structures (Agmon-Fruchtman 1980), students are required to adhere to concord rules. Moreover, school-type language usage is often in the written register, hence: "The increased amount of time available to a writer, the editability of writing . . . make it possible for a writer to arrange sequences of idea units in ways that are impossible for a hard-pressed speaker on the run" (Chafe 1985:111).

Thus, when P-initial structures are produced in writing, the writer is able to go back from the noun to the right of the initial predicating nucleus and make sure it agrees with the noun. The young high-SES subjects, bound by the more conservative nature of the written language, were more likely to pay attention to subject-verb concord under the semi-formal circumstances of the test than adults. Many of the morphophonological features that characterized other test categories could not be expressed in writing, since in most cases they involved either vowel alternation (shown only in vocalized script), or stop/spirant alternation (represented by the same letter); whereas subject-verb concord changes the structure of the word by the *addition* of number and gender suffixes, easily perceived in writing.

The re-analysis of presentative subjects as direct objects follows from the typological propensities of Hebrew and is one of the clearest domains of ongoing language change. But at the same time it is a typical marker of monitored vs. non-monitored discourse: It is very common in spoken Hebrew, but rarer in the written register, which allows the writer enough leisure to check agreement. It characterizes to a large extent the unselfconscious language of children and of the less educated who rely heavily on natural dispositions, and to a lesser degree the monitored speech of educated adults, though immediately apparent in their relaxed conversation.

Regularizations

The main concern of this work is with patterns, but a single lexical item may be revealing of general tendencies. Below I discuss two separate lexical items: *yaxol* 'can', and *tistakel* 'look'. They are the only items in their respective categories (Lexical Exceptions and Verb-Governed Prepositions) where prescribed Norm and Standard differ, and so both represent a changing Standard.

yaxol *'Can'*

It would be best to compare *yaxol* to another item in *Lexical Exceptions—yaSna* 'slept,Fm'. Both items indicate changing standards, yet *yoSénet* 'she sleeps' is still perceived by literate speakers as Nonstandard, while *yaxal* 'could' indicates Language Change. The difference can be assessed in terms of Cost.

Both *yoSénet* and Normative *yeSena* represent a class of items which Transparency marks for the state/nonstate distinction. In the case of *yaxol*, Semantic Transparency distinguishes two tense-forms: past and present tense. It seems that separating tenses is more compelling than marking semantic classes separately, being more relevant to the verb in Hebrew (Bybee 1985). The first meets a stronger resistance from Literacy and Markedness. Moreover, *yaxol* is the only representative of a small class of *Pa'al* verbs that took the form *CaCoC* in past and present tense (Bergstrasser 1982, Blau 1981c, Rosén 1956). As such, there is no group coherence to back it up, and the *CaCoC* past/present tense vowel pattern is idiosyncratic in *Pa'al*.

Given this, it is "inexpensive" to follow Transparency in creating a distinct past-tense form in this case: Unlike the childish *miCaCeC* present-tense reanalysis, which, if retained, would obliterate the typical characteristics of a *binyan* pattern, *yaxol* is a single item whose form is atypical anyway, so that there is no danger of creating problems in other systems. One might ask then how speakers tolerate the idiosyncratic form of *yaxol*. My answer would be that it is a highly frequent, familiar, daily verb, whose entire exceptional paradigm is learnt by Rote early on and thus resists change; and it belongs in the ancient paradigm of *Pa'al*, full of exceptional forms (Blau 1981), all learnt by rote early on. Moreover, it is a modal verb, close to adjectives in semantics, and sharing the *CaCoC* pattern with them (compare *gadol* 'big', *yarok* 'green'). To preserve Transparency, speakers choose one of two ways: (i) Many older high-SES subjects (which accounts for the unusually large number of Nonstandard responses in those groups) combine it with the copula *haya* to indicate past tense, treating it like modal adjectives such as *carix* 'should', *muxrax* 'must', while keeping the rote-learned *yaxol* intact. In this way they both eat the cake and still have it: They preserve Transparency while holding on to a marked form. Option (ii) is regularizing past-tense *yaxol* to *yaxal*. This was the option favored by younger and less literate speakers, and again it is successful, since it follows not only Transparency but also Formal Consistency in conforming to the general *Pa'al* past tense pattern (cf. *saraf* 'burned').

This is undoubtedly a case of ongoing change in all age/SES groups. In a sense *yaxal* belongs with other cases of splitting homophonous forms to denote two separate tenses: childish present-tense *mV*- and the diachronic *yaSen/yaSan* 'sleeps/slept' split. The former is not successful because it is too "costly" in terms of causing opacity elsewhere in the system, whereas the latter is established change, since a diminishing class of verbs was regularized against the rest of the verbs in the same paradigm. The case of *yaxol/ yaxal* 'can/could' is similar to the case of *yaSen/yaSan* 'sleeps/slept', as shown in Table 60.

Table 60. Splitting homophonous tense forms

Childish/Transient	Ongoing Change	Established Change
past tense *niCCaC*	*yaxol* 'is able'	*yaSen* 'sleeps'
present tense *miCaCeC*	*haya yaxol/yaxal* 'was able'	*yaSan* 'slept'

tistakel be/al 'Look'

The Verb-Governed Prepositions category is highly stable, due to early rote acquisition. The only exception is *tistakel* 'look'. This verb is Mishnaic, probably borrowed from Aramaic, since it occurs just once in the Bible, in Aramaic, in the Book of Daniel 7,8, with the governed preposition *be-* 'in' (Even Shoshan 1977). Even Shoshan (1979) lists it as *le-histakel be-* 'to-look in', since this is the only preposition governed by *histakel* in all of the Mishnaic examples he cites. But this is not the Standard now. The experimental design is regarded by Landau (1980) as the most reliable way of synchronically testing speakers' knowledge of collocations (1980:96–99). Using this criterion, the Standard form (60–87% of the cases) is *histakel al* 'look on'. As in English *look at her* and *look!*, *histakel* is both transitive, taking a governed object, and a general-purpose intransitive verb. Other options include the Accusative Marker when *tistakel* appears in imperative direct speech in very informal (or childish) colloquial usage, e.g. *staklu et ha-baxur ha-ze!* '(truncated) look Acc this guy!' But the use of *et* is restricted both pragmatically (informal register) and functionally (direct speech, imperative mode). For example, **histakálti et ha-baxur* '(I) looked Acc the-guy' is ungrammatical. Another possibility is a sentential complement, e.g. *histakálnu ex hu metapes al ha-ec* '(we) looked how he climbs on the-tree', which accounted for some of the responses on this item. But the general-purpose preposition in Modern Hebrew, coming up from Non-standard usage, is *al* 'on', which increases the degree of transitivity of the verb (Afek & Kahanman 1985).

In sum: Language change is in most cases inevitable, taking place where change is "cheap" so that no damage is caused outside the subsystem which is re-analyzed. Moreover, such changes are either not resisted by Literacy because the Normative form is inaccessible, or the benefit is so great, and the change so minor, that it is carried out despite Literacy, as in the case of *yaxol/yaxal* 'can/could'.

7

Language Variation
and Language Change:
Some More Answers

It is time to return to the broad research questions that have occupied us in this work. Above I presented a number of questions about the relationship that holds between language-internal factors, such as Opacity, and sociolinguistic factors such as age and literacy, and the way they affect change. We are now in a position to answer these questions and others that constitute the underpinnings of this study. I will do this in the form of question and answer.

Who Initiates (and Perpetuates) Language Change?

Some scholars view children as the principal agents of change (Bach & Harms 1972, Baron 1977, Closs 1965, Halle 1962, Hooper 1979, Jespersen 1922, Kiparsky 1982, Paul 1970, Tanz 1974). Others regard social-class differences and extralinguistic prestige pressures as its main perpetrators (Gal 1978, Householder 1983, Kroch & Small 1978, Labov 1972a, 1980, 1982, Naro & Lemle 1976, Oksaar 1983, Poplack 1980, Sanches 1977, Weinreich, Labov & Herzog 1968). The present study points to the interaction of language-internal factors with cognitive and sociological properties of speakers. Throughout this investigation, we noted that the Nonstandard and Language Change phenomena are not strictly speaking "new." Most correspond to forms already found in Biblical, Mishnaic or Rabbinical sources. Moreover, present-day "errors" have not arisen arbitrarily out of the blue or in response to some foreign influence: Similar forms are noted in early studies of child language in pre-state

Israel (e.g. Avineri 1946, Bar-Adon 1959, Barles 1937, Dolzhansky 1937, Rivkai 1933–34). One of the ways to interpret these facts is to refer to the theory that relates ontogeny and phylogeny (Gould 1977), whose linguistic version would claim that children recapitulate the history of their language in their personal development (Baron 1977). Yet it is not clear how children are supposed to be aware of the history of their language and what theoretical framework could allow this. Moreover, if any recapitulation is done by children, it is not of a particular language but of the development of the general human language-making capacity in generations of children, shaped by the typology of the language involved.

A weaker version would claim that children's reactions to their input are mainly universal in nature. True, they seize upon language-particular elements (such as salient *m-* or *t*) in response to Opacity, but the way in which they respond to surface opacity is the same in all languages (Slobin 1985c). As a result, their errors may indicate ignorance of language-particular features of their mother tongue. This is the main reason why truly childish errors do not participate in language change: they do not "fit in" as well as language-particular (Nonstandard and Language Change) phenomena. While childish errors arise out of universal underpinnings, Nonstandard and Language Change phenomena occur along ancient morphological fault lines (Bates & MacWhinney 1982) that are inherent in Hebrew. Thus it is not children's ontogenetic recapitulating of phylogenetic features that introduces language change, but rather cognitive structures in older children, adolescents, and adults that respond to certain areas of instability in Hebrew.

Low-level erosion of phonetic distinctions between related classes such as ?-final and *y*-final roots, coupled with semantic drift, are natural changes in any living language (Aitchinson 1974, Aronoff 1976, Bybee 1985, Labov 1981, Venemann 1975). Such phonetic and semantic changes are either the product of time, and/or the result of extra-linguistic factors such as cultural and social changes. Speakers react to these temporally and culturally induced non-grammatical changes by inducing grammatical changes following the introduction of opacity-eliminating measures. Hebrew speakers have been reacting to Opacity in the same manner for millennia, producing the same "deviations" along the same morphological fault lines. Thus young children do not cause Language Change: It is the population of older children and naive (both temporarily, as in ongoing conversation and other non-monitored registers, and permanently, as in the less literate section of the population) adult speakers who both provide the pool of possible variation necessary for change and induce change.

Why Indeed Are Naive Speakers More Apt to Produce Deviations Than Others?

Children and uneducated adults produce more deviations because they are linguistically naive, that is they adhere more closely to innate propensities than educated adults. This is due to the fact that only fully literate speakers have access to all possible registers and levels of linguistic usage, are sensitive to school-taught norms and have an enhanced awareness of abstract underlying structures which otherwise appear idiosyncratic. Moreover, naive speakers have less tolerance towards violations of Transparency while literate speakers easily accept the fact that much of language is idiosyncratic and has to be learnt by rote. In Hebrew, moreover, access to the orthography is even more valuable than in many other languages since distinctions are retained in the orthography which have disappeared from the spoken language, and these provide the motivation for the behavior of spoken forms.

Why Are Certain Changes "Successful" Whereas Others Are Blocked?

Certain changes are more successful than others because they are less costly, that is, they cause merely local changes and do not cause trouble in larger systems. Language change occurs only when it is inexpensive and locally beneficial. Otherwise the natural tendency to change is blocked. What holds Language Change at bay is Cost, a factor that weighs the profit from language change against damage to the global system or against the conservative forces of Literacy and markedness.

Why Are Some Changes Restricted to Certain Segments of the Speech Community, Especially Less Educated Speakers and Children, While Others Spread Quickly throughout the Whole Population?

This is, in fact, the motivation for the three types of deviations presented above: Transient deviations consist of costly juvenile adherence to Operating Principles which lessens with maturation and a fuller grasp of general linguistic systems. Transient phenomena represent adherence to Operating Principles at its crudest, with no regard for problems outside the local system being repaired. They are aborted attempts at language change that do not succeed because their initiators do not know enough about their native tongue. These changes thus do not last long enough to influence the language of the present-day generation of adult speakers.

Literacy-related deviations characterize the sociolect spoken by the less literate segment of population which tends towards a shallower grammar, and are usually absent from the language of more literate speakers who are able to perceive deeper relationships which motivate surface phenomena, except in casual, non-monitored speech. Nonstandard phenomena provide a major source of the synchronic variation found in every living language, so that marked, idiosyncratic forms exist side by side with forms adhering to Transparency, Consistency and Simplicity. They constitute language change in action, and may spread from a restricted environment to the general speech community through unselfconscious speech sociolectally typical of the less-educated and registerially of educated but non-monitored speech.

And Language-Change phenomena indicate that it is no longer possible for any non-professionally tutored speaker to discern the underlying representation, so that previously distinct forms merge in the whole population. Such forms represent change in its final stages, where a new kyriolexia is already in existence, and where speakers are no longer aware of any alternative to the form they are using.

What Is an "Error"?

An error, or deviation, assumes a departure from some fixed homogeneous norm in the language. But what if such norms are non-existent? What would be considered an "error" in the fluid, dynamic, synchronically varied language model presented above? Givón (1985) describes this problem in the following terms: "We tend to typologically characterize some version of an official normative grammar of the adult 'language' as described by linguists, then tacitly assume that we have therefore characterized the input. Nothing is further from the truth" (Givón 1985:1007).

As noted above, the official, Normative grammar of Modern Hebrew does not take synchronic variation into account. Moreover, this study has shown that speakers' notion of educated Standard Hebrew is different from that of the Hebrew Language Establishment. A solution is suggested by Ochs's (1985) scalar characterization of "errors" along the following lines: "Types of error in the language of young children can be distinguished in terms of whether or not the "error" exists as a variant in the adult speech community and if so, the value attached to that variant by the community" (Ochs 1985:784). From this perspective, an error in Modern Hebrew would first and foremost be a childish error, a Transient phenomenon. This study indicates that juvenile deviations are rejected as such by speakers of all backgrounds. They are indeed errors, since they violate typological maxims of Hebrew, such as its bound morphological structure, and major typological patterning such as consonantal root and affixal patterns.

In contrast, Nonstandard deviations, let alone Language Change phenomena, can hardly be counted as "errors." (In a community without the pressures of literacy, scholarly and academics which promote standardization, their effect would be one and same!) They often involve variations in stem-internal vowels, repeatedly shown to carry less weight in Hebrew than consonants or stem-external vowels. Moreover, they have a language-internal basis, being due to the gradual attrition of (mainly) phonological distinctions between classes of segments, which has undermined the motivation for morphophonological alternations, attested to in Biblical and Mishnaic sources. Such processes were further accelerated by special circumstances attending the revival of Hebrew as a spoken language. Recall that high- and low-SES speakers sometimes apply different strategies to solve the same problem. For example, children and uneducated adults resolve the phonetic identity of *Het-* and *xaf*-derived *x* by regularizing to the general *é-e* structure (e.g. *lokéxet* for *lokáxat* 'takes,Fm', root *l-q-H*), whereas literate adults are attracted to the more marked *a-a* sequence (producing colloquial *doráxat* for *doréxet* 'steps,Fm', root *d-r-k*). The first type of *x*-treatment is rejected as an "error" by the literate adult community, while the second may pass unnoticed. But the only difference is sociolinguistic in nature—which variant is predominant in the prestige dialect (Labov 1972a). For the linguist, then, Nonstandard and Language Change phenomena are both grammatical manifestations of Modern Hebrew, each acceptable in its respective sociolect, and they share a large area of overlap where they differ merely in quantity.

Language, Literacy, Register

In conclusion, I would like to present a triangular model of the interactive relationships which determine the occurrence of Liteacy and Language-Change phenomena (see above). This model has three foci, which relate to three different facets of the interaction that leads to language change: The first focus is on *Speaker:* Specifically, it is his/her *age* and *sociolect,* or the SES background that determines the amount of material resources dedicated in the home and in the educational system to fostering Literacy. Older, more literate speakers can handle language opacity more easily than younger and less educated ones. The second variable is the *Register,* a situational component that determines the *degree of linguistic control* the speaker is able to exercise on linguistic performance. The more detached, less intimate, threatening or upsetting the situation, the easier will it be for the speaker to handle opacity. Finally, there is the third locus of *Language* itself, the degree of *linguistic opacity,* or the extent to which the underlying structure is accessible to the speaker. When opacity crosses a certain boundary, neither personal capacities nor linguistic control can check the reanalysis of linguistic components that we term language change. These three factors constitute the mechanism that governs language variation and language change (Table 61).

Table 61. Language, Literacy, Register

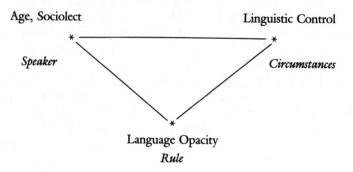

Age, Sociolect   Linguistic Control

Speaker   *Circumstances*

Language Opacity
Rule

Notes

1. According to Sivan (1976) 66% of the words in Contemporary Hebrew are Biblical; 14% are Mishnaic; 4% are Medieval; 16% are Modern Hebrew innovations.

2. The pronunciation adopted eventually was a combination of the Sephardic and Ashkenazi pronunciations (Avineri 1964, Rosén 1956, Wexler 1990).

3. Moreover, we cannot be sure about the Biblical phonological system, since the *nikud* vocalizing apparatus is a creation of the end of the first millennium, and is thus an approximation only of Classical phonetics (Klar 1951).

4. This term, a euphemism for the underpriviledged section of Israeli society, which especially denotes children, was coined in the early 1970s with the increasing awareness of the disparity between social classes in Israel, often motivated by ethnic background.

5. The only exceptions are Donag-Kinrot (1978), Nahir (1978) and Schwarzwald (1981).

6. Which is why playing Scrabble in Hebrew is no big deal.

7. In order to prevent such ambiguity, nonvocalized spelling uses the letter ו to indicate the vowels *o* and *u*, and ' to indicate the vowel *i*, as in קידם kidem, קודם *kodem, Kódem, kudam.*

8. However, these specific forms continue to be taught and drilled for the school-leaving examination and are part of the Hebrew curricula for teachers' colleges.

9. See a list of authors in Ravid (1988).

10. See a list of authors in Ravid (1988).

11. The singular form of 'mattress' favored by the HLE is *mizran,* but it is hardly ever used.

12. A mother tongue: A language acquired in childhood up to puberty in natural settings without formal instruction.

13. Special circular #10, issued by the Director General of the Ministry of Education, Jerusalem, May 1980.

14. "Oriental" is used in Israel in the sense of Mideastern, North African extraction.

15. Actually, *menumas* is an existent word meaning 'polite' (cf. *nimus* 'manners').

16. Nouns optionally take pronominal endings signifying possession, e.g. *giSa/ giSatxa* 'approach/your approach'. This option is limited to the written literate mode, although a number of formulaic expressions in daily interaction such as *tori* 'my turn', *axoto* 'his sister' are used colloquially.

17. 19 out of 61 items, 3 out of 10 test categories.

18. Vowel length is debatable. Qualitative distinctions between *serey/segol*, *pattaH/qamas* were neutralized as well.

19. The 3 mid/low vowels (*e,o,a*) are denoted by at least 3 diacritic forms, signifying three historical quantities: A long, short and very short vowel. In some cases (e.g. *o*), there is special vocalization for a very long vowel as well.

20. The letter *he* represents *two* historical phonemes: (i) the root-final glide *y*, which deleted between vowels, as in the root *g-b-y* 'collect money', and (ii) true *h*, as in *g-b-h* 'grow taller'. At word-final position, the two forms merge due to loss of word-final true *h*, as in *gava* 'collected money/grew taller'. In word-medial position the difference between historical *y* and true *h* is more pronounced: *gavita* '(you) collected money' vs. *gavahta* '(you) grew taller'.

21. As a rule roots with a medial letter *waw* would be represented with a medial underlying glide, e.g. *q-w-m* for *kam/yakum* 'rose/will rise', however *k-v-n* is a new root deriving (by sophisticated derivation) from words containing the old *k-w-m* root such as *naxon* 'ready, right'. As a new root it occurs only in *Pi'el, Pu'al* and *Hitpa'el*, and the middle radical is always consonantal (Ravid 1990).

22. *?*-final and *y*-final roots have alternated in Hebrew since Mishnaic times. The root *q-r-?* 'call,read' yields two perfect forms: *karu* 'guest = one who has been called' and *karuy*, analogous to *y*-final forms (e.g. *panuy* 'unoccupied' root *p-n-y*), meaning 'named'.

23. The HLE form is *li-rkov*, but it is not in use.

24. The *e* following the initial *m*- is an epenthetic vowel inserted to break a cluster beginning with a sonorant (compare *kxulim* 'blue,Pl', *Svurim* 'broken,Pl').

25. The Nonstandard sociolect marks the durative, e.g. *ani hayíti oxel* 'I was eating' vs. *axálti* which is ambiguous between 'I ate' and 'I was eating', but this distinction is not found in the established sociolect (though *ani hayíti oxel* is Standard in *kSe-gárnu be-Yahud hayíti oxel kol yom be-mis'ada aravit* 'When (we) lived in Yehud (I) used to eat every day in an Arabic restaurant'). The durative/nondurative distinction is made in the literate dialect in temporal clauses on a high register, typical of formal usage, e.g. *bihiyoto oxel* 'while being in the state of eating'. A distinction is also made between the perfective and the non-perfective in passive forms, e.g. *nixtav* 'is being written' vs. *katuv* 'is written'. However these are all peripheral to Hebrew, and as a rule Hebrew does not inflect verbs for aspect (Rosén 1956).

26. *Ába* 'dad' is a colloquial form, a sort of diminutive for *av* 'father' (compare *em/íma* 'mother/mummy'). In the same way *sába* is the familiar, colloquial form for *sav* 'grandfather'.

27. I did not give the feminine plural form of the 2nd and 3rd person (*et-xen, ot-an* respectively), which rarely occur in spoken Hebrew (Levy 1982).

28. The Normative form is *et-xem*, but it rarely occurs in spoken Hebrew.

29. In fact, there are possible forms: Normative *mi-kem* and *me-itxem* and Nonstandard but widespread *mim-xem*.

30. Another possible form is *me-itam*.

31. In this case, three verbs have no Nonstandard correspondents: *tetapel* 'treat', *tarbic* 'hit', *tefaxed* 'be afraid', *tix'as* 'be angry'.

32. This category had a statistical "freak" item (no 27 in Appendix B), *higía* 'arrived', which was found to bear almost no statistical relationship to any other item on the test. When this one item is eliminated, the reliability of *Hif'il* Vowel Alternation rises to 0.67. From the point of view of formal structure this stem is, however, a typical example of *n*-initial defective roots, and is very common in everyday use.

33. ˆ indicates the construct state, where the first element often undergoes formal change, e.g. *mila/milatˆkavod* 'word/ wordˆ(of) honor'. Here, *Snáyim* 'two' changes its form to *Sneyˆ* in the construct state.

34. Where there was no single common deviation, the least marked inflected form was chosen as the Expected response, Following the Principle of Formal Simplicity (Clark 1980, 1981), as in *bat/batot* (Normative *banot*) 'girl/s'.

35. See Ravid (1988) for a detailed report of the test results.

36. Beta weights indicate the relative importance of the independent variables in predicting Normative scores.

37. Multiple R^2 equals the amount of variance explained by age and SES, and their interaction.

38. However, in Verb-Governed prepositions the overall score for the older, more literate population is lower than in Stem Change, due to one specific item (*tiStameS* 'use') which is undergoing radical language change.

39. The situation, however, is more complex, as becomes evident in my later discussion of language-change phenomena.

40. For each example, the specific age by year and month is given in square brackets. For instance, [3;8,SAM] refers to a recorded sample of the free speech usage of a child aged 3 years and 8 months.

41. However, the last two Lexical Exceptions items required the task of changing a verb into future-tense, accounting for the lower amount of Appropriate responses on this category.

42. Durative aspect may be marked in Nonstandard, e.g. *hu haya oxel kSe-hi bá'a* 'he *was eating* when she came'.

43. The past-tense of *mefaxed* 'fears', *pixed* 'feared', is absent in the Normative lexicon, so this form is Nonstandard in addition to the spirantization error.

44. The situation at the time of the revision of this work (1992) has changed, however, with the influx of about 400,000 ex-Soviet immigrants to Israel, many of whom are older people.

45. The Italian plural suffix *-i* resembles the Hebrew plural suffix *-im*, therefore *macaroni* in Hebrew is usually *makaronim*.

46. I myself used the same tactic in administering the last items of the test to young children under 6, asking about the Masculine form of domestic animals using the words *íma* 'mummy' and *ába* 'daddy', e.g. *hine íma para, u-mi ze? ze ába.* . . . 'Here's mummy-cow, and who's this? This is daddy. . . .'

47. *marim* 'picks us' in itself is a Normatively deviant form of the *Hif'il* Vowel Alternation type.

48. *kafu* 'frozen' also contains a spirant alternant of *p*, which occurs in the cue-item *hikpía* '(she) froze', and an open final syllable, deriving from the root *q-p-?*.

49. The picture-card showed a birthday cake with candles on it.

50. Actually, there are 4 possible types of language change, using 2 parameters: phonetic vs. lexical change, and abrupt vs. gradual change, so that change can be, for example, lexically abrupt or gradual, phonetically abrupt or gradual.

51. Metathesis probably started out as a phonetically conditioned rule. The rule must have morphologized later.

52. Metathesis is followed by a rule of voicing assimilation when the metathesizing radical is *z*, e.g. /hitzaken/ ———> /hiztaken/ ———> *hizdaken* 'got old'. A historical rule of emphatic assimilation left its impression in the orthography, so that the -*t*- in the verb *hictaref* 'joined' is spelled with *T* (*TeT*), formerly an emphatic dental stop (Blau 1981c, Ornan 1983).

53. A small class of *y*-initial verbs, where the initial radical *y*- is followed by *ṣ* and then by a third radical belonging to a restricted class of 6 consonants, conjugates like *n*-initial roots, e.g. *nibat* 'looked on', root *n-b-T*, and *nicav* 'stood guard', root *y-ṣ-b* ; or *makir* 'knows', root *n-k-r*, and *macig* 'performs', root *y-ṣ-g* (Blau 1981c).

54. My young son Itamar (3;8) corrects me every time I read a story to him in which the form *biglalex* 'because of you,Fm' occurs—he protests loudly and insists on childish *biglalax*.

55. Word-initial clusters which start with gutturals or pharyngeals are impossible in Hebrew, and a low vowel is inserted to break them up, hence the plural form *xadar-im* 'rooms'.

56. *CéCeC/CóCeC* and *CiCCa/CaCCa* alloforms with roots containing low gutturals or pharyngeals have lower vowels, e.g. *kémax* 'flour', root *q-m-H*, *bóhak* 'brilliance', root *b-h-q; emda* 'position', root *y-m-d*, *lahaka* 'group', root *l-h-q*.

57. Word-initial clusters cannot start with a sonorant element, hence *re'al-im* 'poisons'.

58. *CéCi/CCi* and *CóCi* alloforms of *CéCeC* and *CóCeC* respectively have *y*-final roots, e.g. *béxi/bxi* 'crying', root *b-k-y*, *Sóvi* 'worth', root *S-W-y*.

59. *CáyiC* alloforms derive from glide-medial roots, e.g. *Sáyit* 'cruise', root *S-w-T*.

60. Normatively *góvah*, root *g-b-h*, with a true *h* rather than the more common root-final -*y*, which also appears in the written form as *he*, e.g. root *g-b-y* 'collect money'.

61. The additional root radical in brackets signifies an underlying middle geminate radical, accounting for the non-reduction of the first *a* in plural forms of these patterns (Berman 1981c, Rosén 1956, Ornan 1973). Compare *davar/dvarim* 'thing/s', root *d-b-r*, noun pattern *CaCaC*, with *davar/davarim* 'postman/postmen', root *d-w-r*, noun pattern *CaC(C)aC*.

62. When my older children were 3;2 and 2;1 respectively, the younger boy said, looking at a row of streetlights, *hine orot* 'here (are) lights,Fm'. This was the correct form, *orot* being an exceptional form of a masculine noun *or* taking a feminine plural suffix -*ot*. The older girl immediately said *hine orim* 'here (are) lights,Masc.', a deviant form. Obviously, the younger child was using rote-learned information, while the older one was working by rule [*OBS*].

63. This verb, like the other verbs bearing negative semantic content in this category (*tefaxed, tix'as* 'be afraid, be angry') were presented in negative form so as to enable the child to generate a well-formed sentence (one cannot be commanded to be afraid and to be angry) as well as to maintain an agreeable atmosphere.

64. An older high-SES subject gave me, though, three alternative literary forms, all meaning 'rooster': *sexvi, kore, géver*.

65. In fact, this girl performed a change in the stem (*cel/cil-im* 'shadow/s') which shows an awareness of the underlying structure: the vowel change from *e* to *i* is typical of the underlying "double" root *s-l-l* (cf. *xec/xic-im* 'arrow/s', root *H-s-s*).

66. The northern city Haifa is surrounded by a number of satellite-towns, called *krayot*, literally 'towns', e.g. *Kiryat-Hayim, Kiryat-Bialik, Kiryat-Ata* etc. They are often called simply *ha-krayot* 'the-towns'.

67. As far as I can remember, backformed *klaya* was the common form up to about fifteen years ago, since the basic form of 'kidneys' was the plural one. However, recently it has given way back to Normative *kilya*, due to the invention and use of *ha-kilya ha-melaxutit* 'the artificial kidney = the dialysis machine', and *haStalat kilya* 'kidney transplantation'—both of which focus on singular *kilya*.

68. This observation has no grounds in Normative distinctions.

69. In fact, *vilon* is marked for a minor rule which attaches the feminine plural suffix *-ot* to masculine nouns ending in *-on* and *-an*, e.g. *xalon-ot* 'windows', *Sulxan-ot* 'tables'.

70. I have a rare and interesting example from my youngest child, Itamar, who at the age of 2;3 said *mazuz* '(is) moving' for adult *zaz*, root *z-w-z*, following precisely the same road as described above for *Pi'el* verbs, so that he created the following paradigm for 'move' in *Pa'al*: Past-Tense *zaz*; Present-Tense *mazuz*; Future-Tense *yazuz*.

71. Childish *marim*.

72. *mesim*, root *s-y-m*, does exist in *Hif'il*, however its use is mostly formulaic in collocation meaning 'pretend', e.g. *hesim acmo ke-lo Some'a* 'pretended not to hear'. This is formal, even literary Hebrew, and for the young child, non-existent.

73. A high-school teacher of Hebrew grammar told me that her students were amazed to learn that *yaxal* was 'not correct'.

74. In fact, *CCuC(C)-*, since the radical next to the *u-* becomes double; or alternatively *CCuC-* (if the last radical is *b/p/k*, it becomes a stop, as in *cahov/cehuba* 'yellow,Fm'.

75. This does not mean, however, that the *o/u* alternation occurs only in color *CaCoC*; rather, it is found in other *o*-forms with underlying "double" roots (e.g. *tof/ tupim*, 'drum/s', root *t-p-p*, *ma'oz/mauzim* *y-z-z* 'military outposts').

76. I have checked these forms in large classes of students, including those specializing in Hebrew grammar. Less than 1% of these literate native speakers are aware of the Normative forms, since these rare words are even rarer in inflection, and are learnt *from non-vocalized written texts* which do not make explicit the distinction between *u* and *o*.

77. Radical nouns are those noun patterns that start with the initial root radical, e.g. *CéCeC, CCaC, CaCaC*, as opposed to those patterns that start with prefixes, e.g. *tiCCóCet, maCCeC*, etc. (Avineri 1976).

78. For a fuller discussion of the Backformation category items, see Ravid (to appear).

79. A radical *t* is also possible, as in *taskit* 'radio play', root *s-k-t*.

80. I should say *used to occur*, for in the few years since the study was carried out records and record players have disappeared, to yield their places to tape recorders, cassettes and disc players!

81. I thank Eduardo Feingold for these examples.

82. In fact, *ze* 'this' differs from the other items of this category in being deictic and non-predicating. It was included among the test items since it manifests the

same type of lack of agreement as the predicating elements represented by the other members of this test category.

83. Past and future-tense verbs agree with their subjects in number, gender and person, e.g. *nixáSti, nixaSt* 'I-guessed, You,Fm-guessed'. Present-tense verbs and other elements agree in number and gender, e.g. *ani/at/hi oxélet* 'I,Fm/you,Fm/she is-eating'.

84. *CaC(C)aC* allows introducing another root radical if the root is quadri-literal, e.g. *zamar* 'singer', root *z-m-r*, *sartat* 'draftsman', root *s-r-T-T*.

85. The Normative form is *sane*.

86. *alóhi* is childish *aléha* 'on-me' (also occurs as 'on-her'); but it occurred as 'on-him' in a Hebrew dialect of the 4/5th century A.D., evidenced in the Dead Sea Scrolls (Kutscher 1959).

87. *meitánu* 'from-us' is interesting, a suppletive form meaning literally 'from-with-us'. The 'with' *im* paradigm uses a suppletive stem *it-*, e.g. *itxem* 'with-you,Pl', which is also used in *meitánu*.

88. In fact, the Normative form does nor exist any more: nobody says *mile* 'filled', except for Hebrew language specialists. The ubiquitous form is *mila*.

89. Normatively, this process is limited to non-verbs, that is, to nouns, adjectives and present-tense (*benoni*) verbs, e.g. *motéax* 'stretching,Tr', *mitmatéax* 'stretching,Int', but Normative *hitmatax* 'stretched,Int', root *m-t-H*.

90. See Item-Analysis for the results of *mefazéret* '(she) scatters', with root-initial *p-*: in the low-SES adult group, 65% gave the Expected deviant form *fizra* for Normative *pizra* 'she scattered'.

91. While my subjects had to grammatically manipulate a given form, Schwarz-wald's had to read a given verb, often so rare it was a nonce form for them (e.g. *puxsam* 'was chewed'). In the common verbs, her subjects had a base form to relate to in their linguistic competence, but this was not the case in the nonce verbs. I believe that the psycholinguistic process involved in natural production is closer to my test procedure.

92. In fact, *qamaṣ* itself stands for two kinds of *a:* An originally long *a*, as in *lakóax* 'customer', which does not delete (cf. plural *lakoxot*), and another *a*, which deletes when unstressed (e.g. *Sakuf/Skufa* 'transparent/Fm').

References

Adams, V. 1973. *An Introduction to Modern English Word-Formation*. London: Longman.

Afek, E., & I. Kahanman. 1985. The function of *al* 'on' in Israeli Hebrew. *Leshonenu La'am* 35:2, 3–4, 8–10. [in Hebrew]

Agmon-Fruchtman, M. 1980. *Hebrew Syntax*. Tel-Aviv: UPP. [in Hebrew]

Aitchison, J. 1974. Phonological change: some causes and constraints. In: J. M. Anderson & C. Jones (eds.) *Historical Linguistics. Vol III: Theory and Description in Phonology*. Amsterdam: North-Holland.

Akademia, 1950. Establishing the Academy for the Hebrew Language: Protocol of the General Assembly. [in Hebrew]

Aksu-koc, A., & D. I. Slobin. 1985. Acquisition of Turkish. In D. I. Slobin (ed.). *The Cross-Linguistic Study of Language Acquisition*. Hillsdale, N.J.: Lawrence Ehrlbaum, Associates.

Algrably, M. 1975. Measures for sociological characterization and budgeting of schools. *Megamot* 21:219–227. [in Hebrew]

Allon, E. 1984. Reading non-vocalized Hebrew. Doctoral dissertation, Tel-Aviv University. [in Hebrew]

Alvarez Nazario, N. 1961. El elemento afronegroide en el Espanol de Puerto Rico. San Juan, ms.

Andersen, H. 1973. Abductive and deductive change. *Language* 49:765–793.

Andersen, H. 1974. Toward a typology: Bifurcating changes and binary relations. In: J. M. Anderson & C. Jones (eds.) *Historical Linguistics*. Amsterdam: North-Holland.

Anderson, J. R. 1983. *The Architecture of Cognition*. Cambridge: Cambridge University Press.

Anderson, J. R., P. J. Kline & C. Lewis. 1977. A production system model for language processing. In P. Carpenter & M. Just (eds.) *Cognitive Processes in Comprehension*. Hillsdale, N.J.: Lawrence Erlbaum.

Anderson, L. 1982. The 'perfect' as a universal and as a language-particular category. In P. Hopper (ed.) *Tense and Aspect*. Amsterdam: John Benjamins.

Anisfeld, M., & G. R. Tucker. 1968. English pluralization rules of six-year-old children. *Child Development* 38:1201–1217.

Antinucci, F., & R. Miller. 1976. How children talk about what happened. *Journal of Child Language* 3:167–189.

Ariel, S. 1971. Active, Passive, Reflexive and Reciprocal sentences in spoken Hebrew. *Hebrew Computational Linguistics* 3:67–82. [in Hebrew]

Aronoff, M. 1976. *Word Formation in Generative Grammar*. Cambridge, Mass.: The MIT Press.

Aronoff, M. 1985. Orthography and linguistic theory: the syntactic basis of Masoretic Hebrew punctuation. *Language* 61:28–72.

Attias, T. 1981. Adjective order in Israeli Hebrew. M.A. thesis, Tel-Aviv University.

Avineri, I. 1946. *The Conquests of Modern Hebrew*. Merchavia: Sifriyat Hapo'alim. [in Hebrew]

Avineri, I. 1964. *Yad Halashon*—A Lexicon of Linguistic ProblemsTel Aviv: Izre'el. [in Hebrew]

Avineri, I. 1976. *The Palace of Patterns*. Tel Aviv: Izre'el. [in Hebrew]

Avrunin, A. 1924. Correcting children's language. *Hachinuch* 4, 5, 7. [in Hebrew]

Azar, M. 1972. A study of governing verbs. *Leshonenu* 36:282–286, 220–227. [in Hebrew]

Bach, E., & R. T. Harms. 1972. How do languages get crazy rules? In R. P. Stockwell & R. K. S. McCaulay (eds.) *Linguistic Change and Generative Theory*. Bloomington, Ind.: Indiana University Press.

Bachi, R. 1957. Statistics of the revival of Hebrew. *Leshonenu* 20:65–82; 21:41–68. [in Hebrew]

Badri, F. 1983. Acquisition of lexical derivation rules in Moroccan arabic. Doctoral dissertation, UC Berkeley.

Bailey, C-J. N. 1973. *Variation and Linguistic Theory*. Arlington, Virginia: Center for Applied Linguistics.

Bar-Adon, A. 1959. The spoken language of Israeli children. Doctoral dissertation, Hebrew University. [in Hebrew]

Bar-Adon, A. 1963a. The language of the young generation as an object for study. *Hachinuch* 35/a:21–35. [in Hebrew]

Bar-Adon, A. 1963b. Urban and rural child language. *Leshonenu La'am* 14:21–28. [in Hebrew]

Bar-Adon, A. 1967. The vocabulary of Israeli children. *Leshonenu La'am* 18:35–64. [in Hebrew]

Bar-Adon, A. 1971. "Analogy" and analogic change as reflected in contemporary Hebrew. In A. Bar-Adon & W. F. Leopold (eds.) *Child Language: A Book of Readings*. Englewood Cliffs, N.J.: Prentice-Hall.

Bar-Adon, A. 1975. *The Rise and Decline of a Dialect: A Study in the Revival of Modern Hebrew*. Mouton: The Hague.

Bar-Adon, A. 1977. *Shay Agnon and the Revival of Hebrew*. Jerusalem: The Bialik Institute. [in Hebrew]

Baratz, J. C. 1970. Teaching reading in an urban Negro school system. In

F. Williams (ed.) *Language and Poverty: Perspectives on a Theme*. New York: Academic Press.

Barkai, M. 1972. Problems in the phonology of Hebrew. Doctoral dissertation, University of Illinois, Urbana.

Barkali, S. 1962. *Verb Table*. Jerusalem: Mass. [in Hebrew]

Barles, A. 1937. The language of children. *Leshonenu* 8:185–198. [in Hebrew]

Baron, N. 1977. *Language Acquisition and Historical Change*. Amsterdam: North-Holland.

Bates, E., & B. MacWhinney. 1982. Functionalist approaches to grammar. In E. Wanner & L. R. Gleitman (eds.).

Bauer, L. 1983. *English Word-Formation*. Cambridge: Cambridge University Press.

Ben Asher, M. 1969. *The Consolidation of Normative Grammar in Modern Hebrew*. Tel Aviv: Hakibbutz Hame'uchad. [in Hebrew]

Ben Asher, M. 1973. *Modern Hebrew Syntax*. Tel Aviv: Hakibbutz Hame'uchad. [in Hebrew]

Ben Asher, M. 1974. Prepositions in Modern Hebrew. *Leshonenu* 38:285–294. [in Hebrew]

Ben Hayyim, Z. 1953. An old language in a new reality. *Leshonenu La'am* 4:35–37. [in Hebrew]

Ben Hayyim, Z. 1955. Describing spoken Hebrew. *Tarbitz* 24:337–342. [in Hebrew]

Ben Hayyim, Z. 1985. The historical unity of Hebrew. In M. Bar-Asher (ed.) *Studies in Language 1*. Jerusalem: Hebrew University. [in Hebrew]

Ben Horin, G. 1976. Aspects of syntactic preposing in Modern Hebrew. In P. Cole (ed.) *Studies in Modern Hebrew Syntax and Semantics*. Amsterdam: North-Holland.

Ben Horin, G., & S. Bolozky. 1972. Hebrew *bkp*—rule opacity or data opacity? *Hebrew Computational Linguistics* 5:E24–E35.

Ben Tolila, Y. 1984. *The Pronunciations of Hebrew: Social Phonology*. Jerusalem: Hebrew University. [in Hebrew]

Ben Yehuda, N., & D. Ben Amotz. 1973. *Dictionary of Spoken Hebrew*. Jerusalem: Levin-Epstein. [in Hebrew]

Bendavid, A. 1967. *Biblical Hebrew and Mishnaic Hebrew*. Tel Aviv: Dvir. [in Hebrew]

Bendavid, A., & H. Shay. 1974. *A Linguistic Guide for Radio and T.V.*. Jerusalem: Training Center. [in Hebrew]

Bentur, E. 1978. Some effects of orthography on the linguistic knowledge of Hebrew speakers. Doctoral dissertation, University of Illinois, Urbana.

Bereiter, C., & S. Engleman. 1966. *Teaching Disadvantaged Children in the Pre-school*. Englewood Cliffs, N.J.: Prentice-Hall.

Bergstrasser, G. 1982. *Grammar of Hebrew*. Jerusalem: Magnes. [in Hebrew]

Berko, J. 1958. The child's learning of English morphology. *Word* 14:150–177.

Berkowitz, R. & M. Wigodski. 1979. On interpreting non-coreferent pronouns: A longitudinal study. *Journal of Child Language* 6:585–592.

Berlowitch, Y. 1964. Hebrew slang. *Am Vasefer* 26/27:14–17. [in Hebrew]

Berman, R. A. 1975a. How verbs, roots and *binyanim* are entered in the lexicon. In U. Ornan & B.-Z. Fischler (eds.) *Sefer Rosen*. Jerusalem: Hamo'atza Lehanchalat Halashon. [in Hebrew]

Berman, R. A. 1975b. The realization of syntactic processes in the *binyan* system. *Hebrew Computational Linguistics* 9:25–39. [in Hebrew]

Berman, R. A. 1978a. *Modern Hebrew Structure*. Tel Aviv: University Publishing Projects.

Berman, R. A. 1978b. How a child uses her first words. *International Journal of Psycholinguistics* 5:1–25.

Berman, R. A. 1979. Form and function: Impersonals, passives and middles in Modern Hebrew. *BLS* 5:1–27.

Berman, R. A. 1980a. The case of an (S)VO language: Subjectless constructions in Modern Hebrew. *Language* 56:759–776.

Berman, R. A. 1980b. Child language as evidence for grammatical description: preschoolers' construal of transitivity in the Hebrew verb system. *Linguistics* 18:667–701.

Berman, R. A. 1981a. Regularity vs. anomaly: the acquisition of Hebrew inflectional morphology. *Journal of Child Language* 8:265–282.

Berman, R. A. 1981b. Language development and language knowledge: evidence from the acquisition of Hebrew morphophonology. *Journal of Child Language* 9:169–190.

Berman, R. A. 1981c. Children's regularizations of plural forms. *Stanford Papers and Reports on Child Language Development* 20:34–44.

Berman, R. A. 1982a. Verb-pattern alternation: the interface of morphology, syntax and semantics in Hebrew child language. *Journal of Child Language* 9:169–190.

Berman, R. A. 1982b. Early discourse: the stories of a six-year-old. In S. Bloom-Kolka et al. (eds.) *Studies in Discourse*. Jerusalem: Akademon. [in Hebrew]

Berman, R. A. 1983. Establishing a schema: children's construal of verb-tense marking. *Language Sciences* 5:61–78.

Berman, R. A. 1984a. From nonanalysis to productivity: interim schema in child language. *Working Paper #31*. Tel Aviv University Unit for Human Development and Education.

Berman, R. A. 1984b. On the study of first language acquisition. In A. Z. Guiora (ed.) *An Epistemology for the Language Sciences*. Detroit: Wayne State University Press.

Berman, R. A. 1985. Acquisition of Hebrew. In D. Slobin (ed.) *The Cross-linguistic Study of Language Acquisition*. Hillsdale, N.J.: Lawrence Erlbaum.

Berman, R. A. 1986a. A step-by-step model of language acquisition. In I. Levin (ed.) *Stage and Structure: Re-opening the Debate*. Norwood, N.J.: Ablex.

Berman, R. A. 1986b. A crosslinguistic perspective: morphology/syntax. In P. Fletcher & M. Garman (eds.).

Berman, R. A. 1986c. Cognitive components of language development. In C. Pfaff (ed.) *First and Second Language Acquisition Processes*. Rowley, Mass.: Newbury House.

Berman, R. A. 1987a. Hebrew construct state structures. Talk given at Theoretical Linguistics conference, May, Bar Ilan.

Berman, R. A. 1987b. Studying and teaching Modern Hebrew. *Prakim* 7:84–96. [in Hebrew]

Berman, R. A. 1987c. Productivity in the lexicon: New-word formation in Modern Hebrew. *Folia Linguistica* 21:225–254.

Berman, R. A. 1988. On the ability to relate events in narrative. *Discourse Processes* 11:469–497.

Berman, R. A. 1989. Children's knowledge of verb structure: data from Hebrew. Paper given at Boston University Conference on Language Development, October 1989.

Berman, R. A. 1990a. On new-root formation in Hebrew: a psycholinguistic view. Paper given at Workshop on Modern Hebrew, Israel Theoretical Linguistics Society, Hebrew University, Jerusalem, February 1990.

Berman, R. A. 1990b. On acquiring an (S)VO language: subjectless sentences in children's Hebrew. *Linguistics* 28:1135–1166.

Berman, R. A. 1992a. Child language and language change. In U. Ornan, R. Ben-Shachar & G. Turi (eds.) *Hebrew: A Living Language*. Haifa: Haifa University Press. [in Hebrew]

Berman, R. A. 1992b. The development of language use: Expressing perspectives on a scene. In E. Dromi (ed.) *Language and Cognition: A Developmental Pespective*. Norwood, N.J.: Ablex Publications.

Berman, R. A. 1993. Marking of verb transitivity by Hebrew-speaking children. *Journal of Child Language* 20:641–669.

Berman, R. A., & E. V. Clark. 1989. Learning to use compounds for contrast. *First Language* 9:247–270.

Berman, R. A., & E. Dromi. 1984. On marking time without aspect in child language. *Papers and Reports on Child Language Development* 23:23–32.

Berman, R. A., & D. Ravid. 1986. Lexicalization of compound nouns. *Hebrew Computational Linguistics* 24:5–22. [in Hebrew]

Berman, R. A., & I. Sagi. 1981. On early word formation. *Hebrew Computational Linguistics* 18:32–62. [in Hebrew]

Bernstein, B. A. 1960. Language and social class. *British Journal of Sociology* 11:271–76.

Bernstein, B. A. 1964. Elaboratedand restricted codes: their social origins and some consequences. In J. J. Gumperz & D. Hymes (eds.) *The Ethnography of Communication (American Anthropologist* 66:6, part 2, 55–69).

Bernstein, B. A. 1970. A sociolinguistic approach to socialization with some reference to educability. In F. Williams (ed.).

Bernstein, B. A. 1975. Language and socialization. In H. Sinclair (ed.) *Language and Children*. London: Oxford University Press.

Bever, T. G., & D. T. Langendoen. 1971. A dynamic model of the evolution of language. *Linguistic Inquiry* 2:433–463.

Bickerton, D. 1981. *Roots of Language*. Ann Arbor, Michigan: Karoma.

Bickerton, D. 1990. *Language and Species*. Chicago: University of Chicago Press.

Bickerton, D., & T. Givón. 1976. Pidginization and syntactic change: from SOV and VSO to SVO. In S. S. Mufwene, C. A. Walker & S. B. Steever (eds.) *Papers from the Parasession on Diachronic Syntax*. CLS.

Bin-Nun, Y. 1983. On an interim phase in the acquisition of inflected pronouns: data from 3 to 4-year-old Hebrew usage. Tel Aviv University ms.

Blanc, H. 1954. The growth of Israeli Hebrew. *Middle Eastern Affairs* 5:385–392.

Blanc, H. 1957. Hebrew in Israel: trends and problems. *The Middle East Journal* 11:374–410.

Blank, M. 1970. Some philosophical influences underlying preschool intervention for disadvantaged children. In F. Wiliams (ed.).

Blau, Y. 1973. Indirect objects and adjuncts. *Leshonenu* 37:202–204. [in Hebrew]

Blau, Y. 1976. *A Grammar of Biblical Hebrew*. Wiesbaden.

Blau, Y. 1981a. Weakening of the gutturals. *Leshonenu* 45:32–39. [in Hebrew]

Blau, Y. 1981b. *Hebrew Phonology and Morphology*. Tel Aviv: Hakibbutz Hame'uchad.

Blau, Y. 1981c. *The Renaissance of Modern Hebrew and Modern Standard Arabic: Parallels and Differences in the Revival of 2 Semitic Languages. Near Eastern Studies Vol 18*.

Bloom, L., K. Lifter & J. Hafitz. 1980. Semantics of verbs and the derivation of verb inflections in child language. *Language* 56:386–413.

Bloom, L., D. Miller & L. Hood. 1975. Variation and reduction as aspects of competence in language development. In A. Pick (ed.) Minnesota symposium on child psychology. Vol. 9. Minneapolis: University of Minnesota Press.

Bloomfield, L. 1933. *Language*. New York: Holt, Rinehart & Winston.

Blount, B. G., & M. Sanches. 1977. *Sociocultural Dimensions of Language Change*. New York: Academic Press.

Bolinger, D. 1975. *Aspects of Language*. New York: Harcourt, Brace & Jovanovich.

Bolozky, S. 1978. some aspects of Modern Hebrew phonology. Chapter 2 in R. A. Berman.

Bolozky, S. 1980. Paradigmatic coherence: evidence from Modern Hebrew. *Afro-Asiatic Linguistics* 7/4:2–24.

Bolozky, S. 1991. Affixation of Hebrew *-an:* Continuous or Discontinuous? NACAL Conference, San Francisco, March 1991.

Bolozky, S. 1982. Strategies of Modern Hebrew verb formation. *Hebrew Annual Review* 6:69–79.

Bolozky, S. to appear. Israel: Hebrew Phonology. In A. S. Kaye (ed.) *The Phonology of Selected Asian and African Languages*. Wiesbaden: Otto Harrassowitz.

Bolozky, S., & O. Schwarzwald. 1992. On the derivation of Hebrew forms with the *-ut* suffix. *Hebrew Studies* 33:51–69.

Borer, H., & Y. Grodzinsky. 1986. Syntactic cliticization and lexical cliticization: the case of Hebrew dative clitics. In H. Borer (ed.) *Syntax and Semantics, Vol 19: The Syntax of Pronominal Clitics*. New York: Academic Press.

Borokovsky, E. 1984. Imitation in early speech. *Hebrew Computational Linguistics* 22:5–24. [in Hebrew]

Bourne, L. E., R. L. Dominowski & E. F. Loftus. 1979. *Cognitive Processes*. Englewood Cliffs, N.J.: Prentice-Hall.

Bowerman, M. 1978. Systematizing semantic knowledge: Changes over time in the child's organization of word meaning. *Child Development* 49:977–87.

Bowerman, M. 1981. The child's expression of meaning: expanding relationships among lexicon, syntax and morphology. In H. Wintz (ed.) *Proceedings of the New York Academy Conference on Native Language and Foreign Language Acquisition*. New York Academy of Sciences.

Bowerman, M. 1982a. Starting to talk worse: clues to language acquisition from children's late speech errors. In S. Strauss (ed.) *U-Shaped Behavioral Growth*. New York: Academic Press.

Bowerman, M. 1982b. Reorganizational processes in lexical and sytactic development. In E. Wanner & L. R. Gleitman (eds.)

Bowerman, M. 1985. What shapes children's grammars? In D. I. Slobin (ed.)

Bresnan, J. W. (ed.) 1982. *The Mental Representation of Grammatical Relations*. Cambridge, Mass.: The MIT Press.

Bronchart, J., & H. Sinclair. 1973. Time, tense and aspect. *Cognition* 2:107–130.

Brown, R. 1973. *A First Language: The Early Stages*. Cambridge, Mass.: Harvard University Press.

Brown, R., & C. Fraser. 1963. The acquisition of syntax. In C. N. Cofer & B. Musgrave (eds.) *Verbal Behavior and Learning: Problems and Processes*. New York: McGraw-Hill.

Brown, R., C. Cazden & U. Bellugi-Klima. 1968. The child's grammar from I to III. In J. P. Hill (ed.) *Minnesota Symposium on Child Psychology, Vol II*. Minneapolis: University of Minnesota Press.

Bryant, B., & M. Anisfeld. 1969. Feedback vs. no-feedback in testing children's knowledge of English pluralization rules. *Journal of Experimental Child Psychology* 8:250–255.

Bybee, J. L. 1985. *Morphology: A Study of the Relation between Meaning and Form*. Amsterdam: John Benjamins.

Bybee, J. L. 1988. Morphology as lexical organization. *Theoretical Morphology: Approaches in Modern Linguistics*. New York: Academic Press.

Bybee, J. L., & C. L. Moder. 1983. Morphological classes as natural categories. *Language* 59:251–270.

Bybee, J. L., & D. I. Slobin. 1982. Rules and schemas in the development and use of the English past tense. *Language* 58:265–289.

Bynon, T. 1977. *Historical Linguistics*. Cambridge: Cambridge University Press.

Cais, J. 1981. The language of deprived and established children. *Iyunim Bachinuch* 19:131–151. [in Hebrew]

Cais, J. 1983. Social and verbal behavior: an Israeli example. In J.A. Fishman (ed.).

Carey, S. 1982. Semantic development: the state of the art. In E. Wanner & L.R. Gleitman (eds.).

Carrier-Duncan, J. 1985. Linking of thematic roles in derivational word formation. *Linguistic Inquiry* 16:1–34.

Cazden, C. B. 1968. The acquisition of noun and verb inflections. *Child Development* 39:433–438.

Czden, C. B. 1972. *Child Language and Education*. New York: Holt, Rinehart & Winston.

Chafe, W. L. 1985. Linguistic differences produced by differences between speaking and writing. In Olson, Torrance & Hildyard (eds.).

Charney, R. 1980. Speech roles and the development of personal pronouns. *Journal of Child Language* 7:509–528.

Chayen, M. 1972. The pronunciation of Israeli Hebrew. *Leshonenu* 33:212–219, 287–300. [in Hebrew]

Chayen, M. & Z. Dror. 1976. *Introduction to Hebrew Generative Grammar*. Tel Aviv: UPP. [in Hebrew]

Chen, M., & W. S-Y. Wang. 1975. Sound change: actuation and implementation. *Language* 51:255–281.

Cheshire, J. 1982. Dialect features and linguistic conflict in schools. *Educational Review* 34:53–67.

Chiat, S. 1981. Context specificity and generalizations in the acquisition of pronominal distinctions. *Journal of Child Language* 8:75–91.

Chiat, S. 1986. Personal pronouns. In P. Fletcher & L. R. Gleitman (eds.).

Chomsky, C. 1969. *The Acquisition of Syntax in Children from 5 to 10*. Cambridge, Mass.: The MIT Press.

Chomsky, N. 1965. *Aspects of the Theory of Syntax*. Cambridge, Mass.: The MIT Press.

Chomsky, N. 1979. *Language and Responsibility*. New York: Pantheon Books.

Chomsky, N., & M. Halle. 1968. *The Sound Pattern of English*. New York: Harper & Row.

Clancy, P. M. 1985. *Acquisition of Japanese*. In D. I. Slobin (ed.).

Clark, E. V. 1973. Non-linguistic strategies and the acquisition of word meaning. *Cognition* 2:161–182.

Clark, E. V. 1977. From gesture to word: on the natural history of deixis in language acquisition. In J. S. Bruner & A. Garton (eds.) *Human Growth and Development*. London: Oxford University Press.

Clark, E. V. 1980. Convention and innovation in the acquisition of the lexicon. *Papers and Reports on Child Language Development* 19:1–20.

Clark, E. V. 1981. Lexical innovations how children learn to create new words. In W. Deutsch (ed.) *The Child's Construction of Language*. New York: Academic Press.

Clark, E. V. 1982. The young word-maker: a case-study of innovation in the child's lexicon. In E. Wanner & R. L. Gleitman (eds.).

Clark, E. V. 1985. *Acquisition of Romance, with Special Reference to French*. In D. I. Slobin (ed.).

Clark, E. V., & R. A. Berman. 1984. Structure and use in the acquisition of word formation. *Language* 60:542–590.

Clark, E. V., & R. A. Berman. 1987. Types of linguistic knowledge: interpreting and producing compound nouns. *Journal of Child Language* 14:3.

Clark, E. V., & H. H. Clark. 1979. When nouns surface as verbs. *Language* 55:767–811.

Clark, E. V., & C. J. Sengul. 1978. Strategies in the acquisition of deixis. *Journal of Child Language* 5:457–475.

Clark, R. 1974. Performing without competence. *Journal of Child Language* 1:1–10.

Clark, R. 1977. What's the use of imitation? *Journal of Child Language* 4:341–358.

Clark, R. 1978. Some even simpler ways to learn to talk. In N. Waterson & C. Snow (eds.) *The Development of Communication*. New York: Wiley.

Clark, R. 1982. Theory and method in child-language research. Are we assuming too much? In S. Kuczaj (ed.) *Language Development*. Hillsdale, N.J.: Lawrence Erlbaum.

Closs, E. 1965. Diachronic syntax and generative grammar. *Language* 41:402–415.

Comrie, B. 1976. *Aspect*. Cambridge: Cambridge University Press.

Comrie, B. 1981. *Language Universals and Linguistic Typology*. Chicago: University of Chicago Press.

Comrie, B. 1985. *Tense*. Cambridge: Cambridge University Press.

Cook-Gumperz, J., & J. Gumperz. 1978. From oral to written culture: the transition to literacy. In M. F. Whiteman (ed.) *Writing, Vol 1*. Hillsdale, N.J.: Lawrence Erlbaum.

Corson, D. 1983. Social dialect: the semantic barrier and access to curricular knowledge. *Language in Society* 12.

Craig, C. (ed.). 1986. *Noun Classes and Categorization*. Amsterdam: John Benjamins.

Croft, W. 1990. *Typology and Universals*. Cambridge: Cambridge University Press.

Cromer, R. F. 1976. Developmental strategies for learning. In V. Hamilton & M. D. Vernon (eds.) *The Development of Cognitive Processes*. New York: Academic Press.

Cutler, A., & D. A. Fay. 1982. One mental lexicon, phonologically arranged. *Linguistic Inquiry* 13:107–112.

Dagan, Y. 1973. Mispronouncing Hebrew consonants. Master's thesis, Tel Aviv University. [in Hebrew]

Dahl, O. 1985. *Tense and Aspect Systems*. Oxford: Blackwell.

Davis, L. 1976a. The spoken language of deprived children: a preliminary report. Haifa: School of Education. [in Hebrew]

Davis, L. 1976b. The language of deprived children. *Iyunim Bachinuch* 13:133–138. [in Hebrew]

Davis, L. 1978. Register and teaching deprived-background children. *Iyunim Bachinuch* 15:61–66. [in Hebrew]

Davis, L. 1981. Normative grammar and the language of deprived children. In L. Davis et al. (eds.) *Studies in Linguistics and Semiotics*. Haifa: Haifa University Press. [in Hebrew]

Decamp, D. 1971. Toward a generative analysis of a post-creole continuum. In D. Hymes (ed.).

Demuth, K., N. Faraclas & L. Marchese. 1986. Niger-Congo noun class and agreement systems in language acquisition and historical change. In C. Craig (ed.).

Derwing, B. L. 1976. Morpheme recognition and the learning of rules for derivational morphology. *The Canadian Journal of Linguistics* 21:38–66.

Derwing, B. L., & W. J. Baker. 1977. The psychological basis for morphological rules. In J. Macnamara (ed.) *Language Learning and Thought*. New York: Academic Press.

Derwing, B. L., & W. J. Baker. 1986. Assessing morphological development. In P. Fletcher & M. Garman (eds.).

Deutsch, M. 1965. The role of social class in language development and cognition. *American Journal of Orthopsychiatry* 25:78–88.

Deutsch, M., & T. Pechmann. 1978. Ihr, mir or dir? On the acquisition of pronouns in German children. *Cognition* 6:267–278.

deVilliers, J. G., & P. A. deVilliers. 1973. A cross-sectional study of the acquisition of grammatical morphemes in child speech. *Journal of Psycholinguistic Research* 3:267–278.

deVilliers, J. G., & P. A. deVilliers. 1978. Competence and performance in child language. Are children really competent to judge? In L. Bloom (ed.) *Readings in Language Development*. Toronto: John Wiley.

Dewart, M. H. 1975. A psychological investigation of sentence comprehension by children. Doctoral dissertation, University College London.

Di-Nur, M. 1979. *-an* and *-ani* suffixed forms. In H. Rabin & B.-Z. Fischler (eds.) *Mincha LeKodesh*. Jerusalem: Hamo'atsa Lehanchalat Halashon. [in Hebrew]

Dolzhansky, T. 1937. Children's language solecisms. *Leshonenu* 8:35–48. [in Hebrew]

Donag-Kinrot, R. 1975. Norm and Standard in the language of schoolchildren. *Leshonenu La'am* 26. [in Hebrew]

Donag-Kinrot, R. 1978. The language of Israeli students. Doctoral dissertation, the Hebrew University. [in Hebrew]

Donaldson, M. 1978. *Children's Minds*. London: Fontana.

Dotan, A. 1985. The Hebrew of broadcasting. *Leshonenu La'am* 33/7. [in Hebrew]

Dowty, D. R. 1972. Studies in the logic of verb aspect and time reference in English. *Studies in Linguistics*. Austin, Texas, University of Texas at Austin.

Dromi, E. 1979. More on the acquisition of locative prepositions: an analysis of Hebrew data. *Journal of Child Language* 6:547–562.

Dromi, E. 1982. In pursuit of meaningful words: a case-study analysis of early lexical development. Doctoral dissertation, University of Kansas, Lawrence.

Dromi, E. 1987. *Early Lexical Development,* Cambridge: Cambridge University Press.

Dromi, E., & R. A. Berman. 1982. A morphemic measure of early language development: data from Israeli Hebrew. *Journal of Child Language* 9:403–424.

Dromi, E., & R. A. Berman. 1986. Language particular and language general in developing syntax. *Journal of Child Language* 14:371–387.

Dromi, E., L. B. Leonard & M. Shteiman. 1993. The grammatical morphology of Hebrew-speaking children with specific language impairment: some competing hypotheses. *Journal of Speech & Hearing Research* 36:760–771.

Edwards, A. D. 1975. Speech codes and speech variants: social class and task differences in children's speech. *Journal of Child Language* 3:247–265.

Ephratt, M. 1980. *bkp* after a preposition. *Leshonenu* 45:40–55. [in Hebrew]

Ehri, L. C. 1979. linguistic insight: threshold of reading acquisition. In T. Waller & G. E. MacKinnon (eds.) *Reading Research: Advances in Theory and Practice.* New York: Academic Press.

Ehri, L. C. 1985. Effects of printed language acquisition on speech. In Olson, Torrance & Hildyard (eds.).

Eiger, H. 1975. *Remedial Teaching for Disadvantaged Students.* Tel Aviv: Sifriyat Hapo'alim. [in Hebrew]

Erbaugh, M. S. 1986. Taking stock: the development of Chinese classifiers historically and in young children. In C. Craig (ed.).

Ervin, S. 1964. Imitation and structural change in children's language. In E. H. Lenneberg (ed.) *New Directions in the Study of Language.* Cambridge: Cambridge University Press.

Even Shoshan, A. 1977. *A New Concordance for the Bible.* Jerusalem: Kiryat Sefer. [in Hebrew]

Even Shoshan, A. 1979. *The New Dictionary.* Jerusalem: Kiryat Sefer. [in Hebrew]

Even Zohar, I. 1986. The Hebrew/Yiddish multisystem. *Hasifrut* 3/4 (35–36):46–54. [in Hebrew]

Faber, A. 1986. On the origin and the development of Hebrew spirantization. *Mediterranean Language Review* 2:117–138.

Fay, D. A., & A. Cutler. 1977. Malapropisms and the structure of the mental lexicon. *Linguistic Inquiry* 8:505–520.

Feitelson, D., & S. Krown. 1968. The effects of heterogeneous grouping on pre-school children. Jerusalem: Hebrew University.

Fellman, J. 1973. Concerning the "revival" of the Hebrew language. *Anthropological Linguistics,* May:250–257.

Ferguson, C. A. 1971. Absence of copula and the notion of simplicity: A study of normal speech, baby talk, foreign talk and pidgins. In D. Hymes (ed.).

Ferreiro, E. 1982. Literacy development: the construction of a new object of knowledge. Talk given at the International Reading Association, Chicago.

Fischler, B.-Z. 1975. *bkp* in Israeli Hebrew. In U. Ornan & B.-Z. Fischler (eds.) *Sefer Rosen.* Jerusalem: Hamo'atsa Lehanchalat Halashon. [in Hebrew]

Fischler, B.-Z. 1979. On mispronunciations. In H. Rabin & B.-Z. Fischler (eds.) *Mincha LeKodesh.* Jerusalem: Hamo'atsa Lehanchalat Halashon. [in Hebrew]

Fisherman, H. 1985. Foreign words in contemporary Hebrew. Doctoral dissertation, Hebrew University. [in Hebrew]

Flavell, J. H. 1985. *Cognitive Development.* Englewood Cliffs, N.J.: Prentice-Hall.

Fletcher, P. 1985. *A Child's Learning of English.* Oxford: Blackwell.

Fletcher, P., & M. Garman (eds.). 1986. *Language Acquisition: Studies in First Language Development* (2nd edition). Cambridge: Cambridge University Press.

Flores D'Arcais, G. B. 1975. Some perceptual determinants of sentence construction. In G. B. Flores D'Arcais (ed.) *Studies in Perception.* Milan: Martelli-Guinti.

Frankenstein, C. 1972. *Rehabilitating Intelligence.* Jerusalem. [in Hebrew]

Fromkin, V. A. 1980. *Errors in Linguistic Performance: Slips of the Tongue, Ear, Pen and Hand.* New York: Academic Press.

Furrow, D., & K. Nelson. 1984. Environmental correlates of individual differences in language acquisition. *Journal of Child Language* 11:523–534.

Gal, S. 1978. Variation and change in patterns of speaking: language shift in Austria. In D. Sankoff (ed.).

Garbel, I. 1959. The phonemic status of the *schwa,* the *Hataf* and the fricative *beged/kefet* in Masoretic Hebrew. *Leshonenu* 23:152–156. [in Hebrew]

Garner, W. R. 1974. *The Processing of Information and structure.* New York: Wiley.

Gesenius, 1910. *Gesenius' Hebrew Grammar,* edited by E. Kautzsch, revised by A. E. Cowley. Oxford: Clarendon Press.

Gil, D. 1982. Case marking, phonological size, and linear order. In P. J. Hopper & S. A. Thompson (eds.) *Syntax and Semantics, Vol 15: Studies in Transitivity.* New York: Academic Press.

Giora, R. 1982. A pragmatic analysis of focused sentences. In Bloom-Kolka et al. (eds.). [in Hebrew]

Givón, T. 1976. On the VS order in Israeli Hebrew: Pragmatic and typological change. In P. Cole (ed.).

Givón, T. 1977. The drift from VSO to SVO in Biblical Hebrew: the pragmatics of tense-aspect. In C. N. Li (ed.) *Mechanisms of Syntactic Change.* Austin: University of Texas Press.

Givón, T. 1979a. *On Understanding Grammar.* New York: Academic Press.

Givón, T. 1979b. From discourse to syntax: Grammar as a processing strategy. In P. J. Hopper & S. A. Thompson (eds.).

Givón, T. 1985. Function, structure and language acquisition. In D. Slobin (ed.).

Glinert, L. 1989. *The Grammar of Modern Hebrew.* Cambridge: Cambridge University Press.

Goldenberg, E. 1978. Two Medieval idioms in Modern Hebrew. *Leshonenu La'am* 29/4–5. [in Hebrew]

Goldin-Meadow, S. 1982. The resilience of recursion: a study of a communication system developed without a conventional language model. In E. Wanner & L. R. Gleitman (eds.).

Goshen-Gottstein, M. 1951. Study in spoken Hebrew. *Leshonenu* 17:231–240.

Goshen-Gottstein, M. 1956. Our Hebrew. *Ha'aretz,* 24.2.1956. [in Hebrew]

Goshen-Gottstein, M. 1969. *Introduction to Modern Hebrew Lexicology.* Tel Aviv. [in Hebrew]

Goshen-Gottstein, M., & E. Eitan. 1952. Foundations for language corrections. *Leshonenu La'am* 26:3–10. [in Hebrew]

Goshen-Gottstein, M., Z. Livne & S. Span. 1977. *Functional Hebrew Grammar.* Jerusalem: Shoken. [in Hebrew]

Gould, S. J. 1977. *Ontogeny and Phlogeny.* Cambridge, Mass.: The Harvard Press.

Greenberg, J. H. (ed.) 1966a. *Universals of Grammar*. Cambridge, Mass.: The MIT Press.

Greenberg, J. H. (ed.) 1966b. Some universals of grammar with particular reference to the order of meaningful elements. In J. H. Greenberg (ed.) *Universals of Grammar*.

Gruber, J. S. 1976. *Lexical Structures in Syntax and Semantics*. Amsterdam: North-Holland.

Haiman, J. 1983. Iconic and economic motivation. *Language* 59:781–819.

Hale, K. 1973. Deep-surface canonical disparities in relation to analogy and change: an Austrian example. In T. S. Sebeok (ed.) *Current Trends in Linguistics*. The Hague: Mouton.

Halle, M. 1962. Phonology in generative grammar. *Word* 18:54–72.

Hankamer, J. 1972. Analogical rules. *CLS8:*111–123.

Harrel, L. E., Jr. 1957. An inter-comparison of quality and rate of development of the oral and written language in children. *Monographs of the Society for Research in Child Development* 22.

Harris, Z. 1952. *Hebrew in View of Modern Linguistics*. *Leshonenu* 17:128–132. [in Hebrew]

Harshav, B. 1991. The politics of culture and Israeli identity. Keynote address, 7th Annual Meeting of the Association for Israel Studies, Barnard College, New York, June 1991.

Hess, R., & V. Shipman. 1968. Maternal influences upon early learning. In R. Hess & R. Beer (eds.) *Early Learning*. London: Aldine.

Hocket, C. F. 1965. Sound change. *Language* 41:185–204.

Hoenigswald, H. M. 1963. Are there universals of linguistic change? In J. H. Greenberg (ed.).

Hooper, J. B. 1976. Word frequency in lexical diffusion and the source of morphophonological change. In W. M. Christie, Jr. (ed.) *Current Progress in Historical Linguistics*. Amsterdam: North-Holland.

Hooper, J. B. 1979. Child morphology and morphophonemic change. *Linguistics* 17:21–50.

Hopper, P. J., & S. A. Thompson. 1980. Transitivity in grammar and discourse. *Language* 56:251–299.

Hornstein, N. 1977. Toward a theory of tense. *Linguistic Inquiry* 8:521–557.

Householder, F. W. 1983. Kyriolexia and language change. *Language* 59:1–17.

Hurford, J. R. 1981. Malapropisms, left-to-right listing, and lexicalism. *Linguistic Inquiry* 12:419–423.

Huxley, R. 1970. The development of the correct use of subject personal pronouns in two children. In G. B. Flores d'Arcais & W. J. M. Levelt (eds.) *Advances in Psycholinguistics*. Amsterdam: North-Holland.

Hymes, D. (ed.) 1971. *Pidginization and Creolization of Languages*. Cambridge: Cambridge University Press.

Izre'el, S. 1986. Was the Hebrew revival a miracle? On pidginization and creolization processes in the formation of Modern Hebrew. *PWCJS-9* sect. 4, 1:77–84.

Jackendoff, R. 1975. Morphological and semantic regularities in the lexicon. *Language* 51:639–671.

Jackendoff, R. 1983. *Semantics and Cognition*. Cambridge, Mass.: The MIT Press.

Jensen, A. R. 1969. How much can we boost IQ and scholastic achievement? *Harvard Educational Review* 39:1–123.

Jespersen, O. 1922. *Language: Its Nature, Development and Origin*. London: Allen & Unwin.

Jespersen, O. 1949. *Efficiency in Linguistic Change*. Historisk-Filologiske Meddelelser 27:4 Munksgaard, Kobenhavn, 2nd ed.

Johnston, J. R. 1985. Cognitive prerequisites: the evidence from children learning English. In D. I. Slobin (ed.).

Kaddari, M. Z. 1976. *Studies in Biblical Hebrew Syntax*. Ramat Gan: Bar Ilan. [in Hebrew]

Kaddari, M. Z. 1983. Research in Israeli Hebrew: state of the art. *Min HaSadna: Contemporary Hebrew*. Jerusalem: Hamo'atsa Lehanchalat Halashon. [in Hebrew]

Kaddari, M. Z. 1986. The Hebrew teacher as a decision-maker in linguistic matters. Talk given at the Internation Workshop on Jewish Education—"The Jewish Teacher". School of Education, Tel-Aviv University, 20–22.10.86.

Kalmar, I. 1985. Are there really no primitive languages? In Olson, Torrance & Hildyard (ed.).

Kaplan, D. 1983. Order of acquisition of morpho-syntactic elements in Hebrew-speaking nursery schoolers. Master's thesis, Tel Aviv University. [in Hebrew]

Karmiloff-Smith, A. 1978. The interplay between syntax, semantics and phonology in language acquisition processes. In R. N. Campbell & P. T. Smith (eds.) *Recent Advances in the Psychology of Language: Language Development and Mother-Child Interaction*. New York: Plenum Press.

Karmiloff-Smith, A. 1979. *A Functional Approach to Child Language: A Study of Determiners and Reference*. Cambridge: Cambridge University Press.

Karmiloff-Smith, A. 1986a. Some fundamental aspects of language development after age 5. In P. Fletcher & M. Garman (eds.).

Karmiloff-Smith, A. 1986b. Language and cognitive processes from a developmental perspective. *Language and Cognitive Processes* 1:61–85.

Kay, P. 1977. Language evolution and speech style. In B. G. Blount & M. Sanches (eds.).

Kemp, J. 1984. Native language knowledge as a predictor of success in learning a foreign language, with special reference to a disadvantaged population. Master's thesis, Tel Aviv University.

Kimhi, D. 1928. *Teachers' Association Jubilee*, Jerusalem 1902–1927. [in Hebrew]

King, R. 1969. *Historical Linguistics and Generative Grammar*. New York: Holt, Rinehart & Winston.

Kiparsky, P. 1982. *Explanation in Phonology*. Dordrecht: Foris Publications.

Klar, B. 1951. Medieval Hebrew pronunciation. *Leshonenu* 17:72–75.

Klein, W. 1986. *Second language acquisition*. Cambridge: Cambridge University Press.

Kloisener, I. 1964. Spoken Hebrew pioneers. *Leshonenu La'am* 35 7/8. [in Hebrew]

Kremer, S. 1980. *Rega Sel ivrit:* language corrections broadcast by *Kol Israel*. A. Bendavid (ed.). Jerusalem: Ministry of Education. [in Hebrew]

Kressel, G. 1984. Spoken Hebrew in Turn-of-the century Palestine. *Leshonenu La'am* 35 7/8. [in Hebrew]

Kroch, A., & C. Small. 1978. Grammatical ideology and its effect on speech. In D. Sankoff (ed.).

Kuczaj, S. 1977. The acquisition of regular and irregular past tense forms. *Journal of Verbal Learning and Verbal Behavior* 16:589–600.

Kuczaj, S. 1978. Children's judgements of grammatical and ungrammatical irregular past-tense verbs. *Child Development* 49:319–326.

Kuno, S. 1974. The position of relative clauses and conjunctions. *Linguistic Inquiry* 5:117–136.

Kutscher, E. Y. 1956. Modern Hebrew and 'Israeli' Hebrew. *Conservative Judaism* 9:28–45.

Kutscher, E. Y. 1959. *The Language and the Linguistic Background of the Dead Sea Scrolls*. Jerusalem: Magnes. [in Hebrew]

Kutscher, E. Y. 1982. *A History of the Hebrew Language*. Jerusalem: Magnes.

Labov, W. 1966. The social stratification of English in New York City. Washington, D.C.: Center for Applied Linguistics.

Labov, W. 1969. Contraction, deletion and inherent variability of the English copula. *Language* 45:715–762.

Labov, W. 1970. The logic of nonstandard English. In F. Williams (ed.).

Labov, W. 1971. The notion of "system" in creole languages. In D. Hymes (ed.).

Labov, W. 1972a. *Sociolinguistics Patterns*. Philadelphia: University of Pennsylvania Press.

Labov, W. 1972b. *Language in the Inner City: Studies in the Black English Vernacular*. Philadelphia: University of Pennsylvania Press.

Labov, W. 1972c. The internal evolution of linguistic rules. In: R. P. Stockwell & R. K. S. MaCaulay (eds.) *Linguistic Change and Generative Theory*. Bloomington: Indiana University Press.

Labov, W. 1980. The social origins of sound change. In W. Labov (ed.) *Locating Language in Time and Space*. New York: Academic Press.

Labov, W. 1981. Resolving the Neogrammarian controversy. *Language* 57:267–308.

Labov, W. 1982. Building on empirical foundations. In W. P. Lehmann & Y. Malkiel (eds.) *Perspectives on Historical Linguistics*. Amsterdam: John Benjamins.

Labov, W., & W. A. Harris. 1986. De facto segregation of Black and White vernaculars. In D. Sankoff (ed.).

Landau, R. 1980. *Journalistic Collocations*. Ramat Gan: Bar Ilan. [in Hebrew]

Laufer, A., & I. Condax. 1981. The function of the epiglottis in speech. *Language and Speech* 24:24–39.

Legum, S. E., K.-O. Kim & H. Rosenbaum. 1978. The relation between oral and written comprehension. In D. Sankoff (ed.) *Linguistic Variation—Models and Methods*. New York: Academic Press.

Leket, 1972. A collection of errors and solecisms. Jerusalem: Ministry of Education. [in Hebrew]

Leket Te'udot, 1970. Documenting the Language Committee and the Hebrew Language Academy. Jerusalem: Hebrew Language Academy. [in Hebrew]

Lenz, R. 1926. *El Papiamento: La Grammarica mas Sencilla*. Bacells: Santiago de Chile.

Lerner, Y. 1976. The distinction between an Object and an Adjunct. [in Hebrew]

Levy, Y. 1980. The acquisition of gender. Doctoral dissertation, Hebrew University. [in Hebrew]

Levy, Y. 1982. A note on feminine plural inflection in spoken Israeli Hebrew. *Journal of Psycholinguistic Research* 11:265–273.

Lewis, M. M. 1971. The beginning reference to past and future in child speech. In A. Bar-Adon & W. Leopold (eds.).

Lieberman, P. 1984. *The Biology and Evolution of Language*. Cambridge, Mass.: Harvard University Press.

Lightfoot, D. W. 1979. *Principles of Diachronic Syntax*. Cambridge: Cambridge University Press.

Lightfoot, D. W. 1981. Explaining syntactic change. In N. K. Hornstein & D. W. Lightfoot (eds.) *Explanation in Linguistics*. London: Longman.

Lightfoot, D. W. 1982. *The Language Lottery: Toward a Biology of Grammars*. Cambridge, Mass.: The MIT Press.

Lightfoot, D. 1991. *How to Set Parameters: Arguments from Language Change*. Cambridge, Mass.: The MIT Press.

MacWhinney, B. 1975. Rules, rote and analogy in morphological formations by Hungarian children. *Journal of Child Language* 2:65–77.

MacWhinney, B. 1978. Processing a first language: the acquisition of morphology. *Monographs of the Society for Research in Child Language Development* 43 (1–2).

MacWhinney, B. 1985. Hungarian language acquisition as an exemplification of a general model of grammatical development. In D. I. Slobin (ed.).

Manczak, W. 1980. Laws of analogy. In J. Fisiak (ed.) *Recent Developments in Historical Phonology*. The Hague: Mouton.

Manzur, Y. 1962. Language solecisms. *Leshonenu La'am* 13–17. [in Hebrew]

Maranz, A. 1984. *On the Nature of Grammatical Relations*. Cambridge, Mass.: The MIT Press.

Maratsos, M. P. 1979. Learning how and when to use pronouns and determiners. In P. Fletcher & M. Garman (eds.).

Maratsos, M. P. 1982. The child's construction of grammatical categories. In E. Wanner & L. R. Gleitman (eds.).

Maratsos, M., & M. A. Chalkey. 1980. The internal language of children's syntax: The ontogenesis and representation of sytactic categories. In K. Nelson (ed.) *Children's Language,* Vol. 2. New York: Gardner Press.

Maratsos, M., & S. Kuczaj. 1979. The child's formulation of grammatical categories and rules: the nature of syntactic categories. Talk given at the meeting of the Society for Reasearch in Child Development. 16.3.79.

Martin, J. R. 1983. The development of register. In J. Fine & R. O. Freedle (eds.) *Developmental Issues in Discourse*. Ablex.

Martinet, A. 1955. *Economie des changements phonetiques: Traite de Phonologie diachronique*. Berne: A. Francke.

Martinet, A. 1960. *Elements of General Linguistics* (Translated by E. Palmer). Chicago: University of Chicago Press.

Matthews, P. H. 1974. *Morphology: An Introduction to the Theory of Word-Structure*. Cambridge: Cambridge University Press.

Mayrose, O. 1988. The acquisition of gerunds in Modern Hebrew. Master's thesis, Tel Aviv University. [in Hebrew]

McCarthy, J. J. 1981. A prosodic theory of nonconcatenative morphology. *Linguistic Inquiry* 12:373–418.

Medan, M. 1953. Hebrew and its relatives. *Leshonenu La'am* 33–41. [in Hebrew]

Medan, M. 1969. The Academy of the Hebrew language. *Ariel* 25:40–47.

Menyuk P. 1969. *Sentences Children Use*. Cambridge, Mass.: The MIT Press.

Menyuk P. 1977. *Language and Maturation*. Cambridge, Mass.: The MIT Press.

Meyuchas, Y. 1928. Subject-Verb agreement in Hebrew. *Leshonenu* 1:145–151. [in Hebrew]

Mills, A. E. 1985. *Acquisition of German*. In D.I. Slobin (ed.).

Milroy, J. 1992. *Linguistic Variation and Change: On the Historical Sociolinguistics of English*. Oxford: Blackwell.

Minkowitz, A. 1969. *The Disadvantaged Pupil*. School of Education, Hebrew University. [in Hebrew]

Montes, J. J. 1962. Sobre el habla de San Basilico de Palenque. *Thesaurus* 17:446–450.

Morag, S. 1957. *Pa'al* and *Nitpa'el* in Mishnaic Hebrew. *Tarbitz* 26:349–356. [in Hebrew]

Morag, S. 1959. Planned and unplanned development in Modern Hebrew. *Lingua* 8:247–263.

Morag, S. 1960. Seven times *beged kefet*. *Sefer Tur-Sinai*. Jerusalem. [in Hebrew]

Morag, S. 1963. *The Hebrew Spoken by Yemenite Jews*. Jerusalem: The Hebrew Language Academy. [in Hebrew]

Morag, S. 1973. The vowel system in spoken Israeli Hebrew. *Leshonenu* 37:205–214. [in Hebrew]

Moreshet, M. 1969. Shay Agnon as an enricher of the Hebrew lexicon. *Leshonenu La'am* 29:3. [in Hebrew]

Nahir, M. 1978. Normativism and educated speech in Modern Hebrew. *International Journal of the Sociology of Language* 18:49–67.

Naro, A. 1978. A study on the origins of pidginization. *Language* 54:314–347.

Naro, A., & M. Lemle. 1976. Syntactic diffusion. In S. F. Stever et al. (eds.) *Papers from the Parasession on Diachronic Syntax* 221–239. Chicago: CLS.

Nelson, F. 1973. Structure and strategy in learning to talk. *Monographs of the Society for Research in Child Language Development* 38.

Nelson, N. F. 1988. The nature of literacy. In M. A. Nippold (ed.).

Nippold, M. A. (ed.) 1988a. *Later Language Development: Ages 9 through 19*. Austin, Texas: Pro-Ed.

Nippold, M. A. 1988b. The literate lexicon. In M. A. Nippold (ed.).

Nir, R. 1974. *Teaching Hebrew as a Mother Tongue*. Tel Aviv. [in Hebrew]

Nir, R. 1977. What is an "error" in a mother tongue. *Iyunim Bachinuch* 13:81–92. [in Hebrew]

Nir, R. 1981. What is Normative vs. Acceptable usage in Modern Hebrew. In Davis et al. (eds.). [in Hebrew]

O'Donnell, R., W. Griffin & R. Norris. 1967. Syntax of kindergarten and elementary school children. Champaign, Illinois: National Council of Teachers of English, Research Report No. 8.

Ochs, E. 1979. Planned and unplanned discourse. In T. Givon (ed.) *Syntax and Semantics, Vol. 12: Discourse and Syntax*. New York: Academic Press.

Ochs, E. 1985. Variation and error: a sociolinguistic approach to language acquisition in Samoa. In D. Slobin (ed.).

Oksaar, E. 1983. Sociocultural aspects of Language change. In I. Rauch & G. F. Carr (eds.) *Language Change*. Bloomington: Indiana University Press.

Olson, D. R. 1977. From utterance to text: the bias of Language in speech and writing. *Harvard Educational Review* 47:257–281.

Olson, D. R. 1985. Introduction. In D. R. Olson, N. Torrance & A. Hildyard (eds.).

D. R. Olson, N. Torrance & A. Hildyard (eds.) 1985. *Literacy, Language and Learning: The Nature and Consequences of Reading and Writing*. Cambridge: Cambridge University Press.

Omar, M. 1973. *The Acquisition of Egyptian Arabic as a Native Language.* The Hague: Mouton.

Ornan, U. 1969. *The Hebrew Verb System.* Jerusalem: Hebrew University. [in Hebrew]

Ornan, U. 1971. *binyanim,* stems, inflections and root types. *Ha-Universita* 16:15–17. [in Hebrew]

Ornan, U. 1973. Regular rules and *bkp* phonemic split. In U. Ornan (ed.) *Phonology Reader.* Jerusalem: Hebrew University. [in Hebrew]

Ornan, U. 1977. Hebrew radio pronunciation. *Leshonenu La'am* 28:10. [in Hebrew]

Ornan, U. 1983. Emphatic consonants. *Hebrew Computational Linguistics* 20:5–10. [In Hebrew]

Ornan, U. 1985. The end of the process of l revival. In M. Bar-Asher (ed.) [in Hebrew]

Palermo, D. & D. Molfese. 1972. Language acquisition from age five onward. *Psychological Bulletin* 78:409–428.

Park, T. Z. 1978. Plurals in child speech. *Journal of Child Language* 5:237–250.

Paul, H. 1970. *Prinzipien der Sprachgeschichte.* Reprint of the 5th edition of 1920, Tubingen: Niemeyer; English translation by H. A. Strong, London 1891.

Pennanen, E. V. 1975. What happens in backformation? In E. Hovdhaugen (ed.) *Papers from the 2nd Scandinavian Conference of Linguistics.* Oslo: Oslo University.

Perera, K. 1986. Language acquisition and writing. In P. Fletcher & M. Garman (eds.).

Peters, A. M. 1983. *The Units of Language Acquisition.* Cambridge: Cambridge University Press.

Peters, A. M. 1985. Language segmentation: operating principles for the perception and analysis of language. In D. I. Slobin (ed.).

Phillips, B. S. 1984. Word frequency and the actuation of sound change. *Language* 60:320–342.

Piaget, J. 1926. *The Language and Thought of the Child.* London: Routledge & Kegan Paul.

Piaget, J., & B. Inhelder. 1968. *The Psychology of the Child* . London: Routledge & Kegan Paul.

Pinker, S. 1989. *Learnability and Cognition: The Acquisition of Argument Structure.* Cambridge, Mass.: The MIT Press.

Pizzuto, E., & M. C. Caselli. 1992. The acquisition of Italian morphology: implications for models of language development. *JCL* 19:491–557.

Platt, C. B., & B. MacWhinney. 1983. Error assimilation as a mechanism in language learning. *Journal of Child Language* 10:401–414.

Podolsky, B. 1987. The problem of word accent in Modern Hebrew. *Proceedings of the 5th International Hamito-Semitic Congress.* Vienna.

Poplack, S. 1980. The notion of the plural in Puerto-Rican Spanish: Competing constraints on (s) deletion. In W. Labov (ed.) *Locating Language in Time and Space.* New York: Academic Press.

Popova, M. I. 1973. Grammatical elements in the speech of preschool children. In C. A. Ferguson & D. I. Slobin (eds.).

Rabin, H. 1940. La chute de l'occlusive glottale en hebreu parle et l'evolution d'une nouvelle classe de voyelle. *GLECS* 3:77–79.

Rabin, H. 1958. Middle Hebrew. *Leshonenu La'am* 9–10:88–92. [in Hebrew]

Rabin, H. 1959. What is "correct Hebrew"? School of Education, Hebrew University. [in Hebrew]

Rabin, H. 1972. *History of the Hebrew Language*. Jerusalem: World Zionist Association. [in Hebrew]

Rabin, H. 1977. Normativism and Linguistics. *Hed Ha-Ulpan* 19:6–8. [in Hebrew]

Rabin, H. 1981. Language planning and normativism. In Davis et al. (eds.). [in Hebrew]

Rabin, H. 1986. Normativism as a social phenomenon. In M. Zohari et al. (eds.) *Uma Ve-Lashon*. Jerusalem: Hebrew World Alliance. [in Hebrew]

Rabin, H., & Z. Radday. 1976. *Hebrew Thesaurus*. Jerusalem: Kiryat Sefer. [in Hebrew]

Rabinowitch, S. M. S. 1985. Hebrew knowledge in bilingual children and monolingual children. Doctoral dissertation, Tel Aviv University. [in Hebrew]

Ravid, D. 1977. Modern Israeli Hebrew word order. *Hebrew Computational Linguistics* 11:1–45. [in Hebrew]

Ravid, D. 1978. Word formation processes in Modern Hebrew nouns and adjectives. Master's thesis, Tel-Aviv University.

Ravid, D. 1988. Transient and fossilized phenomena in inflectional morphology: varieties of spoken Hebrew. Doctoral dissertation, Tel Aviv University.

Ravid, D. 1990. Internal structure constraints on new-word formation devices in Modern Hebrew. *Folia Linguistica* 24/3–4:289–347.

Ravid, D. 1994. Cost in language acquisition and language processing. In E. Casad (ed.) *Cognitive Linguistics in the Redwoods*. Berlin: Mouton de Gruyter.

Ravid, D. In press. Spirantization in Modern Hebrew. *Mediterranean Language Review*.

Ravid, D. To appear. The acquisition of morphological junctions in Modern Hebrew: the interface of rule and rote. In H. Pishwa (ed.) *The Acquisition of Inflectional Morphology*. Berlin.

Ravid, D., & I. Shlesinger. 1987a. *a*-deletion in Modern Hebrew. Talk given at annual Theoretical Linguistics conference, Bar Ilan, 13.5.87.

Ravid, D., & I. Shlesinger. 1987b. *-i* suffixed adjectives in Modern Hebrew. *Hebrew Computational Linguistics* 25:59–70. [in Hebrew]

Ravid, D., I. Shlesinger & Z. Sar'el. 1985. Construct state constructions. *Prakim* 5:92–100. [in Hebrew]

Riemsdijk, H., & E. Williams. 1986. *Introduction to the Theory of Grammar*. Cambridge, Mass.: The MIT Press.

Ring, Y. 1976. Indirect objects and adjuncts. New York: Academic Press. *Leshonenu* 40:152–154. [in Hebrew]

Rivkai, Y. 1933–34. On our children's language specificity. *Leshonenu* 3:33–77, 4:231–242, 5:279–294. [in Hebrew]

Roeper, T., & M. E. A. Siegel. 1978. A lexical transformation for verbal compounds. *Linguistic Inquiry* 9:199–260.

Rom, A., & R. Dgani. 1985. Acquiring case-marked pronouns in Hebrew: the interaction of linguistic factors. *Journal of Child Language* 12:61–77.

Romaine, S. 1984. *The Language of Children and Adolescents: The Acquisition of Communicative Competence*. Oxford: Blackwell.

Rosén, H. 1952. Studies in spoken Hebrew phenomena. *Leshonenu La'am* 3:3–32. [in Hebrew]

Rosén, H. 1953. Standard and norm. *Leshonenu La'am* 4, 6, 7, 8–9. [in Hebrew]

Rosén, H. 1956. *Our Hebrew: A Linguistic Analysis.* Tel Aviv: Achad Ha'am. [in Hebrew]

Rosén, H. 1966. *A Textbook of Israeli Hebrew.* Chicago.

Rosén, H. 1977. *Good Hebrew: Studies in Syntax.* Jerusalem: Kiryat Sefer. [in Hebrew]

Rubinstein, E. 1975. Categorial shifts in the spoken language. In In U. Ornan & B.-Z. Fischler (ed.) *Sefer Rosén.* Jerusalem: Hamo'atsa Lehanchalat Halashon. [in Hebrew]

Rubinstein, E. 1981. *Our Hebrew and Old Hebrew.* Ministry of Defense Publishing House. [in Hebrew]

Ruddell, R. B. 1978. Language acquisition and the reading process. In L. J. Chapman & P. Czerniewska (eds.) *Reading: From Process to Practice.* Routledge & Kegan Paul.

Ruke-Drarina, V. 1973. On the emergence of inflection in child Language: A contribution based on Latvian speech data. In C. A. Ferguson & D. I. Slobin (eds.).

Sadka, Y. 1977. *Syntax According to New Theories.* Jerusalem: Akademon.

Samocha, S., & Y. Peres. 1974. The ethnic disparity in Israel. *Megamot* 20:5–42.

Samuels, M. L. 1972. *Linguistic Evolution, with Special Reference to English.* Cambridge: Cambridge University Press.

Sanches, M. 1977. Language acquisition and Language change: Japanese numeral classifiers. In Blount & Sanches (eds.).

Sandbank, A. 1992. The development of text writing in preschoolers and first graders: the writing process and the written product. Master's thesis, Tel Aviv University. [in Hebrew]

Sankoff, D. (ed.) 1986. *Diversity and Diachrony.* Amsterdam: John Benjamins.

Sankoff, D., & W. Labov. 1979. On the uses of variable rules. *Language in Society* 8:3, 189–222.

Sankoff, G., & P. Brown. 1976. The origins of syntax in discourse. *Language* 52:631–66.

Sapir, E. 1921. *Language: An Introduction to the Study of Speech.* New York: Harcourt, Brace & World.

Sappan, R. 1963. *Hebrew Slang.* Jerusalem: Kiryat Sefer. [in Hebrew]

Sappan, R. 1964. Hebrew slang and foreign loans. *Am Va-Sefer* 23–24:37–39. [in Hebrew]

Sappan, R. 1969. Hebrew slang and foreign loan words. *Ariel* 25:75–80.

Sar'el, Z. 1984. Discourse structures in Hebrew textbooks and the communicative competence of teacher students. Doctoral dissertation, Tel Aviv University. [in Hebrew]

Sar'el, Z., Y. Shlesinger & D. Ravid. 1986. Normativism in the linguistic eighties. *Prakim* 6:6–12. [in Hebrew]

de Saussure, F. 1955. Cours de Linguistique Generale. 5th edition. Paris: Payot.

Schmelz, U., & R. Bachi. 1973. Hebrew as a spoken vernacular of Jews in Israel. *Leshonenu* 37:50–68, 187–201. [in Hebrew]

Schmidt, H. D., & H. Sydow. 1981. The development of semantic relations between nouns. In W. Deutsch (ed.) *The Child's Construction of Language.* New York: Academic Press.

Schwarzwald, O. 1976. Concrete and abstract approaches in the analysis of Hebrew *beged kefet. Leshonenu* 40:211–232. [in Hebrew]

Schwarzwald, O. 1978. The influence of demographic variables on linguistic performance. *Quantitative Linguistics* 1:173–197.

Schwarzwald, O. 1979. Number and gender agreement rules and linguistic universals. *Bikoret U-Farshanut* 13–14:251–263. [in Hebrew]

Schwarzwald, O. 1980a. The defective verb. *Applied Linguistics* 2:63–76. [in Hebrew]

Schwarzwald, O. 1980b. Normativism and naturalness in the application of a morphophonemic rule. *Bar Ilan University's Year Book*. Ramat Gan: Bar Ilan. [in Hebrew]

Schwarzwald, O. 1980c. Parallel processes in Mishnaic Hebrew and in Modern Hebrew. In G. B. Zarfati et al. (eds.) *Studies in Hebrew and in the Semitic Languages*. Ramat Gan: Bar Ilan. [in Hebrew]

Schwarzwald, O. 1981. *Grammar and Reality in the Hebrew Verb*. Ramat Gan: Bar Ilan. [in Hebrew]

Schwarzwald, O. 1982a. Feminine formation in Modern Hebrew. *Hebrew Annual Review* 6:153–178. [in Hebrew]

Schwarzwald, O. 1982b. Frequency and regularity in language. *Iyunim Bachinuch* 35:163–174. [in Hebrew]

Scott, C. M. 1988. Spoken and written syntax. In M. A. Nippold (ed.).

Selkirk, E. O. 1982. *The Syntax of Words*. Cambridge, Mass.: The MIT Press.

Shalev, Y. 1974. On sabra slang. *Leshonenu La'am* 25:2–3.

Sharvit, S. 1987. The distribution of feminine morphemes in Contemporary Hebrew *benoni* forms. *Prakim* 7:97–102.

Shatz, M. 1982. On mechanisms of Language acquisition: can features of the communicative environment account for development? In E. Wanner and L. R. Gleitman (eds.).

Shimron, Y. 1983. Semantic development and verbal communication abilities in children. *Iyunim Bachinuch* 37–38:117–142. [in Hebrew]

Shlesinger, Y. 1985. The stylistics of Hebrew journalism. Doctoral dissertation, Bar-Ilan University. [in Hebrew]

Shprinzak, D., & E. Bar. 1987. Our educational system in a statistical mirror. Appendix to the lecture of the Minister of Education. Jerusalem: Ministry of Education. [in Hebrew]

Sivan, R. 1963. Forms and trends in the revival of Hebrew: the verb. Doctoral dissertation, the Hebrew University. [in Hebrew]

Sivan, R. 1976. *Contemporary Hebrew*. Jerusalem: Rubinstein.

Slobin, D. I. 1966. The acquisition of Russian as a native language. In F. Smith & G. A. Miller (eds.) *The Genesis of Language*. Cambridge, Mass.: The MIT Press.

Slobin, D. I. 1973. Cognitive prerequisites for the development of grammar. In C. A. Ferguson & D. I. Slobin (eds.) *Studies in Child Language Development*. New York: Academic Press.

Slobin, D. I. 1977. Language change in childhood and in history. In J. MacNamara (ed.) *Language Learning and Thought*. New York: Academic Press.

Slobin, D. I. 1981. The origins of grammatical encoding of events. W. Deutsch (ed.).

Slobin, D. I. 1982. Universal and particular in the acquisition of language. In E. Wanner & L. R. Gleitman (eds.).

Slobin, D. I. 1985a. Crosslinguistic evidence for the language-making capacity. In D. I. Slobin (ed.).

Slobin, D. I. 1985b (ed.). *The Crosslinguistic Study of Language Acquisition*. Hillsdale, N.J.: Lawrence Erlbaum Associates.

Slobin, D. I. 1985c. Developmental paths between form and meaning: crosslinguistic and diachronic perspectives. Keynote address, Boston University Conference on Child Language.

Slobin, D. I., & T. G. Bever. 1982. Children use canonical sentence schemas: a crosslinguistic study of word order and inflections. *Cognition* 12:299–265.

Smilansky, M., & Y. Yam. 1969. The relationship between family size, father's education and father's ethnic origin and cognitive capacities. *Megamot* 16:248–273. [in Hebrew]

Smith, F. 1978. *Reading* (2nd edition). Cambridge: Cambridge University Press.

Smith, M. E. 1978. Grammatical errors in the speech of preschool children. In L. Bloom (ed.) *Readings in Language Development*. Toronto: John Wiley.

Smith, P. T. 1986. The development of reading: the acquisition of a cognitive skill. In P. Fletcher & M. Garman (eds.).

Smoczynska, M. 1985. Acquisition of Polish. In D. I. Slobin (ed.).

Solomon, M. 1972. Plural endings and the acquisition of inflections. *Language Learning* 22:43–50.

Southworth, F. C. 1971. Detecting prior creolization: an analysis of the historical origins of Marathi. In D. Hymes (ed.).

Stahl, A. 1977. *Language and Thought in Disadvanted Pupils in Israel*. Tel Aviv: Otsar Ha-more. [in Hebrew]

Stemberger, J., & B. MacWhinney. 1985. Frequency of the lexical storage of regularly inflected forms. *Memory and Cognition* 14:17–26.

Stemberger, J., & B. MacWhinney. 1986. Form-oriented inflection errors in language processing. *Cognitive Psychology* 18:329–354.

Stern, A. 1987. Which languages are spoken in Israel? Results of the 1985 census. ILASH Conference, 20.10.87.

Stevenson, H. W., T. Parker, A. Wilkinson, B. Bonnevaux & M. Gonzalez. 1978. Schooling, environment and cognitive development: a cross-cultural study. *Monographs of the Society for Research in Child Development* 43:3.

Strohmer, H., & K. Nelson. 1974. The young child's development of sentence comprehension: influence of events probability, non-verbal context, syntactic form and strategies. *Child Development* 45:567–76.

Sugamoto, N. 1982. Transitivity and objecthood in Japanese. In P. Hopper & Thompson (ed.).

Tal, 1980. Hebrew Language knowledge in elementary schools. Center for curricula, Ministry of Education, Jerusalem. [in Hebrew]

Tannen, D. 1985. Relative focus on involvement in oral and written discourse. In Olson, Torrance & Hildyard (eds.).

Tanz, C. 1974. Cognitive principles underlying children's errors in pronominal case marking. *Journal of Child Language* 1:271–277.

Tanz, C. 1980. *Studies in the Acquisition of Deictic Terms*. Cambridge: Cambridge University Press.

Tené, D. 1969. Israeli Hebrew. *Ariel* 25:48–63.

Tené, D. 1985. The historical unity of Hebrew. In M. Bar-Asher (ed.). [in Hebrew]

Thomason, S. G. 1976. What else happens to opaque rules? *Language* 52:371–381.

Thomason, S. G. 1980. Morphological instability, with and without language contact. In J. Fisiak (ed.) *Historical Morphology, Trends in Linguistics*. The Hague: Mouton.

Tolchinsky-Landsmann, L. 1986. The development of written language in pre-scholers and first graders. Doctoral dissertation, Tel Aviv University.[in Hebrew]

Torrance, N., & D. R. Olson. 1985. Oral and literate competencies in the early school years. In D. R. Olson, N. Torrance & A. Hildyard (eds.).

Traugott, E. C. 1978. On the expression of spatio-temporal relations in language. In J. Greenberg, C. Ferguson & E. Moravscik (eds.) *Universals of Human Languages*, Vol 3. Stanford: Stanford University Press.

Tur-Sinai, N. H. 1954. The historical pronunciation of *beged kefet*. In N. H. Tur-Sinai (ed.) *The Language and the Book: Basic Problems in Linguistics and in the Literary Sources*. Jerusalem: the Bialik Institute. [in Hebrew]

Van Valin, R. 1990. Semantic parameters of split intransitivity. *Language* 66:221–260.

Venemann, T. 1975. An explanation of drif. in C.N. Li (ed.) *Word Order and Word Order Change*. Austin, Texas: University of Texas Press.

Venemann, T. 1972a. Phonetic analogy and conceptual analogy. In T. Vene-mann & T. H. Wilbur (eds.) *Schuchardt, the Neogrammarians, and the Trans-formational Theory of Phonological Change*. Frankfurt: Athenaum.

Venemann, T. 1972b. Rule inversion. *Lingua* 29:209–242.

Vidislavsky, D. 1984. Syntactic and lexical aspects in the spoken Language of pupils of western and Mideastern extraction. *Hebrew Computational Linguistics* 21:9–28. [in Hebrew]

Walden, Z. 1982. The root of roots: children's construal of word-formation pro-cesses in Hebrew. Doctoral dissertation, Harvard University.

Wales, R. 1986. Deixis. In P. Fletcher & M. Garman (eds.).

Wang, W. S.-Y. 1969. Competing residues as a cause of change. *Language* 45:9–25.

Wang W. S.-Y., & C.-C. Cheng. 1977. Implementation of phonological change: The Shuang-Feng Chinese case. In W. Wang (ed.) *The Lexicon in Phonological Change*. The Hague: Mouton.

Wanner, E., & L. R. Gleitman (eds.) 1982. *Language Acquisition: The State of the Art*. Cambridge: Cambridge University Press.

Waterman, P., & M. Shatz. 1982. The acquisition of personal pronouns and proper names by an identical twin pair. *JSHR* 25:149–154.

Weiman, R. 1950. *Native and Foreign Elements in a Language: A Study in General Linguistics Applied to Modern Hebrew*. Philadelphia: Russel Press.

Weinberg, W. 1966. Spoken Israeli Hebrew: Trends in departure from classical phonology. *Journal of Semitic Studies* 11:40–68.

Weinreich, U., W. Labov & M. I. Herzog. 1968. Empirical foundations for a theory of Language change. In W. P. Lehmann & Y. Malkiel (eds.) *Directions for Historical Linguistics*. Austin: University of Texas Press.

Weist, R. M. 1986. Tense and aspect: temporal systems in child language. In P. Fletcher & M. Garman (eds.).

Wells, C. G. 1985. Preschool literacy-related activities and success in school. In D. R. Olson, N. Torrance & A. Hildyard (eds.).

Wexler, P. 1990. *The Schizoid Nature of Modern Hebrew: A Slavic Language in Search of a Semitic Past*. Wiesbaden: Otto Harrassowitz.

Whinnon, K. 1956. *Spanish Contact Vernacular in the Philipine Islands*. London.

Wilcox, S., & D. S. Palermo. 1974/5. 'In', 'on' and 'under' revisited. *Cognition* 3:245–254.

Williams, E. 1980. Argument Structure and morphology. *The Linguistic Review* 1:81–114.

Williams, F. 1970a. Language, attitude and social change. In F. Williams (ed.).

Williams, F. (ed.) 1970b. *Language and Poverty: Perspectives on a Theme*. New York: Academic Press.

Williamson, R. 1986. Formes connectives et cohesion textuelle dans le discours conversationel d'enfants de differentes classes sociales dans la capirale mexicaine. In D. Sankoff (ed.).

Wong-Fillmore, L. 1979. Individual differences in second language acquisition. In C. J. Fillmore, D. Kempler & W. S.-Y. Wang (eds.) *Individual Differences in Language Ability and Language Behavior*. New York: Academic Press.

Yifat, R. 1981. The language abilites of institute children. Master's thesis, Tel Aviv University. [in Hebrew]

Zager, D. 1982. A real-time process of morphological change. Doctoral dissertation, SUNY at Buffalo.

Zemach, S. 1956. Hold back your hands. *Davar* 916.3.1956. [in Hebrew]

Zipf, G. K. 1949. *Human Behavior and the Principle of Least Effort*. Cambridge, Mass.: Addison-Wesley.

Ziv, E. 1976. Acquisition of syntactic structures among Hebrew-speaking grade-school children. Master's thesis, Tel Aviv University.

Ziv, Y. 1982. Discourse analysis and "existence" problems in Modern Hebrew. In S. Bloom-Kolka, Y. Tubin & R. Nir (eds.) *Studies in Discourse Analysis*. Jerusalem: Akademon.

Appendix A

א. הפוך לנקבה:

כרטיס הצגה: אבא מדבר וגם אמא _____.

(1) החלון <u>נפתח</u>, וגם הדלת _____.

(2) הכר הוא <u>רד</u>, וגם המיטה היא _____.

(3) דני <u>שוחה</u> בברכה, וגם רותי עכשיו _____ בברכה.

(4) דני <u>דורך</u> על הדשא, וגם רותי _____ על הדשא.

(5) דני <u>קינא</u> ברותי, וגם רינה _____ ברותי.

ב. הפוך לעבר:

כרטיס הצגה: היום אני מדבר עם רותי וגם אתמול _____ איתה.

(6) דני <u>מחכה</u> לרותי היום, וגם אתמול הוא _____ לה.

(7) עכשיו אני <u>שותה</u> מיץ, וגם מקודם אני _____ מיץ.

(8) רותי <u>מפזרת</u> את הקוביות, וגם מקודם היא _____ אותן.

(9) היום אני <u>מביא</u> לרותי פרח, וגם אתמול _____ לה פרח.

(10) אני <u>משחק</u> טניס וגם מקודם _____ טניס.

(11) דני עכשיו <u>יכול</u> לבוא, וגם אתמול הוא _____.

(12) היום אני <u>מנקה</u> את האמבטיה וגם אתמול אני _____ אותה.

ג. הפוך לרבים:

כרטיס הצגה: 1. הנה סל, והנה שני _____.

2. הנה בובה, והנה שתי _____.

(13) הנה <u>דלי</u>, והנה שלושה _____

(14) הנה <u>אבא</u>, והנה שני _____.

(15) הנה <u>תקליט</u>, והנה הרבה _____.

205

(16) הנה גיר <u>צהוב</u>, והנה שני גירים _____.

(17) הנה <u>עיפרון</u>, והנה הרבה _____.

(18) הנה <u>אישה</u>, והנה שתי _____.

(19) הנה <u>אבן</u>, והנה הרבה _____.

(20) הנה כדור <u>אדום</u>, והנה שלושה כדורים _____.

(21) הנה בת <u>אחת</u>, והנה שתי _____.

ד. הפוך להווה:

כרטיס הצגה: מקודם החתול ליקק חלב. וגם עכשיו מה הוא עושה? הוא _____ חלב.

(22) אתמול הילדים <u>שרו</u> בגן, וגם עכשיו הם _____.

(23) הילדה <u>ישנה</u> אחה״צ, וגם עכשיו היא _____.

(24) השפן מקודם <u>הריח</u> את הגזר, ועכשיו הוא גם _____.

(25) אתה יודע <u>לרכב</u> על אופניים? הנה, מה עושה הילד בתמונה? הוא גם כן _____.

(26) מקודם בלוטו ופופאי <u>רבו</u>, וגם עכשיו מה הם עושים? הם _____.

(27) מקודם דני לא <u>הגיע</u> לדלת, וגם עכשיו הוא מושיט יד והוא לא _____.

(28) אמא <u>הקפיאה</u> את החלב במקרר, ועכשיו הוא _____.

(29) נכון צריך <u>להיזהר</u> בכביש? הנה רואים שבלוטו פה _____.

(30) הגמדים <u>הרימו</u> את הניירות מהרצפה, וגם עכשיו הם _____ אותם.

(31) אתמול דני <u>הפיל</u> את האוטו, וגם עכשיו הוא _____ אותו.

(32) מקודם העכברים <u>נכנסו</u> לחור, והנה גם עכשיו הם _____ לחור.

(33) התינוק <u>שבר</u> את הבקבוק, ועכשיו הבקבוק שלו _____.

(34) האיש <u>קדח</u> חור בקיר, וגם עכשיו הוא _____.

(35) אתמול הסנאי <u>ספר</u> את האגוזים. גם עכשיו הוא _____ אותם.

ה. הפוך לעתיד:

כרטיס הצגה: תמיד הברווז שט במים. גם מחר הברווז _____ במים.

(36) דני <u>כותב</u> מכתב. גם אני עוד מעט _____ מכתב.

(37) הנה השפן <u>לובש</u> את המכנסיים. גם מחר הוא _____ אותם.

(38) הילדים <u>למדו</u> על החג. גם אני מחר _____ על החג.

ו. השלם את המשפטים (בעזרת בובות)

הכרת הבובות: זה דני, זאת רותי, וזה אסף.

(39) דני מספר לרותי שהוא ראה <u>את</u> רותי אתמול בחצר. (תעשה שהוא יגיד לה). תגיד: ״רותי, אני ראיתי _____ בחצר״.

(40) דני רוצה לקחת את האוטו רק <u>מאסף</u>. הוא אומר לו (תעשה שהוא יגיד לו): ״אסף, אני אקח את האוטו רק _____״.

(41) דני לא יחול לסדר את הצעצועים <u>בלי</u> רותי. הוא אומר לה (תעשה שהוא יגיד לה): ״רותי, אני לא יכול לסדר את הצעצועים _____״.

(42) דני גבוה <u>כמו</u> אסף. הוא אומר לאסף (תעשה שהוא יגיד לו): ״אסף, אני גבוה _____״.

(43) רותי לא רוצה לשבת <u>עלי</u>. היא רוצה לשבת רק _____ (הצבעה על בובה־זכר).

ז. השלם את המשפטים (בעזרת בובות)

תן לבובת הוראות. תגיד להן מה לעשות:

(44) תגיד לו: ״תשתמש _____״.

(45) ״תשחק _____״.

(46) "תטפל _____".

(47) "אל תרביץ _____".

(48) "אל תפחד _____".

(49) "תסתכל _____".

(50) "אל תכעס _____".

ח. שנה את המשפטים:

(51) <u>יש</u> כאן כמה ילדים. גם מקודם _____ .

(52) מתחילה <u>לכאוב</u> לי הבטן. גם מקודם _____ .

(53) נכון כל דבר יכול <u>להישבר?</u> הנה רואים בתמונה ש _____ .

(54) אמרו לנו <u>להשאיר</u> בוטנים, והנה, כמעט לא _____ .

(55) <u>זאת</u> רצפה, <u>זה</u> נר, ו _____ . (הצבעה על עוגה).

ט. גזירה לאחור:

כרטיסי הצגה: 1. הנה <u>אמא חתולה</u>, והנה אבא _____ .

2. הנה <u>כדורים</u>, והנה _____ אחד.

(56) הנה <u>עצמות</u>, והנה _____ אחת.

(57) הנה <u>אמא פרה</u>, והנה אבא _____ .

(58) הנה <u>צדפים</u>, והנה _____ אחד.

(59) הנה <u>אמא כבשה</u>, והנה אבא _____ .

(60) הנה <u>דמעות</u>, והנה _____ אחת.

(61) הנה <u>אמא תרנגולת</u>, והנה אבא _____ .

II. THE TEST QUESTIONNAIRE TRANSLATED
FROM HEBREW

A. Change into feminine gender:

Introductory picture-card: Daddy *is talking* and mummy _____ too.

    (1) The window *is opening,* and the door _____ too.
    (2) The pillow is *soft,* and the bed is _____ too.
    (3) Danny *is swimming* in the pool, and Ruthie is also _____ now.
    (4) Danny *is stepping* on the grass and Ruthie _____ on the grass too.
    (5) Danny *envied* Ruthie, and Rina _____ Ruthie too.

B. Change into past tense:

Introductory picture-card: Now I'm *talking* to Ruthie and yesterday I _____ to her too.

    (6) Danny *is waiting* for Ruthie, and yesterday he _____ for her too.
    (7) Now I'm *drinking* juice and before I _____ too.
    (8) Ruthie *is scattering* the blocks, and before she _____ them too.
    (9) Today I'm *bringing* Ruthie a flower and yesterday he _____ too.
    (10) I'm *playing* tennis, and before I _____ too.
    (11) Danny can *come* now, and yesterday he _____ too.
    (12) Today I'm *cleaning* the bath, and yesterday I _____ the bath too.

C. Change into the plural:

Introductory picture-cards:

    (i) Here's a *basket,* and here are two _____.
    (ii) Here's a *doll,* and here are two _____.
    (13) Here's a *bucket,* and here are three _____.
    (14) Here's one *daddy,* and here are two _____.
    (15) Here's a *record,* and here are many _____.
    (16) Here's some *yellow* chalk, and here are a lot of _____ chalks.[1]
    (17) Here's a *pencil,* and here are many _____.
    (18) Here's a *woman,* and here are two _____.
    (19) Here's one *stone,* and here are many _____.
    (20) Here's a *red* ball, and here are three _____ balls.
    (21) Here's a *girl,* and here are two _____.

[1] *Chalk* is a count noun in Hebrew.

D. Change into present tense:

Introductory picture-card: The cat has *licked* its milk. And now too, what is it doing? It _____.

(22) Yesterday the children *sang,* and now they _____ again.
(23) The girl *slept* in the afternoon, and now she _____ again.
(24) The rabbit has *smelled* the carrot before, and now it is also _____.
(25) Can you *ride* a bike? What is the child in the picture doing? He _____ his bike.
(26) Bluto and Popeye *fought* before, and now, what are they doing again? They _____.
(27) Danny couldn't *reach* the door before, and now he's stretching out his hand but he still can't _____.
(28) Mummy *froze* the milk in the refrigerator, and now it's _____.
(29) You know we have to *be careful* in the street. Here we see that Bluto is being _____.
(30) The dwarfs have *picked up* the papers from the floor, and now the _____ again.
(31) Yesterday Danny *dropped* his toy car and now he _____ again.
(32) The mice have *entered* their hole before and now they _____ again.
(33) The baby *broke* his bottle and now it is _____.
(34) The man *drilled* a hole in the wall and now he _____ again.
(35) Yesterday the squirrel *counted* its nuts, and now it _____ again.

E. Change into future tense:

Introductory picture-card: The duck always *swims* in the water. Tomorrow it _____ again.

(36) Danny *is writing* a letter. I also _____ in a while.
(37) The rabbit *is putting on* his pants. Tomorrow he _____ too.
(38) The children have *learnt* about the festival. I also _____.

F. Complete the following sentences (using dolls)

Introducing the dolls: This is Danny, this is Ruthie, and this is Assaf.

(39) Danny tells Ruthie that he saw ACC Ruthie yesterday. Make him tell her. Tell her: "Ruthie, I saw. . . ."
(40) Danny wants to take the car only *from* Assaf. Make Danny tell Assaf. "Assaf, I will take the car only _____."
(41) Danny can't put the toys away *without* Ruthie. Make him tell her. Tell her: Ruthie, I can't put the toys away _____."

(42) Danny is as tall *as* Assaf. He tells Assaf (Make him do it): "Assaf, I'm as tall _____."

(43) Ruthie doesn't want to sit *on* me. She only wants to sit _____ (gesture at an unnamed boy doll).

G. Complete the sentences using prepositions:

Tell Danny and Assaf what to do. Tell them:

(44) Use _____.
(45) Play _____.
(46) Take care _____.
(47) Don't hit _____.
(48) Don't be afraid _____.
(49) Look _____.
(50) Don't be angry _____.

H. Change the sentences (output—VS word order)

(51) Here *are* some children. Before there _____ also some children here.

(52) His stomach is beginning to *ache*. Before it _____ too.

(53) Anything can *break*, right? Here, you can see that the plate _____. (picture of broken plate).

(54) We were told to *leave* some peanuts, but almost none _____.

(55) *This,*Fm is the floor, this,Masc is a candle and _____ (picture of birthday cake).

I. Backformation: (plural to singular, feminine to masculine)

Introductory picture-cards:

(i) Here is *mummy cat,* and here's daddy _____.
(ii) Here are some *balls,* and here's one _____.
(56) Here are some *bones,* and here's one _____.
(57) Here's *mummy cow,* and here's daddy _____.
(58) Here are some *shells,* and here's one _____.
(59) Here's *mummy sheep,* and here's daddy _____.
(60) Here are some *tears,* and here's one _____.
(61) Here's *mummy hen,* and here's daddy _____.

Appendix B

CODING OF TEST ITEMS

Test items are given in groups as they appear in the original test

			Response Type		
Item#	Item	Gloss	Normative	Expected	Other-Acceptable[1]
1	*niftax*, V	is opening	*niftáxat*, Fm	*niftéxet*	*ptuxa* 'is open, Fm'
2	*rax*, Adj	soft	*raka*, Fm	*raxa*	ráxa
3	*soxe*, V	is swim-ming	*soxa* 'she is swimming'	*soxétet*	*soxévet*
4	*dorex*, V	is stepping	*doréxet* 'she is stepping'	*doráxat*	*dorxa*
5	*kine*, V	envied	*kin'a* 'she envied'	*kinta*	
6	*mexake*, V	is waiting	*xika* 'waited'	*xike*	
7	*Sote*, V	am/is drink-ing	*Satíti* '(I) drank'	*Satáti*	
8	*mefazéret*, V	is scatter-ing, Fm	*pizra* '(she) scattered'	*fizra*	
9	*mevi*, V	is/am bring-ing	*hevéti* '(I) brought'	*hevíti*	*hivéti*
10	*mesaxek*, V	am/is play-ing	*sixákti* '(I) played'	*hisaxákti*	

211

			Response Type		
Item#	Item	Gloss	Normative	Expected	Other-Acceptable[1]
11	*yaxol*,V	can	*yaxol* 'could'	*yaxal*	*haya yaxol* 'was able'
12	*menaka*,V	am/is cleaning,Fm	*nikíti* '(I) cleaned'	*nikéti*	*nikáti*
13	*dli*,N	bucket	*dlayim* 'buckets'	*dliim*	*dlilim*
14	*ába*,N	daddy	*avot* 'fathers'	*ábaim*	*avim*
15	*taklit*,N	record	*taklitim* 'records'	*takliyot*	*taklitot*
16	*cahov*,Adj	yellow	*cehubim*,Pl	*cehuvim*	*cahovim*
17	*iparon*,N	pencil	*efronot* 'pencils'	*iparonim*	*ipronim*
18	*iSa*,N	woman	*nasim* 'women'	*iSot*	*naSot*
19	*éven*,N	stone	*avanim* 'stones'	*évenim*	*evanim*
20	*adom*,Adj	red	*adumim*,Pl	*adomim*	
21	*bat*,N	girl	*banot* 'girls'	*batot*	*batim*
22	*Sáru*,V	(they) sang	*Sarim* 'are singing'	*maSirim*	*meSirim*
23	*yaSna*,V	(she) slept	*yeSena* 'is sleeping,Fm'	*yoSénet*	
24	*heríax*,V	smelled,Tr	*meríax* 'is smelling'	*maríax*	
25	*li-rkav*,V	to-ride	*roxev* 'is riding'	*rokev*	
26	*rávu*,V	(they) fought	*ravim* 'are fighting'	*marivim*	*merivim*
27	*higía*,V	reached	*magía* 'reaches'	*megía*	
28	*hikpía*,V	froze,Tr	*kafu* 'frozen'	*kapuy*	*kafuy*
29	*nizhar*,V	was careful	*nizhar* 'is being careful'	*mizaher*	
30	*herímu*,V	(they) raised	*merimim* 'are raising'	*marimim*	
31	*hipil*,V	dropped,Tr	*mapil* 'drops'	*mepil*	
32	*nixnesu*,V	(they) entered	*nixnasim* 'enter,Pl'	*mikansim*	*nixnesim*
33	*Savar*,V	broke,Tr	*Savur* 'broken'	*Sabur*	*niSbar*
34	*kadax*,V	drilled	*kodéax* 'is drilling'	*kodex*	

			Response Type		
Item#	Item	Gloss	Normative	Expected	Other-Acceptable[1]
35	*safar*,V	counted	*sofer* 'is counting'	*soper*	
36	*kotev*,V	is writing	*extov* '(I) will write'	*yixtov* '(he) will write	*yiktov*
37	*loveS*,V	is wearing	*yilbaS* 'will wear'	*yilboS*	*yilvaS*
38	*lamdu*,V	(they) studied	*elmad* '(I) will study'	*yilmad* '(he) will study'	*yilmod*
39	*et*,P	Accusative Marker	*otax* 'Acc-you,Fm'	*otex*	
40	*me-*,P	from	*mimxa* 'from-you'	*me-ata*	*miméxa*
41	*bli*,P	without	*biladáyix* 'without-you,Fm'	*biladex*	*bli at*
42	*kmo*,P	like	*kamóxa* 'like-you'	*kmo ata*	*kmoxa*
43	*al*,P	on	*alav* 'on-him'	*alo*	*aléhu*
44	*tiStameS*,V	use	+ *be* 'in'	+ *im* 'with'	+ *me* 'from'
45	*tesaxek*,V	play + *be* 'in'	+ *im* 'with'		
46	*tetapel*,V	take care (of)	+ *be* 'in'		
47	*al tarbic*,V	don't hit	+ *le* 'to'		
48	*al tefaxed*,V	don't be afraid	+ *me* 'from'		
49	*tistakel*,V	look	+ *be* 'in'	+ *al* 'on'	*et* Acc
50	*al tix'as*,V	don't be angry	+ *al* 'on'		
51	*yeS*,V[2]	there are	*hayu* 'there were'	*haya* 'there was'	
52	*li-x'ov*,V	to-hurt,Int	*ko'évet* 'hurts,Fm'	*ko'ev*,Masc	*kaava* 'hurt,Fm'
53	*le-hiSaver*,V	to-break,Int	*niSbera* 'broke,Fm'	*niSbar*	*niSvar*
54	*le-haS'ir*,V	to-leave	*niSaru* '(they) remained'	*niS'ar* '(it) remained'	*niSeru*
55	*ze/zo*,PRO	this (is)/Fm	*zo/zot*,Fm	*ze*,Masc	
56	*acamot*,N	bones	*écem* 'bone'	*acama*	*écema*
57	*para*,N	cow	*par* 'bull'	*para*	*Sor* 'ox'
58	*cdafim*,N	(sea) shells	*cédef* '(sea) shell	*cdaf*	*cdafa*

| | | | Response Type | | |
| | | | | | Other- |
Item#	Item	Gloss	Normative	Expected	Acceptable[1]
59	*kivsa*,N	sheep,Fm	*kéves*,Masc	*kivs*	*kvas*
60	*dma'ot*,N	tears	*dim'a* 'tear'	*dma'a*	*déma*
61	*tarnególet*,N	hen	*tarnegol* 'rooster'	*tarnególet*	

[1] One example of an Other-Acceptable response is given each time. Others are possible, and can be found in Ravid (1988).

[2] *yeS*, signifying existence and possession, is a suppletive component of a paradigm whose main member is the verb *h-y-y* in *Pa'al,* e.g. *haya/yeS/yihye zman leSeelot axár-kax* 'There was/is/will be time for questions later'.

Item Analysis: Mean percentages[1] of Appropriate response types (Normative, Expected and Other) out of total responses, by age and SES[2]. Nor=Normative Response; Exp=Expected (Non-Normative) Response; Oth=Other Appropriate Response.

Group ID>

Input Item #	3 year olds			5 year olds a			5 year olds b			8 year olds			12 year olds a			12 year olds b			16 year olds			Adults a			Adults b		
	Nor	Exp	Oth	Nor	Exp	Oth	Nor	Exp	Oth	Nor	Exp	Oth	Nor	Exp	Oth	Nor	Exp	Oth	Nor	Exp	Oth	Nor	Exp	Oth	Nor	Exp	Oth
(1)[3]	23	36	5	48	33	5	25	20	4	71		5	67	10	21	57	33	19	**95**		5	81		5	53		29
(2)	78	4		81	19		45	35		79		10	**95**	5		33		67	**90**	10		**95**		5	47		53

[1] Ceiling scores 90% and over are given in bold. Figures in each cell that do not add up to 100% are accounted for by Inappropriate responses. Percentages are rounded to the nearest point.

[2] The two sub-groups of Younger Adults a and Older Adults a are collapsed here, since they were shown to share the same statistical domain on all test categories.

[3] Item number refers to Appendix B.

Input Item #	3 year olds			5 year olds a			5 year olds b			8 year olds			12 year olds a			12 year olds b			16 year olds			Adults a			Adults b		
	Nor	Exp	Oth	Nor	Exp	Oth	Nor	Exp	Oth	Nor	Exp	Oth	Nor	Exp	Oth	Nor	Exp	Oth	Nor	Exp	Oth	Nor	Exp	Oth	Nor	Exp	Oth
(3)	35	9	9	67	10	5	15	15	15	100		15	100			90		10	100		10	100			59	6	6
(4)	41	14	23	90	10	10	60			100			100			100			100			100			82		6
(5)	18	14	27	48	38	10	10	15	45	75	13	13	95		5	90		5	80	5	15	90	5	15	53	6	35
(6)	22	22	22	38	52	10	15	40	20	63		38	86	14		29		71	90		10	100			18	77	
(7)	74	17		100			75		20	92		8	95		5	100	5		95	5		96		4	77		23
(8)	5	37	33	5	81		5	75		58		42	100			67		33	100			100			47	41	
(9)	11	6	5	67	14	9	32	5		42	17	8	71	8		67		29	70	5	15	72	5		35	18	
(10)	46	18	5	91	4	5	70	5	10	100		10	100			100			100			100			100		
(11)	39	9		76	24		40	25		92	4		100			81		19	95		5	100			47	23	

216

Input Item #	3 year olds			5 year olds a			5 year olds b			8 year olds			12 year olds a			12 year olds b			16 year olds			Adults a			Adults b		
	Nor	Exp	Oth	Nor	Exp	Oth	Nor	Exp	Oth	Nor	Exp	Oth	Nor	Exp	Oth	Nor	Exp	Oth	Nor	Exp	Oth	Nor	Exp	Oth	Nor	Exp	Oth
(12)			5	14		19				38		50	81		19	57	19		60	24	35	57		43	6		71
(13)	50		5	5	86			55		21	79		76	24		19	81		100			95	5		29		65
(14)	14	27	32	33	29	24	15	20	60	63	17	17	86	10		62	29	5	70	10	30	86	10	4	24	41	35
(15)	59	5	9	95	5		75	25		92	8		95	5		95	5		100			100			47		35
(16)	35	26	9	57	38		25	45	15	100			100			86	10		100			100			71		24
(17)		22	33	62	10		6	22		63	25		100			33	57		95		5	100			47		35
(18)	65	4		95			30		65	100			100			100			100			100			94		6
(19)	74	4		100			90	5		96			100			100			95		5	100			94		
(20)	39	39	17	24	9	67	15	85		67	33		95		5	52		48	100			100			47		53
(21)	48	26		67	29		60	30	5	63	37		57	43		38	48	14	70		30	28	62	10	20		70

Input Item #	3 year olds			5 year olds a			5 year olds b			8 year olds			12 year olds a			12 year olds b			16 year olds			Adults a			Adults b		
	Nor	Exp	Oth	Nor	Exp	Oth	Nor	Exp	Oth	Nor	Exp	Oth	Nor	Exp	Oth	Nor	Exp	Oth	Nor	Exp	Oth	Nor	Exp	Oth	Nor	Exp	Oth
(22)	35	4		76	10		35	5		42	42		62	29		48	19		65	35		37	63		35	18	
(23)	55			24	62	62	65		5	54	46		86	14		43	52		65	35		96	4		41	29	
(24)	9	48		10	81		11	68		54	42	5	71	29		43	57		55	45		86	14		24	53	
(25)	48		5	91		5	95			96			100			100			100			100			100		
(26)	48	4		91			95			96			100			100			100			100			100		
(27)	68	5		86	5		85	5		100			100			91		9	85		15	95			94		
(28)	22	13		67	5	24	45		25	88		25	100		8	91			100			91			47		
(29)	48	19		100		19	80		5	100		5	100			100			100			100			94		
(30)	5	10	33	19	10	52	10	10	65	50	25	25	81	14	5	57	14	29	70	20	10	95			18	24	

Input Item #	3 year olds			5 year olds a			5 year olds b			8 year olds			12 year olds a			12 year olds b			16 year olds			Adults a			Adults b		
	Nor	Exp	Oth	Nor	Exp	Oth	Nor	Exp	Oth	Nor	Exp	Oth	Nor	Exp	Oth	Nor	Exp	Oth	Nor	Exp	Oth	Nor	Exp	Oth	Nor	Exp	Oth
(31)	10	10	29	14	43	19	20		65	71	21	4	81	14	5	52	43	5	80	20		100			35		9
(32)	44	13	17	67		5	5	50	5	100		5	100			100			95		5	100			100		
(33)	4	65	9	5	91		65	15	5	46	50	5	95	5		52	48		95	5		100			59	29	12
(34)	22		26	10	67	10	65		10	75	13	10	100		4	86			100			100			77		6
(35)	23		9	33	33	14	42		5	75	17	5	100		8	81	5	14	85	10	5	100		5	65	29	
(36)	4	70	4	14	76	43	95	35	45	29	71		43	57		29	71		70	30		100			12	77	
(37)	17	13	26	38	10		35	15		58	13	29	76		24	43	5	52	85		15	96		4	24	6	41
(38)	14	5	5	14	19			16		21	38	25	38		24		5	43	15	80	5	24	9	43	6	47	
(39)	50	11	6	62	33	5	32	53		100			100			100			100			91	9		82	12	
(40)	5	5	42	29	5	19	12	12	6	83		6	100		8	100			100			100			77		6

#	3 year olds			5 year olds a			5 year olds b			8 year olds			12 year olds a			12 year olds b			16 year olds			Adults a			Adults b		
	Nor	Exp	Oth	Nor	Exp	Oth	Nor	Exp	Oth	Nor	Exp	Oth	Nor	Exp	Oth	Nor	Exp	Oth	Nor	Exp	Oth	Nor	Exp	Oth	Nor	Exp	Oth
(41)	32	5	18	52		24	30	15	50	58		21	95			38			80	14		91			71		6
(42)	13	13	6	19	14	10	6	17	6	74		6	100			52			95	5		95			65		
(43)	13	13	20	10	25	20			17	42	8	21	81		5	43		5	80	24	5	86		5	24	6	18
(44)	85		5	67	29		95	5		96	4		100			95		5	90		5	100			82		6
(45)	65	15	5	57	38		85	15		88	13		100			100			80			86	10	4	77		18
(46)	94			91			100			100			100			100			100			100			94		
(47)	88		6	95			95			100			100			100			100			100			94		
(48)	67		11	95	5		71			96			95	5		86		10	100			100			94		
(49)	17	33	25	5	80	15	6	59		8	83		24	76		33	62		25	60		15	76		87		
(50)	50	10		95			60	13		100			100			81			95	19		100			87		7

220

#	3 year olds			5 year olds a			5 year olds b			8 year olds			12 year olds a			12 year olds b			16 year olds			Adults a			Adults b		
	Nor	Exp	Oth	Nor	Exp	Oth	Nor	Exp	Oth	Nor	Exp	Oth	Nor	Exp	Oth	Nor	Exp	Oth	Nor	Exp	Oth	Nor	Exp	Oth	Nor	Exp	Oth
(51)	31	6		48	33		53	21		83	13		100			95			100			100			71	12	
(52)	23	55		47	42		10	70	10	79	21		95	5		71	29		95	5		67	28		35	53	
(53)	48	30	9	86	10	5	45	35	10	83	17		91	10		86	10		35	55	5	57	38		29	59	
(54)	12	24		10	62			35	5	38	38		71	5		48	24		90	5	5	48	29		18	59	
(55)	6			11	5		10	5		17	8		33	5		14	5		95	5		42	5	9	6	6	
(56)	48	55		10	76		5	47		21	71	4	81	10	9	100			70	25	5	77	19	4	88		
(57)	48	22	9	91	9		45	30		100		5	100			76	19		90	5	5	100			88	6	
(58)	10	57		20	65	10		75	5	79	13	4	100		4	67			85	5	10	100			47	29	18
(59)	10			29	5		5			83			81						100			100			47		
(60)	10	5	5	48	5	5	11		11	71	4	11	76	8		81			100			85			65	6	

221

Input Item	3 year olds			5 year olds a			5 year olds b			8 year olds			12 year olds a			12 year olds b			16 year olds			Adults a			Adults b		
#	Nor	Exp	Oth	Nor	Exp	Oth	Nor	Exp	Oth	Nor	Exp	Oth	Nor	Exp	Oth	Nor	Exp	Oth	Nor	Exp	Oth	Nor	Exp	Oth	Nor	Exp	Oth
(61)	77			95			65			100			100			100			100			95			100			

Subject Index

Author Index

229